MW01634668

Secessionist Movements in Comparative Perspective

ICES ETHNIC STUDIES SERIES

Published in the same series:

Robert B. Goldmann and A. Jeyaratnam Wilson (eds), *From Independence to Statehood: Managing Ethnic Conflict in Five African and Asian States*, 1984

Dieter Rothermund and John Simon (eds), *Education and the Integration of Ethnic Minorities*, 1986

R. Siriwardena, *Equality and the Religious Traditions of Asia*, 1987

Neelan Tiruchelvam and Radhika Coomaraswamy (eds), *The Role of the Judiciary in Plural Societies*, 1987

K.M. de Silva, Pensri Duke, Ellen S. Goldberg and Nathan Katz, *Ethnic Conflict in Buddhist Societies*, 1988

Secessionist Movements in Comparative Perspective

Edited by

Ralph R. Premdas,
S.W.R. de A. Samarasinghe
and Alan B. Anderson

INTERNATIONAL CENTRE FOR ETHNIC STUDIES, SRI LANKA
in association with
FRIEDRICH EBERT STIFTUNG

Pinter Publishers, London

First published in Great Britain in 1990 by
Pinter Publishers Limited
25 Floral Street, London WC2E 9DS

British Library Cataloguing in Publication Data

A CIP catalogue record for this book is available from the British Library
ISBN 0 86187 102 2

Typeset by GCS, Leighton Buzzard, Bedfordshire

Printed and bound in Great Britain by
Biddles Ltd, Guildford and King's Lynn

CONTENTS

To Robert B. Goldmann

NOTES ON CONTRIBUTORS

Laura Donnadieu Aguado was Scholar in Residence at the International Centre for Ethnic Studies, Kandy, Sri Lanka, on a United Nations University Fellowship, and also a Researcher at El Colegio de Mexico, Mexico.

Alan B. Anderson is Professor, Department of Sociology and Associate Member, Department of Religious Studies, University of Saskatchewan, Canada.

Pierre Corbeil is Professor of History at CEGEP, Drummondville, Quebec, Canada.

K.M. de Silva is Professor of Sri Lankan History at the University of Peradeniya, Sri Lanka, and Executive Director of the International Centre for Ethnic Studies, Kandy, Sri Lanka.

Nandini Raghavan is a doctoral candidate at Purdue University, West Lafayette, Indiana, USA.

Don Ray is Associate Professor of Political Science at the University of Calgary, Canada.

Harun-or-Rashid is Assistant Professor, Department of Political Science, University of Dhaka, Bangladesh.

Ronald D. Renard is Assistant to the President for Special Projects, Payap University, Chiang Mai, Thailand.

André Montambault is Professor of Economics at CEGEP, Drummondville, Quebec, Canada.

Samuel K. Tan is Professor of History, and Research Fellow, Center for Integrative and Development Studies, University of the Philippines.

Ralph R. Premdas is Professor of Political Science, University of the West Indies, St Augustine, Trinidad and Tobago. Earlier he was Senior Fellow, Center for Developing Area Studies, McGill University, Montreal, Canada, and Visiting Professor in the Department of Government, University of the West Indies, Trinidad.

S.W.R. de A. Samarasinghe is Senior Lecturer in Economics at the University of Peradeniya, Sri Lanka, and Director of the International Centre for Ethnic Studies, Kandy, Sri Lanka. He is spending the current academic year (1989–90) at Swarthmore College, Pennsylvania, USA, as Julien and Virginia Cornell Visiting Professor.

George M. Scott Jr is Adjunct Professor, North Central Regional Centre at Utica, Empire State College, State University of New York, New York, USA, and Research Fellow at International Centre for Ethnic Studies, Kandy, Sri Lanka.

ACKNOWLEDGEMENTS

The present volume contains the revised papers presented at an ICES international workshop on **Secessionist Movements** held in Sri Lanka in the summer of 1987. The editors wish to thank the authors and the workshop participants for their intellectual contribution to the project. They also express their gratitude to the staff of the ICES, particularly to Shama de Zoysa, Kanthi Gamage, Nalini Weragama, Chalani Lokugamage, Sepali Liyanamana, Tilak Jayatilake, H.M. Jayawardena and Samarakoon Bandara, for thier unstinted cooperation to make the project a success.

The ICES acknowledges with thanks the financial support provided by the Friedrich Ebert Stiftung (FES) and the encouragement given by its Director Mr Gerhard Wendler and his successor Mr Arnold Wehmhoerner. The ICES also wishes to thank Dr Wesumperuma and his staff at the Sri Lanka Foundation Institute for providing the conference facilities of the Institute.

Ralph R. Premdas
S.W.R. de A. Samarasinghe
Alan B. Anderson

ICES,
554/1, Peradeniya Road
Kandy
Sri Lanka

May 1990

INTRODUCTION

S.W.R. de A. Samarasinghe

Today the nation-state is being challenged from two sides. From above at the supranational level it is being challenged by forces such as the multinational companies, common markets, satellite communications and global environmental concerns, none of which have much respect for traditional political boundaries and the integrity of the sovereign state. From below at the subnational level the nation-state is being challenged by a new wave of ethnic nationalism that has manifested itself across the globe. This latter phenomenon has been aided by three major developments. The first is the democratisation of hitherto authoritarian societies, which gives ethnic minorities in those countries the freedom to express themselves. The second factor is the heightened international concern for human rights, including those of minorities. Often the concern of the international community for human rights overrides the conventional respect for sovereignty and non-interference in the internal affairs of a country. Third is the greater scope that emerging regional powers—e.g. Germany, India—enjoy to influence events in neighbouring countries. Given the usual cross-border connections of many ethnic groups, ethnic conflicts in one country can quickly be transformed from a domestic issue to an international issue, especially when the interests of a regional power are involved.

In practice, the three factors that I have identified above have generally worked together to generate the new wave of ethnic nationalism and unrest that we have witnessed across the globe from Canada to the Soviet Union to India, Sri Lanka and China. However, political science has not yet adequately incorporated this phenomenon into its models of macro-political behaviour. Most models of the state assume a strong centralised state that would promote socio-economic development so that ethnicity, a pre-modern primordial anachronism, would wither away gradually. Now that this is no longer happening, political scientists will have to pay more attention than they did in the past to pluralist behaviour in general and ethnic nationalist behaviour in particular.

The principal objective of the present collection of essays is to set out the ethnic conflict issue and more particularly the separatist/

secessionist issue in comparative perspective, by examining case studies from many different parts of the globe. Most of the chapters deal with ethnic conflicts that at one time or another have veered from separatism to secession. Here separatism is defined as an attempt that seeks some degree of self-government short of total independence for a minority in conflict with the existing state. Secession is defined as an attempt to establish a separate sovereign state. The intensity, nature and length of time of the campaign for separation or secession has varied a great deal from case to case. For example the campaign of the French Canadians in Quebec has been generally peaceful with only a few incidents of violence. The campaign in Sri Lanka by the Tamils has been more violent. Most separatist/secessionist campaigns have fluctuated in intensity. For example, the Quebec campaign was intense in the 1970s, quietened down in the early and mid-1980s and again picked up in the late 1980s. Some campaigns, such as that of the Kurds, have a long history, whereas the secessionist sentiments in, say, Papua New Guinea (PNG) are of more recent origin. In general, the dynamics of ethnic conflicts suggest that given the appropriate conditions—a culturally homogeneous group, a 'homeland', a common set of grievances, political leadership and political mobilization etc.—a separatist movement with modest aims that do not extend beyond devolution of power within the existing state can easily evolve into a full-blown secessionist movement. That indeed is the central theme that binds together most of the case studies presented in this monograph.

In Chapter 1 Ralph Premdas provides a conceptual framework to understand separatism and secession. He identifies the principal characteristics of separatist and secessionist movements. They include, *inter alia*, the claim to a separate territory, the 'we–they' dichotomy underpinned by racial, cultural and religious differences and a strong belief in the doctrine of self-determination. Premdas discusses several alternative hypotheses and methodologies—ranging from the modernisation paradigm, internal colonialism theory, political economy models to the 'phases-and-stages' school—that have been proposed to understand ethnic separatism and secession. However, he sees serious shortcomings in every such theory and model and proposes his own analytical framework that attempts a synthesis of several of the existing theories.

The Premdas framework makes a distinction between primordial factors—language, religion, race etc.—and secondary factors—economic and political grievances—that lead to separatism and secession. However, most importantly, he emphasises the role of 'collective ethnic consciousness' that triggers off a separatist/ secessionist movement. As Premdas notes, no ideology or ism (be it capitalism or socialism, democracy or authoritarianism) or type of country (developed or underdeveloped) is today free of the threat of separatism or secession. However, the evolution of any given separatist/ secessionist movement will be fashioned by its organisation, ideology and leadership, the response of the state and the conflict-management techniques it deploys and the attitude of the international community. Given a process of such complexity and dynamism, it is not easy to generalise about separatism and secession. Thus the case studies presented in this volume must be viewed as an attempt both to study each in its own unique environment as well as to draw some generalisations from a comparative perspective so as to develop a fuller theory of ethnic separatism and secession.

Part II of this monograph deals with six case studies from Asia. The first two, by K.M. de Silva and S.W.R. de A. Samarasinghe respectively, deal with Sri Lanka's Tamil secessionist movement, one of the most violent that the world has witnessed in recent times. In essence the 2.0 million Sri Lankan Tamils who are about 12 per cent of the island's population of 16.9 million have been fighting for a separate Tamil state—Eelam—comprising the northern and eastern provinces of the country and covering about one-third of Sri Lanka. De Silva discusses the Tamil claim for a 'traditional homeland' in the north-east. The author, who is a historian, traces the historical antecedents of the Tamil claim and finds little historical basis to support it, especially in the eastern province. However, as de Silva notes, whether historically valid or not the Tamil homeland concept has become a powerful driving force in Tamil separatism. Furthermore, when the territory claimed as a homeland also contains Muslims and Sinhalese, who do not share the Tamil secessionist sentiments, the situation can become very complicated.

Samarasinghe's chapter on the Sri Lankan conflict focuses on the dynamics of separatism. Given the primordial factors, the author describes the principal secondary factors that triggered off the conflict. What is noteworthy in the Sri Lankan case is the manner in which the conflict evolved through several distinct but interrelated phases from a moderate separatist movement to a bloody and violent secessionist movement that also got internationalised especially with the involvement of India. It is a debatable point whether the internationalisation of the Sri Lankan conflict eventually helped in its resolution. Be that as it may, Samarasinghe makes two useful points. First, at the theoretical level separatism has to be studied within a dynamic framework. Secondly, at the practical level the international community still prefers the settlement of separatist disputes through devolution of power within the existing state boundaries rather than through a redrawing of state boundaries.

In Chapter 4 Samuel Tan deals with the Moro secessionist movement in the Philippines. Moros are adherents of Islam and constitute only about 4.5 per cent of the country's population, which is almost 95 per cent Christian, primarily Catholic. Like the Sri Lankan Tamils the Moros occupy their own homeland in the South and South-western part of Mindanao island. Tan makes the important point that the Moros are essentially fighting to preserve their Islamic identity. The author, who is a historian, describes Moro hostility to Christian domination, which has deep historical roots going back to the Spanish occupation of the Philippines in the sixteenth century. Thus, while the contemporary political economy—denial of political rights, economic discrimination etc.—might have aggravated the Moro battle with the Philippino government that began in the 1960s, the conflict is best understood in primordial terms in its historical context.

Harun-or-Rashid in Chapter 5 deals with the creation of Bangladesh in 1971. Bangladesh produced the only successful secessionist movement since World War II that achieved its ultimate objective of establishing a new state. In the popular perception the role of India, especially of its army, looms large in the creation of the country. Rashid acknowledges the importance of the Indian contribution. However, the chapter focuses attention on domestic factors that the author believes made the division of Pakistan in 1947 inevitable. Pre-1971 Pakistan was an example where religion (Islam) alone was not a sufficient primordial binding force. Other primordial factors such as ethnicity, culture, language and history sharply divided the two wings of Pakistan. Thus, when economic exploitation and political dominance by West Pakistan created grievances in the East, the latent Bengali nationalism took over as the driving force of the Bangladeshi secessionist process. The intervention of the Indian army simply facilitated its quick resolution.

The last two chapters on Asia deal with South-east Asia. Chapter 6, by Ronald D. Renard, discusses the Karen rebellion in Burma (Myanmar). Tracing the origins of the Karen secessionist movement, the author notes that the British colonial administration emphasised the division between the Burmans and the Karens, a policy which ancient Burmese rulers also followed. Under the British rule, Karens who became Christians—in contrast to the Buddhist Burmans—began to develop a sense of nationhood. The post-independence rebellion of the Karens that started in 1948 has defied a solution to date. It is economically costly to the Burmese. But the Karens have managed to achieve in their own territory in Burma's eastern border region a virtually independent state but without the usual trappings—seat in UN, ambassadors etc.—of a sovereign state. Ironically, given the important role played by the Karens in the troubled Burmese economy as suppliers of scarce goods that the Karens 'import' (smuggle) from Thailand, even Rangoon probably sees some virtue in the present arrangement.

George M. Scott Jr's chapter on Hmong separatism focuses on the 'messianic impulses' for nationhood of a comparatively weak tribal group in north-central Laos in Indo-China. The Hmong have had a long history of conflict with groups that were economically and technologically superior to them. Scott discusses the latest episode in that history, when some Hmong allied themselves with the United States and some others with the Communists during the Vietnam war in the hope of achieving their age-long dream of nationhood. This is an example of yet another failed internationalised 'secessionist' movement. Outsiders who required Hmong assistance to fight their own wars gave false promises to the latter that help would be given to the Hmong to realise their ambition for a separate state. But that help never materialised.

Part III of the monograph deals with three case studies from North Africa, the Pacific Islands and the Middle East respectively. Chapter 8, by Nandini Raghavan, discusses the Southern Sudanese secessionist movement that has waged a bloody war for the last twenty years. Here again, as in Burma, we find that British colonial policy reinforced precolonial divisions that existed between the Islamic north—two-thirds of the population—and the non-Islamic (animist and Christian) south. Raghavan stresses state policy controlled by the north on the economy, education, religion, language and so forth that has left the south dissatisfied. The Addis Ababa Agreement (1972) was an attempt to arrive at a political solution. But it failed partly because of external pressures that can be traced to the strength of Pan-Arabism and partly because of objective domestic factors that are at least in part an integral element of underdevelopment.

In Chapter 9 Ralph Premdas discusses the issue of decentralisation and its political implications for secession using Papua New Guinea (PNG) as a case study. Many consider decentralisation as an effective method to promote genuine development in the Third World. Premdas notes that the Australians established a highly centralised colonial administration in PNG. However, when it was time to grant independence the Australians opted to decentralise the system of government, which, as the author points out, led not to national integration but to a threat of national disintegration. The copper-rich island of Bougainville wanted to go its own way, a story familiar to us from Nigeria (Biafra), Britain (Scotland) and elsewhere, which have had to contend with regions relatively rich in high-priced natural resources. Although PNG averted Bougainville secession by conceding a highly devolved system of government, Premdas is very critical of the supposed economic and political benefits of decentralisation. At least in the case of PNG it has created more government that costs more but without corresponding economic benefits. Moreover, decentralisation has also encouraged more parochial ethnic disunity.

In Chapter 10 Laura Donnadieu Aguado discusses the national liberation struggle of the 20 million Kurds in the Middle East who are not only a nation without a state but also inhabit several states. Today Kurds are found in contiguous areas in Turkey, Iran, Iraq and the Soviet Union. Thus, the Kurdish struggle for a separate state is automatically internationalised. However, in this case the international fragmentation of the Kurdish community as well as the divisions within the liberation movement have greatly weakened the Kurdish struggle for a separate state. On several occasions in the present century the Kurds have been the willing allies of one or the other of the Middle Eastern powers in the hope of gaining a measure of independence for themselves. However, that hope has never been realised, primarily due to the political and military weakness of the Kurds. Indeed, today they suffer in varying degree as an oppressed minority with not much hope for improvement of their conditions.

In Part IV, which deals with case studies from Europe and Canada, Alan B. Anderson (Chapter 11) discusses ethno-nationalism in Western Europe and Canada with special reference to language rights. The author develops several typologies to analyse the language rights of minorities. In general in the last few decades Western democracies have been tolerant of the demands made by minorities for language rights. An important point made by Anderson is the link between the system of government and language rights. Usually, minorities in countries that have a relatively weak central government and relatively strong regional governments enjoy more ethnic rights, including language rights, than those in countries with strong central governments.

The last two chapters of the monograph discuss the separatist issue in Canada. Pierre Corbeil and André Montambault provide a historical account of the Quebec separatist movement. Ralph Premdas and Don

Ray discuss the separatist sentiments that exist in Western Canada. The strong separatist feelings in French Quebec are underpinned by linguistic and cultural factors that separate the French Canadians from the English Canadians. As Corbeil and Montambault note, in the past Quebec and the French Canadians complained of ethnic discrimination by English Canada. Premdas and Ray tell us that the western provinces of Canada also entertained a historical grievance along similar lines against central Canada, mainly Ontario. However, in the last ten years economic prosperity in Canada has spread more evenly. In particular Quebec has caught up with Ontario and the French Canadians no longer feel that they have an economically inferior status. The irony is that today it is that very strength that provides encouragement to Quebec separatists who are seriously thinking of leaving the Canadian Federation if the Meech Lake Accord that gives a 'special' constitutional status to Quebec is not approved. However, even if that happens the account in the chapter by Premdas and Ray does not suggest that western Canadian separatist sentiments will be strong enough to promote a successful separatist movement in that part of the country. But then one lesson that the case studies in this monograph teaches us about separatism is to appreciate its volatility. Thus even in the case of Canada nothing is impossible when it comes to ethnic sentiments.

Finally, there are some lessons that we can draw from the different case studies that we have reviewed above. However, before we do that a note regarding generalisations on ethnic conflicts for theory building is required. Our case studies are good examples of how some factors—e.g. internationalisation of ethnic conflicts—influence each situation differently. Thus, it is essential to study each case in its own unique environment. It would be a hazardous enterprise to draw conclusions, especially policy conclusions, from one case to apply to another. Given that important qualification, we can make some useful generalisations on separatist and secessionist movements from a comparative perspective using the case studies in the present monograph.

First, all the case studies confirm the already well-known fact that primordial factors—history, race, ethnicity, religion, language, culture etc.—play a major role as mobilisers of ethnic nationalism. What our studies also reveal is that even in economically prosperous societies primordial identities are a powerful factor in shaping group behaviour. For example, in Western Europe linguistic ethnicity survives. In Canada, one of the richest countries in the world, French Canadian nationalism not only persists but is threatening to break up the country. Our case studies also reveal that ethnicity is not an unchanging phenomenon. The relative importance of the different primordial factors as ethnic mobilisers changes in response to changes in circumstances. For example, at independence in 1947 Islam was the principal binding force of West and East Pakistan *vis-à-vis* Hindu-dominated India. Twenty years later, Islam notwithstanding, language, ethnicity, history and culture set the Bengali East Pakistanis apart from the West Pakistanis. Similarly, the Hmong identity in Laos changed depending on the group with whom they interacted.

A basic distinction can be made between ethnic groups with a territorial base and those without. In the case of the latter, demands for minority rights do not involve separatism/secession. Hence the integrity of the state is not threatened. The civil rights demands of the Afro-Americans in the United States and the demand for equal opportunity made by new immigrant groups in Western Europe are examples. For separation or secession a claim to one's own territory is an essential precondition. A strong indisputable claim, as in the case of Bangladesh, facilitates separation or secession. Indeed, as the Karens have shown, if a minority can secure its territory they can enjoy *de facto* secession without the trappings of *de jure* secession. However, if the territorial claim of a minority is disputed by another group — as has happened in Sri Lanka — it becomes that much more difficult to resolve the conflict.

Our case studies also show the complicated and dynamic manner in which primordial and secondary factors that encourage ethnic mobilisation interact over time. For example, in Quebec the French Canadians rallied round the ethnic flag in response to perceived economic and political discrimination against them by the majority English Canadians. Although remedies were found for most of the complaints made by the French Canadians, the separatist sentiments in Quebec have not subsided. This seems to suggest that once an ethnic group with a territorial base is mobilised to win demands related to political and economic conditions, the challenge to the integrity of the state cannot easily be overcome.

As regards the process of separatism and secession in ethnic conflicts, our case studies reveal four important features. First, separatist and secessionist movements are dynamic and change over time. Peaceful movements could eventally turn to violence (e.g., Sri Lanka) and violent movements could become peaceful (e.g., Quebec, although violence there had only been moderate) depending on the response of the state, the ideology and the resources of the minority group and so forth. Also separatist movements can turn into secessionist movements and secessionist movements could settle for something less than a sovereign state.

Secondly, violence—both by the minority group that is fighting and by the state—almost certainly prolongs and complicates the conflict. This is true of the Philippines, Sudan, Sri Lanka and elsewhere. Violence makes the conflict bitter, hardens attitudes on both sides and generally detracts attention from the original causes of the dispute to new immediate issues concerning state and non-state terrorism, third-party involvement, arms supplies and so forth. Once violence takes a grip on the conflict, the state is reluctant to compromise because that would be considered bad in principle. The minority group that is fighting may consider the state's unwillingness to compromise as further evidence of oppression.

It is harder to judge whether the internationalisation of a separatist or secessionist movement helps or hinders the resolution of ethnic conflicts. In the case of Bangladesh the Indian military involvement helped to end the conflict quickly. In Sri Lanka the Indian intervention failed to end the conflict quickly. In point of fact, there was more bloodshed following the arrival of the Indian military. However, arguably, some conditions—for example, the establishment of the provincial councils—that were created by the Indian initiative would have been helpful to the eventual peaceful resolution of the conflict. The involvement of outsiders in the Hmong and Kurdish struggles have not been helpful to either group. In general, one lesson that can be learnt is that outside aid for separatists and secessionists comes, like most foreign aid, with strings attached. More often than not outsiders have, as in the case of Indians in Sri Lanka and the United States and the Communists in Laos, multiple objectives for getting involved in separatist and secessionist movements and some of these objectives may be in conflict with those of the groups concerned.

Finally, most of the case studies that we have discussed here identify devolution as a principal political solution to meet ethnic minority demands without conceding secession. It appears to be an effective method of securing not only the political rights of minorities but also that of language and other primordial identity-based rights. However, as the experience of Quebec shows, devolution also has its limits as a solution to ethnic nationalism when the minority is not satisfied with what has already been conceded and the majority is reluctant or unwilling to yield more because it is 'going too far'. Moreover, as the PNG case study shows, devolution can unleash further disintegrative forces and may also fail to yield the expected socio-economic benefits by way of more efficient government.

PART I: THEORETICAL ISSUES

1 SECESSIONIST MOVEMENTS IN COMPARATIVE PERSPECTIVE

Ralph R. Premdas

Secession, like divorce, is an ultimate act of alienation. Committed against an existing state, secession may result in the emergence of an international unit possessing all the attributes of a sovereign state—territory, people, government and autonomy. Or it may, as a temporary measure, settle for internal self-government within an extensively decentralised system such as a federal or confederal state. As an act of territorial and political assertion, a secessionist struggle is usually prolonged, punishing and prohibitively costly. Often badly beaten and savagely brutalised, rarely is it totally and finally annihilated. At times, it may appear moribund and may even be forgotten in the preoccupation with other problems, but over time, given the right circumstances, the movement will be awakened in all its old fury. It comes and goes, ebbs and flows in a logic of its own. It dies hard, if ever.

Secession can also be conceived as a social process constituted of steps and stages, cumulative and precipitating causes, displaying patterns of accommodation and intransigence. It may originate from nothingness in a fabricated and mythical claim built around an invented self-differentiating group, but its energies and objectives are real and can become a menace to a material pre-existing entity. More often than not, its target of territorial autonomy is only reluctantly relinquished by an antecedent state. Bloodshed, chaos and suffering tend to accompany the birth of the secessionist child. It is likely to be illegitimate, spawned in conspiracy and the result of rape. The mother country must be dismembered. Maimed fractions must now become healthy wholes. Territory is lost, and with it, tenacious memories, people and vitality. Prolonged struggle demoralises all sections in the conflict equally, polarises and demoralises nearly all members, creates a garrison

---

Note: The author wishes to thank several people for helpful comments on this chapter: Professor K.M. de Silva, Dr Sam Samarasinghe, and Dr George Scott at the International Centre for Ethnic Studies in Kandy, Sri Lanka, and Professors Cynthia Enloe and Don Rothchild.

mentality, cripples democratic institutions, breeds fanaticism and helplessly accepts a distorted existence as normal and inevitable.

Should it succeed, a secessionist movement legitimates its claim to an autonomous territorial survival on the 'natural right' as a unique nation to determine its own destiny. Self-determination of nationality groups is an enshrined sacred right. It is often asserted as an absolute and unqualified right. But rights are never unequivocal and unrestrained. The right to secede and determine a group's destiny is asserted in diametrical opposition to another sacred right, that of a state to safeguard its sovereignty and territorial integrity. The latter is also a right sanctioned by the United Nations. Secession, then, is not an uncontested moral claim made in a vacuum and yielded to without argument and challenge. Its success, it seems, depends less on an inscrutable moral imperative and more on superior physical power and unsurrendering persistence. The right to secede is as valid as the capability of forcibly wresting territory and people from another state. No state dismembers itself willingly; no separatist movement has been proferred victory on a platter.

Secession can be seen as a solution, then, to an intransigent struggle between a state and an assertive sub-state nationality unit. The parties may negotiate, entertain each other, double talk and deceive, but often in the end, they remain irreconciled, each seeing itself as self-righteous and the other as evil. In moments of communal passion, irreconciliability may provoke the state to attempt desperate solutions, such as genocide, mass expulsion, totalitarian repression and, most dreaded of all, assimilation of the ethnic enemy. Secessionist leaders rise to the challenge equalling the level of inanity, barbarism and outright insanity of its adversary.

Characteristics of a secessionist movement

Any study of secession must identify its characteristic features. The object of secessionist quest is first to affirm a boundary between 'its people' and 'others'. The 'we–they' dichotomy is essential to its identity. This is often followed by a claim to territory for self-government. Where the 'people' and 'territory' are both clearly distinguishable and separable, the claim to autonomy is in part validated and reinforced by these facts. Often, however, neither people nor territory can be disaggregated, easily reassembled and homogenised without strong counter-claims and acrimonious controversy. Regardless, the secessionist claim cannot be contained by these practical objections. Its aim, however, can be attained either in the form of a proper sovereign state or in a semi-sovereign segment (such as a province) of a decentralised state (federal or unitary).

In the demand for separation, the critical test resides in the acquisition of political power by a group to determine its way of life without external interference. It may be problematic to attain this ideal within the bosom of the pre-existing state, although a formula for the devolution of extensive and entrenched powers to a sub-state unit can be designed that satisfies both centre and periphery. At nearly all times in such an arrangement, life is potentially filled with frustrations and lived on a razor's edge, the relationship persistently buffeted by suspicion, fear and misunderstanding. To sever all ties with the existing state is an inviting, tempting, next step. Taking the entire pie—instead of a compromised part—cannot always be resisted, especially in the context of modern mass politics where extremist chauvinists may be expected to hover in a perpetually disgruntled mood.

It is critical that we specify the basic traits of the secessionist phenomenon before describing the related literature and proposing an analytic scheme. I shall distinguish five components which I believe capture the essence of the secessionist creature:

(*a*) *An organised struggle.* A secessionist movement may have several contending factions each claiming the mantle of legitimacy to represent the aspirations of the group. Nevertheless, as a movement it is not an amorphous cluster of sentiments drifting towards a haphazard end. It is organised; its energies and vision are directed. The word 'movement' contains a dynamic element suggesting struggle and resistance. If there is no struggle, there is no need for a movement. A secessionist struggle embodies action, tension and resistance. In the idea of struggle inheres a contest between two entities, each claiming to be coterminous communities, striving for people, territory and autonomy. The gain of one group is the loss of the other. The struggle can be deadly and tantamount to total war, cast in an uncompromising zero-sum game. That is why secessionist struggles tend to be fanatical. The longer the struggle, the more likely that the history of the movement, with its heroes and legends, will become part of the added baggage of emotional claims to be defended and upheld.

(*b*) *Territorial self-government.* A secessionist movement invariably seeks a territorial base, which is often enshrined in the claim to a 'homeland' in which to govern itself, avoid exploitation and preserve its way of life. A movement that seeks to obtain recognition of its cultural values, but does not seek a separate territory, cannot be regarded as secessionist. The territorial factor is essential. Similarly, a movement that merely seeks a separate territory, but does not wish to govern itself and determine its destiny cannot be a *bona fide* separatist cause. A high level of autonomy—especially over collective decision-making affecting culture and local affairs—is critical to our definition. Some questions are bound to crop up with regard to territory, autonomy and way of life. For instance, how much territory and how much autonomy are minimally required for a region to survive as a viable separate entity? Our answer is that feasibility or viability does not bear on the validity of a group's claim to an autonomous territorial existence. Minimal autonomy is required over cultural and local affairs. It is in this latter factor that the idea of 'way of life' inheres. The phrase 'way of life' embodies alleged primordial values of a group that confirm its uniqueness as a nation. The forced loss of the values of a nation is the true meaning of being vanquished. It is the moral equivalent of genocide.

(*c*) *Facilitated by primordial and secondary factors.* A secessionist movement may be sustained in its claims by alleged underlying unique factors such as common language, religion, race and values. These primordial features may be mythical or apply only to a core within the claimed population. It may lack objectivity or historical authenticity. Similarly, a secessionist group may be bound together by a claim that it is the subject of discrimination, neglect, exploitation, repression or domination. These too may lack objective basis. What is significant is that the movement believes that these factors are true, and together this belief bestows a collective consciousness of group identity that sustains the momentum of the movement. A secessionist movement can be based either on primordial or secondary factors alone, thereby being designated ethno-national, ethno-linguistic, ethno-religious or ethno-regional. More often however, it is nurtured on numerous interlocking claims.

(*d*) *The doctrine of self-determination as a right.* A secessionist movement is involved in a moral quest. It affirms a right to self-determination as God-given and natural. It is asserted as a collective group right. This position is doctrinal, neither right nor wrong as measured by a universal standard. It is a 'claim' right. It confers obligations on others. In this sense, its operational validity depends on the willingness of others to accede to it. Without a recognised and widely accepted doctrine of self-determination, few secessionist movements would arise. It is the availability of this doctrine and its enshrinement in the international moral order as a right that has facilitated, if not created, many separatist movements. Further, the demonstration effect of one group winning autonomy has led in the twentieth century, especially after World War II, to an avalanche of nationality groups being formed, each claiming the right to self-determination.

(*e*) *The state as a unit of international organisation.* Finally, secessionist movements occur in an international environment, where the state is the established unit of sovereign existence. The nation state is only a recent invention of Europe, but it has become the norm of contemporary international organisation. The state is free, contains people and territory, and is subordinate to no one. It is this ideal organisation that embodies the highest form of the self-determination quest. Many secessionist movements may, however, have to settle for something short of full sovereignty such as may be found in a federal or confederal arrangement.

The empirical evidence and some classifications

The peoples of the world are distributed over 164 states in the international system. While at an earlier time, the ideal state was conceived as being coterminous with a single nation so that the term 'nation-state' expressed a reasonable equation, in today's world only a minority of states can claim to be repositories of a single homogeneous nation. The word 'state' refers to a legal entity; 'nation' pertains to a sociological entity. Most states are multinational. When nations in a state evolve a consciousness of themselves as distinct identities, they then become 'ethnicised'.

In the contemporary state, internal ethnic cleavages are the source of secession. Indeed, in every cleavage lurks a potential separatist movement. The fissures in the state can be many, ranging from language, religion, race and region to discontent stemming from alleged neglect, discrimination or exploitation. Some cleavages are deeper than others and some states possess only one major cleavage, while others contain multiple, coinciding, divisions. These cleavages have prompted specialists to classify the states in the international system by the number of fissures they possess. A further classification can be made by simply identifying the nationality elements in each of the divided countries on the continents of the world. These categories suggest that we live in a divided world where cleavages abound and where secessionist claims for a separate autonomous existence are more 'normal' than are often perceived. It is the homogeneous state that is the deviant case. It is clear, then, that we are not dealing with a peripheral phenomenon, but with one that is indeed predominant in the world and one from which a good part of today's violent news emanates.

It needs to be equally emphasised that these 'minorities' and 'sub-national societies' are not merely a Third World phenomena which signal underdevelopment. Only as recently as a decade ago the literature on political integration focused on nationalist 'aberrations' in the Third World, but today—in a diametrical swing—it is part of the new orthodoxy that the developed countries are not only the historical products of separatist claims, but that they themselves continue to be bedevilled by their own nationalist movements. Audrey and David Smock noted: 'No continent and virtually no nation is now immune to the impact of claims for special status and privileges made on behalf of communal groups.'[1] New works, anthologies in particular, are published annually pointing to internal ethno-national, ethno-regional and ethno-linguistic challenges to the integrity of the United Kingdom, France, Italy, Spain, Belgium, Canada, the Soviet Union and elsewhere in the developed North. The Third World literature on integration, secession, repression and instability is being re-examined with a view to applying its insights to the developed countries. Cross-national comparisons across the North–South divide are now being undertaken because, as Glaser and Moynihan have noted, 'ethnic identity has become salient, ethnic conflict more marked everywhere in the last seventy years'.[2]

Focuses and methodologies in the study of secession

In the literature on methodologies and theories of secession, several frameworks are available from which to choose. In this review I have highlighted five, including my own framework, developed over several empirical case studies. The criteria on which I base my selection are (1) simplicity of the model; and (2) comprehensibility. At once, a good working model should involve the relationship between a few key variables or processes and comprehend in its scope most of the secessionist cases in both the developed and underdeveloped world.

1. Secession and integration in modernisation theory

It used to be held by most Western scholars that with the achievement of modernisation, ethnic cleavages would be ironed out and an integrative homogenisation process established. Cleavages were regarded as signs of underdevelopment. They were aberrations to be eradicated by industrialisation and urbanisation. Professor Arend Lijphart has taken Karl Deutsch, Samuel Huntington and Cyril E. Black to task for their frameworks which associated social mobilisation and development with national assimilation in the process of industrial transformation.[3] The early writers on ethno-nationalism espoused 'a melting pot' hypothesis concluding that 'modernisation is not only homogenising, it is also an irreversible process'.[4]

Integration through modernisation is now a thoroughly discredited proposition. The experience of proliferating separatist movements seeking autonomous existence has become commonplace, especially provoked in many instances by galloping modernisation. In effect, the opposite hypothesis is now held to be true; namely, that modernisation in multi-ethnic states tends to activate assertions for self-determination. Notes Lijphart: 'if modernisation leads to rapidly increasing social transactions and contacts among diverse groups, strain and conflict are more likely to ensue than greater mutual understanding.'[5] It is noteworthy that not all groups that have discovered their unique identities have proceeded to seek an autonomous territorial existence. No one knows for sure what causes some ethnic groups to drift towards separatism and others not. Theories abound, ranging from internal factors such as unique values to external forces such as the infectious demonstration effects of other movements.

Modernisation brings disparate peoples closer together. The impact of change varies from ethnic group to ethnic group, conferring advantages on some and severely disadvantaging others. The differential impact of modernisation stimulates sentiments of relative deprivation which are amplified by another dimension of modernisation: better communications. Disparities in development breed jealousy and may spawn fears of ethnic domination (internal colonialism). Claims of discrimination and exploitation then become rife. Democratic mass politics feeds on these raw materials of the modernisation process, fuelling the fires of ethnic militancy. Ethnic consciousness breeds responses of the same kind, producing more ethnic groups. In an escalating crescendo of intensifying ethnic competition, a critical mass of fury is unleashed threatening to split the state asunder at its ethnic seams. Ethnic group formation and emergent separatist movements stem in the main from the modernisation experience of both the developed and underdeveloped world.

2. The colonialism/internal colonialism school

Generally, this school argues that oppression and imperialism by a dominant internal 'nation' over another inevitably trigger claims for autonomy and separate development. A nation refers to a community that believes that it shares a unique set of values and customs. The name of Michael Hechter is most closely associated with internal colonial 'nationalist' school, although the idea of an internal colony is an old one. Basically, the internal colonialism school gives a subordinate place to the nationalist, subjective factor and a paramount place to objective exploitation and relative deprivation variables.

In the internal colonialism explanation, claims of oppression and exploitation tend to be argued and accentuated by a heavy dose of spurious and fabricated data. What is more important than objective facts, however, is the belief among an ethnic group that it is oppressed. The negative motif of oppression is combined with a positive claim that the group is superior and more virtuous than its oppressor. The package is powerfully impregnated with a mixture of half-truths and valid claims concocted into a separatist potion.

3. The political economy school

Often associated with Marxism, the political economy school posits that below the symbolism and rhetoric of subjective ethnic claims for autonomy lurk objective material motivations. Political economy analysts use this line of argument to uncover the 'real reasons' for separatism. Fundamentally, the political economy school relies heavily on an explanation that argues that objective rational factors are manipulated by a self-interested class or elite to attain the end of territorial autonomy. One variant of this school stresses the conspiracy of cross-communal elites in provoking ethnic animosity so as to prevent the emergence of inter-communal class ties among workers. Should workers discover that the cause of their alienation resides not in their 'ethnic belly-button', but in their relation to the owners of the means of production, then they will unite and eliminate their oppressors. In this vision of things, ethnicity is viewed as an epiphenomenon, a diversion that must be jettisoned to inaugurate a new order of justice based on socio-economic and class solidarity. Like the early modernisation theorists, the Marxist adherents of the political economy school see ethnic cleavages as residual remnants of a moribund capitalist and feudalist age.

Another variant of the political economy school is less doctrinaire about the underlying objective factors that account for ethnic assertiveness. Its adherents compile elaborate statistical data to show disparities in the distribution of resources, jobs and privileges among ethnic communities. They hold that when these disparities, which may be caused either by deliberate policy design or by an accident of history, are eliminated, the ardour of the separatists will be diffused and the march to intercommunal harmony will proceed without further digression.

All the political economy theorists are optimists and rationalists. They underestimate the psychological aspects and symbolic power of the secessionist claims. They are often shocked when a secessionist sentiment persists and deepens in the face of policy palliatives and generous concessions to redress the objective disparities.

4. The phases-and-stages school

The analysts in this school generally orient to the internal aspects of a secessionist movement pointing to processes and phases in its life. External aspects may occupy a secondary place in their internal stage theory. These authors tend to be highly eclectic, drawing their data and supportive hypotheses from interdisciplinary sources.

John Wood sets out five processual phases:[6] (1) the preconditions of secession; (2) the rise of secessionist movements; (3) the response of central governments; (4) the direct precipitants of secession; (5) the resolution of secessionist conflicts by armed conflict. Under 'preconditions of secession', Wood discusses such factors as the separability of a piece of territory, the role of race, language and religion; the differential distribution of resources and relative deprivation of various ethnic groups; the cohesiveness of the state; the legitimacy of the ruling regime; the institutions of conflict resolution available; and the intensity of motivation of the secessionists. Under 'the rise of secessionist movements', he explores the role of ideology, leadership and organisation, noting that it is often difficult to pin-point when and how such a movement begins. Under the rubric of 'the response of central governments', the author explores the capability and ingenuity of the ruling regime in confronting or accommodating the secessionists. Finally, under 'the resolution of the secessionist crises by Armed Conflict', Wood evaluates the armed solution, also noting the role of external actors who may come to the aid of either side.

Wood's study contains no new ingredients, borrowing and bringing together his categories from an assortment of scholars.[7] His contribution has been in the area of assembling the various aspects of a secessionist movement, but without specifying linear causative links. In this, I believe his analysis is yet to prove valuable. It has no set of interconnected variables possessing predictive power. The individual segments in the model possess useful insights, however, and can be usefully applied to empirical case analyses.

Anthony D. Smith has also offered a processual model of a secessionist movement.[8] He notes that separatist movements vary in intensity, duration, extent, force and clarity. With these criteria in mind, he classifies movements into degrees of maturity. Under his analysis, four aspects are treated: (a) political dimension involving organisation and institutionalisation of the movement; (b) a social variable relating to its mobilisation capability; (c) a cultural core that diffuses and creates new communal values in the target population; and (d) symbolic component dealing with cases of a movement's ideology becoming a religious surrogate.

A mature secessionist movement for Smith is one that displays all four components in a high level of articulation. A sense of shared nationalist bonding is required to inaugurate, control and interpret the movement through all levels of its evolution. Smith adds another level of complexity to his developmental formulation. This relates to factors necessary to sustain them and bring them to fruition. Smith argues that nationalist-imbued secession represents a quest for dignity and security originating 'as a passionate reaction against state power and authority'. Smith's theory falls within the rationalist school of thought.

There are other phases-and-stages theories including that of Donald L. Horowitz on 'Patterns of Ethnic Separatism' where he discusses the interplay between 'relative groups position' and 'relative regional position' as the determinant of separatism.[9] Horowitz's categories on 'backward' and 'advanced groups' in backward and advanced economies fall again within a rationalist framework.

Overall, the phases-and-stages analysts provide a rich lode of insight into aspects of a secessionist movement's behaviour. None of the frameworks, however, has been tested against an actual movement studied in detail. Rather the stages and phases were defined and proved against selective data gathered from an assortment of movements everywhere.

5. *Primordial and secondary factors in secession: a suggested analytic framework*

The framework that I have designed to study secessionist movements has been applied empirically over several cases which have been published over the past decade.[10] In my own framework, I have divided the causes of secession into two broad categories: primordial and secondary. Primordial causes refer to those cleavages in a society that are deep and serve to define the very identity of a group. Primordial variables are usually part fact and part myth. They include: (i) language; (ii) religion; (iii) race; (iv) values or culture: (v) territory or homeland or region.

A secessionist movement that has one or several of these variables serving as the underlying cause of discontent usually casts its arguments in absolute terms. These are primal features which are deeply entrenched in the character of the group and its membership. It is the stuff of which 'nation' or 'tribe' is constituted.

Secondary factors are features which have been recently acquired or experienced. They serve as the triggering mechanism of collective consciousness felt by a group as it proceeds to define its demands. Secondary factors can be equally fabricated as well as primordial ones. They include: (i) neglect; (ii) exploitation; (iii) domination and internal colonialism; (iv) repression and discrimination; and (v) forced annexation.

The primordial and secondary factors vary from movement to movement. In some cases, only a combination of a few of these factors are present. In the history of a movement, the claims of a group may change the emphasis from one factor to another. The usual situation is that a movement rarely stands up on the pedestal of a single cause. A major difference between a primordial and secondary factor is the latter's susceptibility to compromise. Generally, primordial factors represent a deep and very difficult cleavage; they do not lend themselves to division, splitting and negotiations. Secondary factors are acquired traits and usually they are amenable to bargaining. They tend to deal not with symbolic but pragmatic issues. In practice, the primordial causes are intermixed with the secondary. Over a length of time, secondary and primordial factors can be so interwoven that negotiators may find it difficult to disaggregate them. Racism may result from the confounding of the secondary factor with a primordial one.

In my scheme of analysis, the presence of primordial and secondary factors does not automatically transform the movement into a separatist one. A catalytic factor is required for the transformation process. It is 'collective consciousness'. When a group of people come to view themselves consciously as being endowed with a unique language, race, religion or region and see that this is threatened because of one of the secondary factors, then and only then, they become a 'nation' and 'an ethnic group'.[11] It is the psychological collective factor of group consciousness, which is often activated by contact and competition with another group, that stirs life into a group transforming it into an ethno-linguistic, ethno-regional or ethno-national movement. It is imperative, then, that the analyst of separatist movements should examine the history of a movement to establish the reasons for the emergence of collective consciousness.

In a state of agitation, a nationalist or ethnic group attempts to rediscover its roots. It will need to anoint its language, religious or regional claims with mythical history and 'rediscover' the origins that confer uniqueness upon it. This is all a subjective solidarity process. The scholar who seeks to question the legitimacy of a movement on the basis of the objectivity of the primordial and secondary causes will misunderstand what separatist movements are all about. What is significant is the shared belief of a group that its identity and survival are defined by these factors. Usually in conferring uniqueness on itself, a nationalist group resorts to stereotypes. Stereotypes serve as defence mechanisms to protect group identity. They portray members of the in-group in glorious positive terms and denigrate the out-group in the worst possible light. Stereotypes must be studied, for they also serve to perpetuate inter-group prejudice and provoke intransigence. Mass mobilisation of a group is often facilitated by invoking stereotypes that tend to dehumanise an ethnic opponent, permitting murder and various forms of atrocities. In communal conflicts, the intensity of passions and barbarism in behaviour flourish under the blind cover of stereotypes.

Examination of the primordial and secondary causes of a separatist movement inevitably involves extensive field work, field observation, interviews and familiarity with the language and culture of the groups in question. Other categories of analysis are used in my framework. These include:

(*a*) *The organisation, ideology and leadership of the movement.* The researcher of the separatist phenomenon must be familiar with the literature on mass movements. In particular, not only should the modes of mass mobilisation in a movement be studied, but also the critical role played by charismatic leaders. Analysis must be made of the background, interests and role of intellectuals in the movement, especially in relation to their articulated right of self-determination. Membership of the movement must be examined for levels of activism and commitment. The general tendency is for movements to be splintered and unified at different phases in their life. Internal factionalism is an important area. The resource base of the movement, its solidarity appeals and its persistence are all critical in explaining the life of the movement.

(*b*) *The governing regime.* A description of the regime in power and the governmental institutional structure is essential. Often the government in power has enormous resources compared with the separatists. This may make them overly arrogant, leading to the slighting of the claims of the separatists who may be viewed as common criminals, terrorists or power-hungry persons. Evidence is abundant to show that separatism grows in ardour because the avenues of official access are limited or denied. The inept manner with which a government deals with the demands of a movement may validate its cause. Just as a separatist movement is analysed organisationally, so must a ruling regime be analysed for its leadership, ideology, resources and tactics.

(*c*) *Modes of conflict management.* This factor has been alluded to in (b) above. It needs special treatment, however. What is noteworthy is that the bases of a group's complaints can carry it only a short to moderate distance towards winning a fray. Usually, the additional momentum is generated by the nature of the interaction between the movement and the ruling regime in trading demands and settling issues. In the styles of leadership and conflict resolution a residue of independent goodwill or bitterness is accumulated leading to the tractability or intractability of the ongoing dispute. Trust and treachery, like openmindedness and inflexibility, can sustain or restrain a movement. This dimension requires research.

(*d*) *The international dimension.* Separatist movements tempt foreign intervention. As the dispute protracts, each side may seek external allies, resources and support. In a number of cases, because the secessionist group may straddle borders, foreign intervention is built into the problem from the start. Other factors can invite alien interest in the conflict, such as strategic location or ideological affinity. Foreign intervention may intensify the issue, adding new levels or weaponry and inserting new issues and interests into the dispute. The addition of foreign forces tends to draw in yet more participants regionalising and internationalising that which originated as a domestic dispute.

Summary of the approaches and the associated literature

Looking at all five of the perspectives on secession examined in this chapter, it can be concluded that several variables are common to each of them. These variables, in turn, have been the subject of analysis by specialised academic disciplines. This implies that the study of the secessionist phenomena requires interdisciplinary training if a balanced view is to be obtained. It would be useful here to identify these common variables and place them within their respective disciplines. I also supply a short list of important literature in each area. It is from these disciplinary building blocks that an adequate theoretical edifice of secessionist movements will have to be constructed. The key variables, disciplines and samples of works are in the following bibliographical section.

Notes

1. Audrey and David Smock, *The Politics of Pluralism*, New York, Elsevier, 1975.
2. N. Glazer and D.P. Moynihan (eds), *Ethnicity: Theory and Development*, Cambridge, Mass., Harvard University Press, 1975.
3. A. Lijphart, 'Political Theories and the Explanation of Ethnic Conflict in the Western World', in *Ethnic Conflict in the Western World*, Ithaca, NY, Cornell University Press, 1977, p. 48.
4. Ibid.
5. Ibid., p. 56.
6. Several of Wood's phases are discussed in my earlier work, see R. Premdas, 'Secession and Political Change: The Case of Papua Besena', *Oceania* (June 1977); John Wood, 'Secession: A Comparative Analytic Framework', *Canadian Journal of Political Science*, vol. 14, no. 1 (March 1981), pp. 107–33.
7. I have also developed several aspects of this theme in my work 'Secession and Political Change'. See also Walker Connor, 'Nation-Building or Nation-Destroying', *World Politics*, vol. 24 (1972).
8. A. Smith, 'Introduction: The Formation of Nationalist Movements', in A.D. Smith (ed.), *Nationalist Movements*, New York, Macmillan, 1976, pp. 5–12.
9. D.L. Horowitz, 'Patterns of Ethnic Separatism', *Comparative Study of Society and History*, vol. 23, no. 2 (April 1981), pp. 165–95.
10. See Premdas, 'Secession and Political Change'; 'Secessionist Politics in Papua New Guinea', *Pacific Affairs* (Spring 1977); 'Ethno-nationalism, Copper, and Secession: The Case of Bougainville', *Canadian Review of Studies in Nationalism*, vol. 6, no. 2 (Spring 1977); 'The Western Breakaway Movement in the Solomon Islands', *Pacific Studies* (Summer 1980); 'Vanuatu: Decentralisation and Secession', *Kabar Sebarang* (February 1985).
11. See Walker Connor, 'The Politics of Ethno-Nationalism', *Journal of International Affairs*, vol. 27, no. 1 (1973).

Bibliography

1. *Nationalism:* noteworthy works include: C.J.H. Hayes, *Historical Evolution of Modern Nationalism* (1931) and *Nationalism: A Religion* (1960); Hans Kohn, *The Idea of Nationalism* (1944) and *Nationalism: Myth and Reality* (1955) and *Faces of Nationalism* (1972); L.L. Snyder, *The New Nationalism* (1968) and *Varieties of Nationalism* (1976); K. Deutsch, *Nationalism and Social Communication* (1953): A.D. Smith, *Theories of Nationalism* (1971): and *Nationalism in the Twentieth Century* (1979); K.R. Minogue, *Nationalism* (1970); C. Tilly (ed.), *The Formation of the Nation-State of Western Europe* (1975).
2. *Self-determination:* key works: D. Ronen, *The Quest for Self-Determination* (1979); L.C. Burcheit, *Secession: The Legitimacy of Self-Determination*

(1978); A. Cobban, The Nation-State and National Self-Determination (1969); R.F. Johnson (ed.), *The Politics of Division, Partition and Unification* (1976).

3. *Ethnicity and Ethno-Nationalism:* sociologists and anthropologists predominate: W. Connor, 'The Politics of Ethno-Nationalism', *Journal of International Affairs*, vol. 28, no. 1 (1973); and 'Nation-Building or Nation-Destroying', *World Politics*, vol. 24 (1972); M.J. Esman (ed.), *Ethnic Conflict in the Western World* (1977); C. Enloe, *Ethnic Conflict and Political Development* (1973); N. Glazer and D.P. Moynihan (eds), *Ethnicity: Theory and Experience* (1975); C. Young, *The Politics of Cultural Pluralism* (1976); F. Barth (ed.), *Ethnic Groups and Boundaries* (1969); C. Geertz (ed.), *New States and Old Societies* (1963); W. Bell and W.E. Freeman (eds), *Ethnicity and Nation-Building* (1974); M. Banton, *Race Relations* (1967); A. Rabushka and K.A. Shepsle, *Politics in Plural Societies*; R. Melson and H. Wolpe, 'Modernisation and the Politics of Communalism', *American Political Science Review*, vol. 64 (1970); R.S. Milne, *Politics in Bi-Polar States* (1982); R. Premdas, 'Ethnonationalism, Copper, and Secession', *Canadian Review of Studies in Nationalism*, vol. 4, no. 2 (Spring 1977); A. Fishman (ed.), *Language and Nationalism* (1983); P. Brass, *Ethnicity and Nationality Formation', Ethnicity*, vol. 3 (1978); E. Allworth (ed.), *Soviet Nationality Problems* (1971).
4. *Integration:* the literature is mainly by economists and political scientists: E.B. Haas, *The Uniting of Europe* (1965); B.A. Balassa, *The Theory of Economic Integration* (1961); James Rosenau (ed.), *Linkage Politics* (1969); K. Deutsch (ed.), *Political Community and the North Atlantic Area* (1957); A. Etzioni, *Political Unification* (1968); A.H. Birch, 'Minority Nationalist Movements and Theories of Political Integration', *World Politics*, vol. 30 (1978); and *Political Integration and Disintegration in the British Isles* (1977); C. Geertz, 'The Integrative Revolution', in C. Geertz (ed.), *Old Societies and New States* (1963).
5. *Internal Colonialism:* M. Hecter, *Internal Colonialism* (1975); R.B. Goldmann and A.J. Wilson (eds), *From Independence to Statehood* (1984).
6. *Political Economy Approach:* E.W. Nafziger and W.L. Richter, 'Biafra and Bangaladesh: The Political Economy of Secessionist Conflict', *Journal of Peace Research*, vol. 2, no. 13 (1976); J.G. Williamson, 'Regional Inequality and the Process of National Development', *Economic Development and Cultural Change*, vol. 13, no. 4 (1965); L. Despres (ed.), *Ethnicity and Resource Competition in Plural Societies* (1975); H.B. Davis, *Toward a Marxist theory of Nationalism* (1978); S.W.R. de A. Samarasinghe, 'Ethnic Representation in Central Government Employment and Sinhala–Tamil Relations in Sri Lanka, 1948–81', in *From Independence to Statehood*, edited by R.B. Goldmann and A.J. Wilson (1984).
7. *Secession/Separatism:* Institute of Commonwealth Studies, *The Politics of Separatism* (1969); J. Nagel, 'The Conditions of Ethnic Separatism', *Ethnicity*, Vol. 7, No. 2 (September 1980); D.L. Horowitz, 'Patterns of Ethnic Separatism', *Comparative Studies in History and Society*, vol. 23, no. 2, (April 1981); J. Wood, 'Secession: A Comparative Analytic Framework', *Canadian Journal of Political Science* vol. 14 (March 1981); Oriol Pi-Sunyer (ed.), *The Limits of Integration* (1971): S. Berger, 'Bretons, Basques, Scots, and other European Nations', *Journal of Interdisciplinary*

History, vol. 3 (1973); P.A. Gourevitch, 'The Re-Emergence of Peripheral Nationalism', *Comparative Studies in History and Society*, vol. 21 (1979); A.D. Smith (ed.), *Nationalist Movements* (1976): C.H. Williams (ed.), *National Separatism* (1982); R. Premdas, 'Secessionist Politics', *Pacific Affairs* (Spring 1977); T.V. Sathyamurthy, *Nationalism in the Contemporary World* (1983); F.L. Shields (ed.), *Ethnic Separatism and World Politics* (1983); T. Nairn, *The Breakup of Britain* (1977); R.I. Hall (ed.), *Ethnic Autonomy* (1979); Jacobs, *The Quebec Separatism* (1980); W.H. Wriggins, *Ceylon: Dilemmas of a New Nation* (1960); J. Gerard-Libois, *Katanga Secession* (1966).

8. *Territory:* L.L. Snyder, 'Nationalism and the Territorial Imperative', *Canadian Review of Studies in Nationalism*, vol. 3 (1975); A. Mass (ed.), *Area and Power* (1966); I. Duchacek, *Nations and Men* (1976); M. Esman, 'Defence of Homelands', *Ethnic and Political Studies*, vol. 8, no. 3 (1985). Vidyamali Samarasinghe, 'Spatial Inequalities and the Ethnic Conflict in Sri Lanka', paper presented to the workshop on 'The Economic Dimensions of Ethnic Conflict in Sri Lanka' (August 1985), ICES, Kandy, Sri Lanka; K.M. de Silva, *The Traditional Homelands of the Tamils of Sri Lanka: A Historical Appraisal* (ICES, Kandy, Sri Lanka), Occasional Paper No. 1, 1987.
9. *Decentralisation:* A. Lijphart, *Democracy in Plural Societies* (1976); A. McMahon, *Delegation and Autonomy* (1961); H. Maddick, *Democracy, Decentralisation, and Development* (1966); R. Premdas and S. Pokawin (eds), *Decentralisation in the Pacific* (1980); R. Premdas and J. Steeves, 'Decentralisation and Development in Melanesia', *International Review of Administrative Science* (1985); K.R. Cox and D.R. Reynolds (eds), *Locational Approaches to Power and Conflict* (1974).
10. *Minorities:* J. Laponce, *The Protection of Minorities*; *Minority Rights Group Report* (London: Minority Rights Group); S. Smooha, 'The Control of Minorities in Israel and N. Ireland', *Comparative Studies in History and Society* (April 1980); P. Hintzen and R. Premdas, 'Guyana: Coercion and Control', *Journal of Inter-American Studies and World Affairs* (August 1982).
11. *Conflict Resolution:* A. Lijphart, *Deomocracy in Plural Societies* (1977), M. Esman, 'The Management of Communal Conflict', *Public Policy*, vol. 21 (Winter 1973): H. H. Daalder, 'The Consociational Theme', *World Politics*, vol. 26, no. 4 (1974): B. Barry, 'The Consociational Model and its Dangers', *European Journal of Political Research* (December 1975); R. Premdas, 'Communal Conflict Management', *Ethnic Studies Report* (January 1986); E.A. Azar, 'Management of Protracted Social Conflict in the Third World', *Ethnic Studies Report*, vol. 4, no. 2 (July 1986); D. Rothchild, 'Ethnicity and Conflict Resolution', *World Politics*, (July 1970); R. Premdas, 'Ethnic Conflict in the Caribbean', *Ethnic Studies Report*, vol. 4, no. 2 (July 1986); E. Nordlinger, *Conflict Resolution in Divided Societies* (1972); K.M. de Silva, *Managing Ethnic Tensions in Multi-ethnic Societies: Sri Lanka 1880–1985* (1986).
12. *Group Identity* (mainly by sociologists): H.R. Isaacs, *Idols of the Tribe: Group Identity and Political Change* (1975); Erik Erikson, *Childhood and Identity* (1965); F. Barth (ed.), *Ethnic Groups and Boundaries* (1969).

13. *Internationalisation and Foreign Interference:* A. Suhrke and L.G. Noble (eds), *Ethnic Conflict in International Relations* (1977); S. Neumann (ed.), *Small States and Segmented Societies* (1976); K. Deutsch, 'External Involvement in Internal War', in H. Ekstein (ed.), *Internal War* (1964); F.S. Pearson, 'Foreign Military Intervention and Domestic Disputes', *International Studies Quarterly*, vol. 8 (1974); J.N. Rosenau, *International Aspects of Civil Strife* (1964); J. Bartelsen (ed.), *Non-State Nations in International Politics* (1977).

PART II: ASIA

2 SEPARATISM IN SRI LANKA: THE 'TRADITIONAL HOMELANDS' OF THE TAMILS

K.M. de Silva

I: Introduction

Where an ethnic (or religious) minority is concentrated in a region or regions of a country, and where in addition it constitutes the overwhelming majority of the population there, as is the case with the Tamils of the Jaffna peninsula and Jaffna district in Sri Lanka (and to a lesser extent in the other component districts of the Northern Province), geography and demography combine to provide an ideal breeding ground for a separatist movement.

Ethnic cohesion and a heightened sense of ethnic identity, important ingredients for the emergence of separatist sentiment, had existed in Jaffna and the Jaffna district since the mid-1950s; indeed, some would argue that these had been in existence since the 1940s, in the last decade of British rule. However, the striking feature of the emergence of Tamil separatism in Sri Lanka, in contrast to contemporary separatist movements in Burma or Thailand, is its late development. The transition from expressions of separatist sentiments (in the late 1940s and early 1950s) to a full-fledged separatist movement took over twenty-five years, and that transformation was the result of the operation of a number of factors. These included a perceived threat to the ethnic identity of the Tamils from political, economic and cultural policies; perceived grievances of a political or economic nature or both; and a sense of relative deprivation at the loss of, or the imminent loss of, an advantageous or privileged position.

Separatist agitation went through several stages and phases, beginning with peaceful political pressure, moving on to civil disobedience, and then to violence, and that violence itself from sporadic acts to more systematic attacks directed against state property and police and security forces. The avowed objectives of the agitation could vary from securing greater autonomy for a region or a people within the Sri Lankan polity, to pressure for conversion of its unitary structure to a federal or quasi-federal one. The final phase was a fully developed separatist movement bent on independence.

Many of the essential ingredients of separatism had emerged by the 1970s: a leadership that had taken a public position advocating separatism and, more important, bands of militant agitators intent on converting the traditional political leadership's public utterances and political rhetoric—the leadership was not known for any steadfast adherence to that cause—into a programme of action, to be systematically implemented with the leadership's consent if possible, but without that consent or even acquiescence if necessary, and intent on 'selling' the legitimacy of their political cause to the Tamil masses and to the world at large. Thus, grievances of the literati and the rest of the elite were more than adequate as a substitute for widespread mass social and economic discontent in generating public support for separatism.

The threat that Tamil separatism poses to the Sri Lankan polity is all the greater because of the operation of another factor—once more a potent combination of geography and demography—the existence of a great reservoir of Tamil separatist sentiment and a powerful sense of Tamil ethnic identity just across the narrow and shallow seas that separate Jaffna from Tamilnadu on the Indian sub-continent. Once a separatist movement emerged among the Tamils of Sri Lanka it was fostered, nurtured and protected by Tamilnadu, almost as though it were a surrogate for the independent state which the Tamils of Tamilnadu had been compelled—through a constitutional amendment as the first line of the Indian government's armoury of attack—to abjure in their own country.

The case for Tamil separatism in Sri Lanka was built upon the modern doctrine of self-determination of people, and linked with it came, in time, the concept of the 'traditional homelands' of the Tamils, 'homelands' that needed to be protected from 'outsiders', themselves citizens of the same country. The concept of the Tamil 'traditional homelands' was itself based, as we shall see, on a fragile foundation of pseudo-historical data and demography of the 'homelands', past and present.

The Sinhalese, the majority group, and the Sri Lankan Tamils, the island's most significant minority, have sharply different perceptions of the nature of the Sri Lankan state; and diametrically opposed attitudes to decentralisation and devolution of power to regional units of administration. Although the early proponents of decentralisation (from the 1920s onwards) were Sinhalese, the situation has changed since independence. The main political parties of the Sri Lankan Tamils have become the principal if not the sole advocates of decentralisation and devolution. These demands have provoked strong opposition. The opposition has been strongest from the Sinhalese both in the mainstream political parties, as well as pressure groups representing Sinhalese-Buddhist opinion, many of whom fear, if not believe, that schemes for devolution of power are likely to lead to political fragmentation of the island, and are therefore a potent threat to the island's territorial integrity through the re-emergence of a separate Tamil state and the linkage of such a state to Tamilnadu in South India.

The processes of centralization vigorously pursued by the British during their rule in the country (1796–1947) have proved to be a formidably stable political legacy, and one that post-independence regimes have been both reluctant and unable to repudiate. Initiated in 1815–18 by the subjugation of the Kandyan kingdom and fusion of its territories with the coastal strip the British had conquered from the Dutch in 1795–6, this unified political system was the first such structure since the first half of the fifteenth century when a Sri Lankan (Sinhalese) ruler last had effective control over the whole island for any considerable length of time. One has to go further back into the history of Sri Lanka to identify a period of political control from the national capital comparable in length and in the consistent pursuit of centripetalism as a desirable objective of state policy to the period of British rule in Sri Lanka. The years 1815–18 were thus a decisive turning point in the history of Sri Lanka.

However, it was not till 1832 that a unified administrative system for the whole island was set up. In this process the existing regional and sub-regional administrative boundaries were eliminated, and replaced by new provincial boundaries, a radical change amounting in effect to the division of the island into five zones of administration in the form of the Northern, Southern, Eastern, Western and Central provinces.[1] The objective behind all this was avowedly political: to hasten the break-up of the Kandyan kingdom and to weaken national feeling in this last independent Sinhalese kingdom,[2] and one which had successfully resisted Western invaders since the mid-sixteenth century, by attaching its low-lying and littoral regions to the maritime territories conquered from the Dutch. In all except one of the new provinces created in 1832 the administrative centre was located on the coast.

When changes in these boundaries came in the course of time, and four such changes were made between 1845 and 1889, with the demarcation of the North-Western, North-Central, Uva and Sabaragamuva provinces, they marked a belated recognition of some traditional regional boundaries. By 1889 there were nine provinces. With only minor adjustments to their boundaries introduced largely for purposes which can only be described as administrative convenience, this structure has survived to the present day. From the 1950s the district—a smaller administrative entity within a province—replaced the province as the largest unit of administration. Even so the province survived, bereft of all administrative energy and purpose, a remnant of a British system that refused to fade away, till it received another lease of life in 1987–8.

II: The Federal Party and the 'traditional homelands' concept

The concept of the 'traditional homelands' of the Tamils of Sri Lanka emerged in the 1950s.[3] Every version of it since that time has been built on a foundation of 'historical' data and has a superstructure of 'historical' data as well. It is also inextricably linked with the political ideology of the Federal Party, and its successor the Tamil United Liberation Front (TULF), and was immanent in the principal resolution adopted when the Federal Party was established in 1949. At the first national convention of the Federal Party in 1951 a claim was made that: 'the Tamil-speaking people in Sri Lanka constituted a nation distinct from that of the Sinhalese in every fundamental test of nationhood' and the 'separate historical past' of the Tamils was emphasised as an essential part of this.

It was a claim based on a hazy 'historical' memory of statehood in centuries past, remembered and newly interpreted (and generally misinterpreted) as a continuous and continuing tradition of independent statehood and an unbroken national consciousness. In less than a decade of its first enunciation, this theory—refined as 'the traditional homelands' of the Tamils—had become an indispensable and integral part of the political ideology of the Tamil advocates of regional autonomy and separatism. At this point, there was very little by way of definition of the boundaries of these 'national areas' of the Tamils except for occasional references to the Northern and Eastern provinces.

The definition of the boundaries came in the mid-1950s and it was based on a single piece of 'historical' evidence, contained in a document prepared by Hugh Cleghorn, a British academic, who had been in the island in the very early years of British rule in the last years of the eighteenth century as a political trouble-shooter, and later on as the island's first colonial secretary. This document, entitled 'Notes from Mr Cleghorn's Minute dated 1st June 1799, on the Administration of Justice and of the Revenues under the Dutch Government', was first published in the government's *Ceylon Almanac and Annual Register* in 1855. It was subsequently reprinted elsewhere, in 1883 and again in 1891. It was known to be a fragmentary, if not defective, version of an original which had disappeared from the records that should have been in Colombo. The original itself was not located till the 1930s. A Sri Lankan scholar Dr (later Professor) Ralph Pieris published this fuller version of the Cleghorn Minute in 1954 under the title 'Administration of Justice and of Revenue on the Island of Ceylon under the Dutch Government (The Cleghorn Minute)'.[4]

It immediately attracted scholarly attention and critical comment. More important, Tamil politicians and ideologues looking for historical data and evidence in support of their case for the 'traditional homelands' of the Tamils seized upon one short extract from the Cleghorn Minute. It read as follows:

> Two different nations, from a very ancient period, have divided between them the possession of the island. First the Cingalese [*sic*] inhabiting the interior of the country, in its southern and western parts, from the river Wallouve [Walawe] to that of Chilow [*sic*], and secondly the Malabars [Tamils], who possess the northern and eastern districts. These two nations differ entirely in their religion, language and manners. The former, who are allowed to be the earlier settlers, derive their origin from Siam, professing the ancient religion of that country.[5]

The last sentence, an egregious solecism, would have alerted readers to the limitations of this extract as historical source material, but ideologues of Tamil separatism generally omitted it in their resolutions and documents on the theme of 'traditional homelands'. They used the rest of this extract. One sees this in claims advanced by the Federal Party, its successor the TULF and by other Tamil separatist activists, in defining the territorial limits of 'the traditional homelands' of the Tamils. This single extract from Cleghorn's minute in support of their territorial claims has gained the status of scriptural sanctity among the advocates of a separate state for the Tamils of Sri Lanka, accepted almost as an act of faith, in the face of scholarly criticism of its reliability as a historical source.

From the outset the concept of the Tamil-speaking peoples of Sri Lanka sought to bring the Muslims, who were Tamil speakers generally, under the umbrella of Tamil politics, on the assumption that a common language linked them, despite a fundamental difference in religion. It was a linkage which the Muslims have persistently rejected because of its assumption of a Tamil tutelage over them, but one which — as we shall see—constantly reappears in Tamil agitational activity. Secondly, it was linked with a purposeful opposition of the Federal Party and its successors in the leadership of Tamil politics, to the entry of Sinhalese into those parts of the country regarded as 'traditional' Tamil areas. Thus, at the inaugural convention of the Federal Party (or Ilankai Thamil Arasi Kachchi in Tamil—ITAK) in April 1951, a resolution urged that

> Inasmuch as the Tamil-speaking people have an inalienable right to the territories which they have been traditionally occupying, the first national convention of the ITAK condemns the deliberately planned policy of action of the Government in colonizing the land under the Gal-Oya reservoir and other such areas with purely Sinhalese people as an infringement of their fundamental rights and as a calculated blow aimed at the very existence of the Tamil-speaking nation in Ceylon.

We shall return to the theme of the Gal-Oya project and settlement of peasants there later on in this chapter (see Part IV). Here we need only to state that charges about the damaging effects of state sponsored peasant colonisation were resumed in the same forthright terms after the general election of 1956 and against the background of the language controversies of that time.

III: The agitation for Eelam—a Tamil state in Sri Lanka

The mid-1970s marked the emergence of separatism as a destabilising factor in Sri Lankan politics. At the beginning the main advocate of a separatist programme was the TULF as the successors of the Federal Party. At a convention held on 14 May 1976 at the village of Pannakam near Vaddukodai, a suburb of Jaffna, the vague and disconnected separatist aspirations of the 1950s were given a more coherent form, and a programme of action for the establishment of 'Eelam', a Tamil state in Sri Lanka, was announced.[6]

The principal resolution there—the Vaddukodai resolution as it came to be called—claimed that the:

> Sinhalese people have used their political power to the detriment of the Tamils by (inter alia) . . . making serious inroads to the territories of the Tamil kingdom by a system of planned and state-aided colonization and large-scale regularization of recently encouraged Sinhalese encroachments calculated to make the Tamils a minority in their own homeland.

As with the Federal Party in the 1950s, now in the 1970s too, the claim for a separate state looked back to the distant past and endeavoured to link the present with that past through a misinterpretation of historical events and data. Once more the emphasis was on a continuing tradition of independent statehood and unbroken national consciousness. Above all, the territorial dimensions of 'Eelam' were defined in the Vaddukodai resolution in terms which clearly showed an—unacknowledged—dependence on Cleghorn:

> Whereas throughout the centuries from the dawn of history, the Sinhalese and Tamil nations have divided between them the possession of Ceylon, the Sinhalese inhabiting the interior parts of the country in its southern and western parts from the river Walave to that of Chilaw and the Tamils possessing the northern and eastern districts . . . [the TULF resolves that] Tamil Eelam shall consist of the Northern and Eastern Provinces [of Sri Lanka].

In its manifesto for the general election of July 1977, the TULF elaborated further the concept of the 'traditional homeland of the Tamils'. The claim now was that 'Even before the Christian era the entire island [of Sri Lanka] was ruled by Tamil kings'. From this claim, which was, in fact, a falsification of history,[7] the manifesto proceeded thus:

> From this background of alternating fortunes [of the Sinhalese and Tamil rulers of ancient Sri Lanka] emerged, at the beginning of the 13th century, a clear and stable political fact. At this time, the territory stretching in the western sea-board from Chilaw through Puttalam to Mannar and thence to the Northern Region, and in the east, Trincomalee and also the Batticaloa Regions that extended southwards up to Kumana or the northern banks of the river Kumbakkan Oya were firmly established as the exclusive homeland of the Tamils. This is the territory of Tamil Eelam.

Tamil Eelam, the manifesto asserted, is the successor to the Jaffna kingdom.

A Tamil kingdom was in fact a historical reality, but its life span had been short—from the thirteenth century to the early part of the seventeenth and, except during the brief heyday of its power in the fourteenth and early fifteenth centuries, it seldom controlled anything more than the Jaffna peninsula and some adjacent regions on the coast and some parts of the interior. Set against Sri Lanka's recorded history of over 2,000 years the independent existence of this kingdom was a brief episode during a period of political decline of the Sinhalese kingdoms of that period. At times the kingdom of Jaffna had been very powerful; at others it had been reduced to the status of a satellite of expanding Dravidian states across the Palk Straits, and at times it had been subjugated by the Kotte kingdom, the principal political entity in the island in the fifteenth and early sixteenth centuries, and generally it acknowledged the suzerainty of the principal Sinhalese kingdom. It disappeared from the historical scene in the early seventeenth century and, while its memory was kept alive in the twentieth century, there was neither an unbroken 'national' consciousness nor a continuing tradition of independent statehood among the Tamils of Jaffna in particular or of Sri Lanka in general.

There were, besides, contradictions and ambiguities in the claims made in the 1970s and 1980s. The Vaddukodai resolution defined the boundaries of Tamil Eelam in terms of people: 'Tamil Eelam shall consist of the people of the Northern and Eastern Provinces': the TULF manifesto of 1977 adopted a territorial definition and the territorial limits were extended to cover part of the North Western province in addition, of course, to the Northern and Eastern provinces. The lack of consistency in these claims was demonstrated afresh in the amendment to the Statement of Government Policy in the national legislature moved on 18 August 1977 by A. Amirthalingam (as the Leader of the TULF and Leader of the Opposition), in which he referred to the 'mandate given by the people of Tamil Eelam to the Tamil United Liberation Front for the restoration and reconstitution of a free sovereign socialist state of Tamil Eelam'. On that occasion there was no reference to the boundaries of the state, no reference to provinces, or to peoples, no reference to the exclusive rights of the Tamils to such territory and no reference implicit or explicit to that extract from the Cleghorn minute which plays such a vital role in the claims of Tamil politicians, but merely a reference to the Tamils' 'traditional occupation of a separate and well-defined territory in the Northern and Eastern parts of Ceylon'.

Eight years later the TULF's reliance on the extract from Cleghorn's minute was at last made explicit, in the TULF's letter dated 1 December 1985 to Prime Minister Rajiv Gandhi of India. That document contained a section with the sub-title 'the Integrity of the Tamil Homeland'. An extract from it is quoted below.

> The Northern and Eastern provinces have been traditionally recognised as Tamil-speaking areas from the days of British rule. This was the position at

> the time of the British conquest of the Maritime Provinces of Ceylon. Sir [sic] Hugh Cleghorn in a report to the Colonial Office in 1799 stated as follows:
>
> 'Two different nations, from a very ancient period, have divided the Island. First, the Sinhalese in its Southern and Western parts, from the river Walawe to that of Chilaw; and secondly, the Malabars in the Northern and Eastern Districts' (Malabars is used to refer to the Tamils).

The TULF's letter was written during negotiations for a political settlement of Sri Lanka's ethnic conflict then being conducted through the mediation of the Indian government and was clearly aimed at influencing the Indian government's policies. One of the immediate consequences of the ethnic disturbances of 1983 in Sri Lanka had been the application of diplomatic and political pressure by India on behalf of the Tamils of Sri Lanka for a more thoroughgoing scheme of decentralization and devolution of power than that introduced in the island through the District Development Councils Act of 1980.

The problem at this stage was the unit of development. This unit had been the district since the decentralization exercise of 1980–1 and indeed in all political negotiations on devolution of power since the early 1960s. The upshot of India's mediatory effort was the presentation of a set of proposals by the Sri Lanka government for a radical restructuring of Sri Lanka's administrative system, in which the key feature was a system of provincial councils, nine in all, based on the provinces of British times but modelled as regards their legislative powers and administrative authority on the states of the Indian union with the significant difference that the Sri Lankan provincial councils would operate within the framework of the country's constitutionally-entrenched unitary system.

One of the most controversial features of this endeavour to reshape the structure of the Sri Lanka polity in the 1980s is the attempt to create a supra-provincial regional unit by the fusion of, or a linkage between, the Northern and Eastern provinces. The pressure for this came from the TULF and various other Tamil separatist groups, in the aftermath of the riots of 1983, and was a revival of a concept of regionalism introduced into the national political debate by the Federal Party in 1956–7. The Bandaranaike government of that latter period had agreed to this but the storm of opposition that erupted from within and outside the government compelled a hasty — and indeed ignominous — withdrawal of the offer. When a proposal to create a regional unit encompassing the Northern and Eastern provinces was introduced by the TULF in late 1983 it immediately won the backing of the Indian government. As in 1956–7, so in 1983–4, the Sri Lanka government found itself hastily abandoning such plans as it had to consider this demand, once it became evident that there was division within the Cabinet on it. There was almost unanimous—and vehement—opposition to it from the principal opposition party and other Sinhalese groups, not to mention powerful sections of the government.

In mid-1987, however, under renewed pressure from India and in the hope that a concession on this would provide a breakthrough to a settlement in Sri Lanka's ethnic conflict, the Sri Lankan government agreed to a temporary merger of the Northern and Eastern provinces, as part of the political package in the Indo-Sri Lankan accord signed in Colombo on 29 July. Provision was made for the people of the Eastern province to decide, through a referendum to be held within a year of the merger, or at any later date to be decided upon by the Sri Lankan government, whether or not they wished to continue as part of this regional unit. The offer of a referendum did not make the merger any the more acceptable to the Sinhalese and the Muslims living in the Eastern Province. The widespread civil unrest—the most ferocious anti-government riots in two decades or in over thirty years if one excludes the JVP insurrection of 1971—that erupted against the Indo-Sri Lankan accord in many parts of the country was, in part at least, a reaction against the decision to create a North Eastern province by a merger of the two provinces. Despite this opposition the North Eastern province was created in 1988; a referendum will be held to determine its fate. The referendum and its results are likely to be as controversial and perhaps as destabilising as the proposal to create a North Eastern province was in July–August 1987.

The TULF's letter to Rajiv Gandhi of 1 December 1985 brought up once again the equivocal concept of the 'Tamil-speaking peoples' in which the Muslims, as a Tamil-speaking group, are involuntarily yoked to the Tamils. The TULF argued that in the Eastern Province '75 per cent of the population have Tamil as their mother tongue [and in] the combined Northern and Eastern provinces the Tamil-speaking people form over 86 per cent of the population'.

From that specious piece of statistical information they proceeded to invoke the Indian experience in support of the claim for a Tamil homeland encompassing the Northern and Eastern provinces: 'In the same way that India has solved its multi-lingual problem by creating linguistic states the Tamil linguistic area, i.e., the Northern and Eastern provinces should be made into one unit'.

IV: The Eastern province

The Eastern Province whether in the form it was in the period 1832 to 1873 or in its present form consists of territories which were integral parts of the Kandyan kingdom at the time it was ceded to the British in 1815. Most of the eastern seaboard had never been part of the short-lived Jaffna kingdom. At the height of the latter's power, part of its southern boundary had extended close to Trincomalee, but this had been only for a very brief period. Nor was the Batticaloa area part of the Jaffna kingdom.[8] Indeed, not only was the eastern seaboard part of the Kandyan kingdom, but also for much of the nineteenth and the early twentieth century the Tamil population there was concentrated in and around Trincomalee and the Batticaloa lagoon. These littoral settlements were—as in the eighteenth century—in the nature of a thin strip of habitation confronting two powerful forces of nature, the sea on the one side and the forbidding wilderness of the almost impenetrable forests of the dry zone on the other. The overwhelming difficulties of access by land intensified the isolation of this region; land communication improved only in the late nineteenth and early twentieth centuries. More important, these settlements had a large Muslim population.

The littoral regions of the present Eastern province are the home of over a third of Sri Lanka's Muslims. Some of them are descended from immigrants from the coasts of South India, but a substantial number perhaps the large majority, are descended from Muslim refugees from Sri Lanka's own west coast, fleeing the persecution of the Portuguese and afforded a safe haven on the east coast—and elsewhere—by Sinhalese kings of the period. While they were, and still are largely, a Tamil-speaking group, they maintain an identity distinct from the Tamils through their religion.

In the 1880s Sir Ponnambalam Ramanathan, a distinguished Tamil lawyer-politician, caused a stir by arguing that the Muslims were, in the main, Tamils who had converted to Islam. Spokesmen for the Muslims passionately rejected this and responded by reasserting their Arab or Indo-Arab origins, and by insisting that their Islamic faith separated them from the Tamils with whom they shared only a common language.[9] Echoes of this controversy reverberated in the aftermath of the language controversies of the 1950s when the concept of the 'Tamil-speaking peoples' of Sri Lanka became part of the political jargon of those tumultuous times. Muslims rejected this concept then as they do now and—as they did at the tail-end of the nineteenth century—because of its implications of a subordinate role for them *vis-à-vis* the Tamils, and the assumption of a Tamil wardship over them.

Nevertheless, we have seen TULF politicians—and radical groups to the left of them—persisting in treating the Muslims as part of the Tamil-speaking population, especially in claims for the 'traditional homelands' of the Tamils encompassing the Northern and Eastern provinces. And this despite the frequency of violent clashes in recent years between the Tamils and Muslims in the Eastern province (and in Mannar in the Northern province, where there is a large Muslim presence). Islamic fundamentalism, which was a potent political force in the politics of the Muslims in the Eastern province in the late 1980s, has sprung up largely as a reaction against the political pressure on the Muslims from Tamil separatist groups operating there.

The interior of the Eastern province was sparsely populated and contained Sinhalese settlements in *purana* (i.e., traditional) villages with its people eking out a hard existence in this forested region. These Sinhalese settlements, although smaller in population than either the Tamil or Muslim ones, and few and far between, were scattered throughout the Trincomalee and Batticaloa districts. (The present Amparai district of the Eastern province was created only in 1960.) Writing in 1921, S. C. Canagaratnam, a Tamil official of the Kachcheri (secretariat) at Batticaloa, observed that:

> One of the saddest features in the history of the [Batticaloa] District is the decay of the Sinhalese population in the West and South. At one time there were flourishing and populous Sinhalese villages here, as is evidenced by the ruins and remains dotted about this part of the country.[10]

Canagaratnam also made the point that 'the whole District formed part of the Kandyan Provinces when the Sinhalese Kings held sway and Batticaloa was then known as Puliyanduwa'.[11]

It is precisely in this part of the present Eastern province that the massive multi-purpose Gal-Oya project—which the Federal Party pointedly refers to in its political resolutions of the 1950s as a prime example of state-sponsored settlement of Tamil homelands—was established. This was the first new major irrigation project and settlement scheme after independence, and the first new major scheme since the eleventh century, the last great age of Sinhalese irrigation engineering. C. W. Nicholas's path-breaking monograph on the *Historical Topography of Ancient and Medieval Ceylon*[12] makes specific reference to the Gal-Oya scheme, and shows it as occupying for the greater part the ancient and important territorial division called Dighavapi-Mandala or Dighavapi-rata. Gal-Oya and most of the other major colonization schemes of the Eastern province are located in areas which in 1921—and at the time of the census of that year—were either the sites of remnant Sinhalese villages or were covered by forests. These settlements had survived several centuries of war and invasion, of pestilence and privation, and the ravages of nature in the forms of droughts, floods and cyclones, till they were revitalized in the years after independence as peasant 'colonies', that is to say village settlements of the Gal-Oya scheme. Nor are the Sinhalese the sole beneficiaries of this scheme. Despite the large number of Sinhalese peasants who were settled in the 'colonies' established under the Gal-Oya project, the then existing Muslim and Tamil village settlements of the Eastern Provinces more than held their own in regard to population growth and agricultural productivity. Indeed, thirty years after the Gal-Oya project was initiated, the Sinhalese are very much a minority of the population there, as the official census of 1981 would show (see Table 2.1).

Table 2.1 Ethnic composition of the Gal-Oya settlement, 1981

	Sinhalese	Tamils	Muslims
Left bank system	61,451	42,114	18,200
Right bank system	12,084	5,975	19,436
River division	3,228	41,085	110,119

Source: Department of Census and Statistics, Government of Sri Lanka.

Furthermore, and here we quote the geographer Professor G. H. Peiris,

> The sparsely settled interior of the Eastern Province of Sri Lanka was not a hinterland of the settlement cluster of the littoral and . . . there is no empirical basis for a theoretical assertion that because there was a numerical preponderance of the Tamils in the coastal areas, the inland areas, regardless of the traditional rights of other ethnic groups, should form a 'traditional hinterland' of the Tamil areas.[13]

V: Retrospect

The 'traditional homelands' of the Tamils theory has, as we have seen, several versions. One of these, as propounded in the TULF's election manifesto of July 1977, speaks of these regions as 'exclusively the homeland of the Tamils'. This claim to exclusivity has caused profound concern among other ethnic groups in the country, indeed more concern than other variants of this theory because of its implications: nearly 30 per cent of the land area of the country and over half of its coastline, with its marine resources, to be reserved for a minority who constitute only 12.6 per cent of the island's population in their entirety. The share of the national resources thus claimed is grossly disproportionate to their numbers *vis-à-vis* the rest of the population, and even more so when two other factors are considered.

Tamil politicians and publicists who protest against alleged Sinhalese encroachments into the 'traditional homelands' of the Tamils have seldom shown any sensitivity to the grievances of the Kandyan Sinhalese over the massive presence of Indian—almost entirely Tamil—plantation workers, a process of demographic transformation which is historically of very recent origin, and one which converted parts of the core area of the old Kandyan kingdom into a poly-ethnic community; in some areas, for example in the Nuwara Eliya district, the Indian Tamils far outnumber the local Sinhalese population. Tamil politicians of the Federal Party and the present TULF see no contradiction in advocating the preservation of the 'traditional homelands' of the Tamils from Sinhalese encroachment while at the same time championing the cause of Indian Tamils settled in Sinhalese areas by British planters, meeting a demand for cheap, regimented labour on the plantations which the local population was unwilling or reluctant to meet. Population increase through immigration of Indian labour was actually greater than natural increase of population during some decades of the late nineteenth and early twentieth centuries. Most if not all of these immigrants moved into the Kandyan areas to the tea and rubber plantations there.

Secondly, there is the demographic reality of a vital Tamil presence in other parts of the island: 29.2 per cent of the Sri Lankan Tamils lived outside the Northern and Eastern provinces in 1971; this figure had increased to 32.0 per cent at the 1981 census. The Tamil areas of the North are poor in economic resources, and since the late nineteenth century have exported labour, generally skilled labour and professionals, to the Sinhalese areas and especially to Colombo city and its suburbs. There are, in fact, more Tamils in Colombo and its suburbs than in the town of Jaffna.

And finally, from the 1930s, when the regeneration of the dry zone of the ancient Sinhalese kingdom—the core of which lies in the present North Central province—and its peripheral regions began on a systematic basis, the Tamils who lived to the north and north-east looked upon this process of economic development with a mixture of fear and anxiety. The ebbing of the jungle tide that had submerged this region for centuries, and the moving frontier of Sinhalese settlement represented, or were seen to represent, a potent threat to the majority status the Tamils enjoyed in the north and some parts of the north-east of the island.

These fears and anxieties became more pronounced after independence and lie at the heart of the myth-making connected with the political pressure for a demarcation of a region or regions as the 'traditional homelands' of the Tamils. That pressure ignores the facts of history as well as the hard economic reality that the forests of these regions could not serve forever as a buffer between the two ethnic groups, the one—the Tamils—anxious to preserve their ethnic dominance of these regions, and the other moving in to do battle with the forests and the anopheles mosquito in a historic return to the heartland of the hydraulic civilizations of old. Resources of land and water are scarce in all the dry zone regions and the preservation of an uninhabited no man's land in the face of unprecedented population pressure is as unreasonable as it is inequitable. Moreover, as Professor Peiris points out, while 'state-sponsorship' has 'admittedly been a vital element in land settlement schemes', this was necessarily so because such schemes

> were meant for the poorest segment of the population—the landless peasantry. But neither in this nor in state responses to . . . encroachment [on state lands] do we find any evidence of discrimination against the Sri Lanka Tamils.[14]

Political myths such as the 'traditional homelands' of the Tamils theory, like any other myth, meet a social purpose, the emotional needs of a people facing rapid change in their fortunes and a perceived threat to their identity. Their capacity to believe in such myths will not be diminished by demonstrations by scholars that the supporting evidence provided is flawed and full of contradictions. The myths will survive; they will change; change will transform them, and even transmogrify them, especially where such myths—like the one we have analysed here—are not peripheral to, but integral parts of, the ideology of a political party, or in this instance, of political parties claiming to represent the interests of an ethnic group.

Notes

1. There were, in all, between thirty-two and thirty-five such units in the period 1815 to 1832. These were reduced to five.
2. For discussion of this see, K.M. de Silva, *A History of Sri Lanka*, London, Berkeley and Delhi, 1981, pp. 315–26.
3. I have discussed this in greater detail in *'Traditional Homelands' of the Tamils of Sri Lanka: A Historical Appraisal,* Kandy, International Centre for Ethnic Studies, Occasional Papers, No. 1, 1987.
4. See the *Journal of the Royal Asiatic Society (Ceylon Branch)* hereafter *JRAS (CB),* n.s. vol. 3 (1954), pp. 125–52.
5. Ibid., p. 131.
6. Most of the documents relating to the years 1976–7 are printed in the Appendix to K.M. de Silva, *Managing Ethnic Tensions in Multi-Ethnic Societies: Sri Lanka, 1880–1985*, Lanham, Md, University Press of America, 1986.
7. There is no evidence of any extensive Tamil settlements in the island earlier than the tenth century AD. Permanent Tamil settlements in parts of the north of Sri Lanka became fairly extensive only in the eleventh century AD. See, K. Indrapala, 'Early Tamil Settlements in Ceylon', *JRAS (CB)*, vol. 13 (1969), pp. 43–63.
8. The discussion here is based on P.A.T. Gunasinghe, *The Tamils of Sri Lanka,* Colombo, 1985, pp. 92–94, and Tikiri Abeysinghe, ed., *A Study of the Portuguese Regimentos of Sri Lanka at the Goa Archives*, Department of National Archives, Colombo, n.d., published probably in 1984, pp. 8–9.
9. See K.M. de Silva, *Managing Ethnic Tensions,* op. cit., pp. 114–23.
10. S. C. Canagaratnam, *Monograph of the Batticaloa District of the Eastern Province, Ceylon,* Colombo, The Government Press, 1921, p. 102.
11. Ibid. p. 2.
12. This monograph was published as a special issue of the *JRAS (CB)*, n.s. vol. 6 (1963), pp. 1–232.
13. G.H. Peiris, 'An Appraisal of the Concept of a Traditional Tamil Homeland in Sri Lanka', a mimeographed paper presented at a conference on 'The Economic Dimensions of Ethnic Conflict in Sri Lanka', 8 August 1985, Kandy, Sri Lanka.
14. Ibid.

Select bibliography

K.M. de Silva, *Managing Ethnic Tensions in Multi-Ethnic Societies: Sri Lanka 1880–1985*, Lanham, Md, University Press of America, 1986.

——, *The 'Traditional Homelands' of the Tamils of Sri Lanka: A Historical Appraisal.* Kandy/Colombo, International Centre for Ethnic Studies, Occasional Papers No. 1, 1987.

Satchi Ponnambalam, *Sri Lanka, the National Question and the Tamil Liberation Struggle,* London, Zed Press, 1983.

Sinha Ratnatunga, *Politics of Terrorism: The Sri Lanka Experience*, Canberra, International Fellowship for Social and Economic Development Inc., 1988.

S.J. Tambiah, *Sri Lanka, Ethnic Fratricide and the Dismantling of Democracy*, Chicago, University of Chicago Press, 1986.

3 THE DYNAMICS OF SEPARATISM: THE CASE OF SRI LANKA

S.W.R. de A. Samarasinghe

Sri Lanka's Sinhalese–Tamil ethnic conflict is a good example of what Wood calls 'a process of dynamic interaction and cumulative effect . . . occurring in stages'.[1] The first stage of the conflict was associated with a Tamil demand in 1937 for constitutionally-guaranteed power sharing at the centre.[2] This was not conceded and in 1949 the demand shifted to separatism — the creation of a federal state with considerable autonomy for the Tamil areas.[3] By 1976, when separatism had also not been realised, the demand was raised to secession — the establishment of a separate Tamil state 'Eelam'.[4] The demands in the first two stages were articulated by peaceful and constitutional means. But the third stage gradually transformed itself into a guerrilla war with acts of terrorism to which the Sri Lankan government responded with a military campaign and repressive measures. After almost eight years of fighting that caused much bloodshed and loss of property, India directly intervened in 1987. Developments since then indicate that the Tamil separatist movement has reached a fourth 'post-secessionist' stage and is apparently willing to give up the demand for a separate state in favour of a high degree of autonomy for the Tamil areas. These four stages were the product of the interaction of a complex set of factors. The first two stages were associated with factors almost exclusively internal in origin and peaceful in nature. The third and fourth stages were associated with increasing violence and were interrupted by external factors in a decisive manner.

Much has been written on the first three stages of the conflict.[5] However, it is only now that we can begin to analyse the fourth stage initiated through the Indo-Lanka Peace Accord and the Indian military intervention that brought the Indian Peace Keeping Force (IPKF) to Sri Lanka in July 1987. The importance of understanding this latest stage of Sri Lanka's ethnic conflict extends beyond the specific case study at hand. For sometime now political theorists have speculated on two major issues in ethnic conflict theory. One is the role of foreign intervention in ethnic conflicts[6] and ethnic civil wars.[7] The other is the nature of the post-secessionist state.[8] On both these issues Sri Lanka offers interesting empirical evidence but subject to one important qualification: that is, as of early 1990, the situation in the north-east is far from settled. The Indian forces who were deployed in the region were withdrawn in full in March 1990. This led to the collapse of the provincial administration run by the Eelam People's Revolutionary Liberation Front that was elected to office in November 1987 with the backing of the Indians. The principal Tamil separatist group, the Liberation Tigers of Tamil Eelam (LTTE), who fought the IPKF and also opened talks with Colombo in April 1989, have taken control of the two provinces on the departure of the Indians. The LTTE has not yet officially renounced its secessionist aims although in their talks with the Sri Lankan government they indicated that they were willing to settle for something less than a separate Tamil state and participate in the electoral process.

The rest of this chapter will be organised as follows. The first section will provide the essential background information to understand the situation that prevailed in July 1987 when the Indians intervened. The second section will discuss the principal factors that internationalised Sri Lanka's ethnic conflict and eventually led to the Indian intervention. The third section will describe the principal developments after July 1987. The fourth will analyse the post-1987 developments and the fifth will discuss some implications of the Sri Lankan case for the understanding of separatist movements in general.

I. Background

Population

About 74 per cent of Sri Lanka's population (total 16.9 million, end of 1989) are Sinhalese and 18 per cent are Tamils: another 7 per cent are Muslims and the balance of 1 per cent belong to small minority groups such as Burghers (Eurasians), Malays, Parsees, Borahs and Sindhis. The Tamils have two distinct sub-groups. One comprises the Sri Lankan Tamils, who account for about two-thirds of the total Tamil population have lived in Sri Lanka from ancient times. The Tamil secessionist movement sprang from this group. The other one-third of the Tamils are usually described as 'Indian' or 'Plantation' Tamils, a reference to their historical origins and their principal occupation. These people originally came to the island from South India, starting about 1830, to work in the coffee and later tea and rubber plantations opened by the British. The Indian Tamils, the majority of whom live in the central and south-western parts of the country, have not been directly involved in the secessionist movement.[9]

Territory

By the early 1980s the Sri Lankan ethnic situation fulfilled almost every textbook precondition—geographic, cultural, economic, political and psychological—to develop a strong separatist movement among the Tamils. A separatist movement must have a territory that they can claim as their own. The Tamils in Sri Lanka have such a territory. About 72 per cent of the Sri Lankan Tamils and a little less than 10 per cent of the plantation Tamils live in the northern and eastern provinces of Sri Lanka that cover about one-third of Sri Lanka's land area. Almost 70 per cent of the population of this region is Tamil. Hence the Tamils claim the north and east as a 'traditional homeland'.

Culture

This geographic divide between the Sinhalese and Tamils has been reinforced by a cultural cleavage. One facet of this is the religious divide. About 94 per cent of the former are Buddhist and 85 per cent of the latter are Hindu. The divide is also partly linguistic: the Sinhalese speak Sinhala, an Indo-European language, and the Tamils speak Thamil, a Dravidian language. However, it must be stressed that there is no significant racial difference between the two groups. Moreover, as Obeyeskere notes, at the level of popular culture and religion the two groups have much in common.[10] Nevertheless, from the time of the Buddhist 'revival' in the late nineteenth century the Buddhist majority among the Sinhalese have been driven by a strong sense of Sinhala-Buddhist consciousness and identity.[11] Although somewhat neglected by many observers—who often blame in some measure the Sinhala-Buddhist consciousness of the Sinhalese for the present conflict—a powerful Hindu-Tamil consciousness also developed in parallel from about the same time. The revival associated with both religions was partly against a common foe, the Christian missionaries. However, the Buddhist revivalist movement also assumed an anti-imperial political character that persisted even after the departure of the British. But after independence it challenged local forces, such as the Roman Catholic church, which were perceived to be a threat to Sinhalese-Buddhist progress. The key issue, however, was language. In 1956 Sinhalese was made the official language replacing English. In practice, of course, the Tamil language, which was spoken by one-quarter of the population, was used as a working language in public administration (especially in the Tamil districts), judiciary, school education and higher education—to which it was entitled as the language spoken by one-quarter of the population.[12] Moreover, a series of legal enactments culminating in the

1978 second Republican Constitution gave legal legitimacy to the official use of the Tamil language which even Tamil observers considered reasonable.[13] These, however, did not fully assuage the Tamils. The inadequacy of resources—shortage of clerks proficient in Tamil, shortage of Tamil typewriters, etc.—to facilitate the use of the Tamil language in administration became a grievance. More importantly the use of Sinhalese as the official language was seen by the Tamils not only as a means of denying them opportunities of government employment but also as an instrument of cultural oppression and a denial of Tamil identity. Thus linguistic nationalism, in combination with several other issues in dispute described below, not only caused the two groups to drift apart after Independence, but also served to overshadow the intra-ethnic divisions that in earlier times made the two groups less monolithic and even helped forge inter-ethnic bonds. Thus, today, the Buddhist–Christian division among the Sinhalese and the Hindu–Christian division among the Tamils matter less. Of course, there are occasions when the ethnic factor is overridden by other considerations. For example, in 1987 a predominantly Sinhalese synod of the Anglican church chose a Tamil priest to be its head. However, in general, when compared to the situation some years ago, Sinhalese Christians and Tamil Christians have drifted apart just as much as the English-speaking elites in the two groups have.

University places

Overlying the primordial differences in language, culture and religion were three major 'secondary' issues that were highly contentious and were also linked to a greater or lesser degree to economic privilege and political power. One of these was the intense competition for relatively scarce university places.[14] In the late 1960s the Sri Lankan Tamils claimed about 40 to 50 per cent of the places in the science-based faculties, engineering and medicine in particular. There were good reasons for this situation. The Jaffna peninsula had a superior secondary-school system matched elsewhere in the country only by Colombo. The Jaffna Tamils had built a tradition of employment in white-collar and technical jobs in the government and private sectors and in the professions, for which a good education was essential. For the Jaffna youth a major incentive ('push factor') to pursue an education came from the shortage of agricultural land and other suitable avenues of employment in the densely-populated peninsula.

Whatever, the objective conditions might have been, basically, the Sinhalese believed the disproportionate allocation of university places for Tamils to be the outcome of Jaffna having a superior secondary-school system, a legacy of colonial Christian missionary work.[15] Of course, those who made this assertion often neglected to point out that Colombo, a predominantly Sinhalese city, also had equally good secondary schools although they catered for a smaller proportion of the Sinhalese population than did the Jaffna schools for the Tamils. In any event, the Tamils attributed their relative good performance in education to factors such as superior intelligence and talent, higher motivation and a stronger work ethic. Thus from the Sinhalese perspective, changing the rules governing, say, university admissions, was to compensate for disparities in educational facilities so that the outcome would be more equal. The Tamils, however, rejected all such steps as manoeuvres designed to discriminate against them. For example, the remedy adopted by the government in 1970 to correct the ethnic imbalance in university admissions was to fix a higher minimum mark for Tamil-speaking students and a lower mark for Sinhalese-speaking students. Thus, in that year the minimum aggregate mark to gain admission to the medical faculty for a Tamil-speaking candidate was 250 and for his Sinhalese-speaking counterpart 229. In 1971 this was replaced by language (and subject) standardisation. This also generally had the effect of requiring a Tamil-speaking student to get a higher minimum aggregate mark than the Sinhalese-speaking student to gain admission to the university. Beginning in 1974 a district quota-system based on population was added to the system of selection. The net result of these changes was to cut the Tamil share of the admissions to science-based faculties from nearly 40 per cent in 1969 to less than 20 per cent in 1974–5. Standardisation was abolished in 1978 by the newly installed Jayewardene administration. District quotas, however, were retained and are still in operation. The district quotas place candidates seeking admissions from both Jaffna (almost entirely Tamil) and Colombo (mainly Sinhalese) at a disadvantage. However, this system has had the support not only of the majority of Sinhalese outside Colombo but also of the Tamils in the north and east outside the peninsula, where educational facilities are poor.[16] Since 1978 the Sri Lankan Tamil share of admissions to the science-based faculties has fluctuated around 25 per cent of the total. This may be a reasonable share for a population group that is only about 12 per cent of the total. However, the events of the 1970s had already done irreparable damage in alienating the Tamil youth, who felt cheated by the government in their efforts to acquire higher education.

Employment

In employment the contentious issue related to jobs in the state sector. Here again, in brief, until about 1960 the Tamils did have a share considerably in excess of their population ratio. This was true not so much of the total share, which probably did not exceed 20 to 25 per cent, but of certain key categories (such as clerks) and professions (such as doctors and engineers).[17] Tamil concern in this matter first arose when Sinhalese was made the official language in 1956, because the lack of Sinhalese proficiency would automatically exclude them from government service. In addition to the language barrier, there were other factors that made it harder than in the past for Tamils to get government jobs. One was increasing competition from the Sinhalese, who also qualified in ever-increasing numbers due to better education. Another was the increasing politicisation of recruitment to state employment, especially to government corporations, which today account for about one-third of total state employment excluding the nationalised tea and rubber estates. Politicisation of recruitment favoured the supporters of the party in power and that inevitably excluded the bulk of the Tamils, especially in the peninsula.

By the mid 1980s, Tamils (excluding estate workers) accounted for about 12 per cent of those employed in the government and government corporations.[18] Their representation in the security forces was minimal and in the police only about 5 per cent. Overall the Tamil share in state employment definitely declined after 1960 and the fear was that if the declining trend of Tamil recruitment continued their share in state employment would drop below their percentage in the population.

Land

The land issue is concerned with the official settlement of Sinhalese families in the 'traditional Tamil homeland' in the north and especially in the east. Since about 1930, in addition to official settlement through the allocation of state land for cultivation, such colonisation has also attracted a large number of informal immigrants. The net result has been a significant change in the ethnic population balance in Trincomalee and Ampara districts in the eastern province. In Trincomalee the proportion of Tamils declined from 53.2 per cent in 1921 to 33.8 per cent in 1981 and that of the Sinhalese increased from 4.5 per cent to 33.6 per cent. In Ampara the Tamil percentage declined from 30.5 per cent to 20.1 per cent and the Sinhalese percentage rose from 8.2 per cent to 37.6 per cent. The Tamils strongly objected to this on several grounds: first, that they have a prior claim to land in their 'homeland' areas; second, that they would be swamped by the Sinhalese; third, that it would alter the electoral balance in these areas against them; fourth, that a homeland in which the Tamils predominate will give them security from ethnic violence.

The Sinhalese for their part do not accept that the Tamils have prior claims, let alone an exclusive claim to any part of the country, especially the east. Moreover, it is asserted that given an acute land shortage in the south and a relative abundance of land in the north and east it is economically justified to alienate land to the landless irrespective of ethnic considerations. Research done by G. H. Peiris and K. M. de Silva shows that the claim of a homeland in the eastern province outside a relatively narrow coastal strip cannot be sustained on historical, geographic or demographic grounds.[19] Nevertheless, the homeland concept remains as one of the most powerful driving forces of the Tamil separatist movement.

Movement towards secession

Given the geographical separation, the cultural cleavage and the economic grievances, the political marginalisation that took place over three decades and the psychological insecurity that the periodic anti-Tamil violence generated fulfilled all the preconditions to give rise to a powerful Tamil separatist movement. Several attempts were made in the past, most notably the Bandaranaike–Chelvanayakam Pact of 1957, the Dudley Senanayake–Chelvanayakam agreement of 1965 and the District Development Councils of 1980 to reach a political accommodation on the ethnic issue. However, for various reasons,[20] none succeeded. On the contrary the Sinhalese and the Tamils embarked on a collision course fuelled, on the one hand, by ethnic violence in 1956, 1958, 1977, 1981 and 1983, when Tamils were the principal victims of Sinhalese mob violence, and, on the other, by the growth of politically-motivated violence by secessionist groups in the north after 1972, but especially after 1980.

Not surprisingly, most Sinhalese and Tamils have different perceptions of the political process that led to the current situation. Many Sinhalese believe that they were the original settlers of Sri Lanka and that they have only that country to preserve the Sinhala culture, language and Buddhism. They also assert that the Tamils have Tamil Nadu in South India. The Sinhalese deny that they want to discriminate against the Tamils. However, most Tamil demands are seen as unreasonable ones that, if granted, would either make them a privileged minority (e.g. conceding one-third of the country as a Tamil homeland while Tamils enjoy full citizenship rights elsewhere also) or help preserve real or imaginary existing privileges (such as a disproportionate share of university places or government jobs), which they have inherited partly owing to colonial historical circumstances.[21]

The Tamils naturally take a diametrically opposite view. To them much of what has happened since 1948—Sinhalese as the official language, university admissions, land settlement, periodic outbursts of ethnic violence, etc.—represents a process in the relegation of their status to that of a second-class citizenry. They consider that peaceful protests and attempts to promote a federal solution to the problem in the past have failed because of Sinhalese intransigence and political opportunism.[22] It is true that the Tamil name for the Federal Party (FP, formed in 1949—the leading Tamil political party from 1956 until the Tamil United Front (TUF) was formed in 1974 with the FP as the major constituent party) was Ilankai Thamil Arasu-Kadchi, meaning Ceylon (Sri Lanka) Tamil State Party, which implies a secessionist position from almost the beginning of Independence. However, the party officially switched from separatism to secession only in 1976, when the Tamil United Liberation Front (TULF, formed in 1976, of which the FP was a constituent party) adopted the now famous Vaddukoddai resolution[23] in May 1976 that resolved to establish a separate Tamil state of 'Eelam'. In the 1977 general election the TULF requested the electorate to give it a mandate for 'Eelam'. The electorate in the Northern province overhwelmingly endorsed the TULF position giving it 68.9 per cent of the total poll and all fourteen parliamentary seats in the province. In the Eastern province, however, they contested only nine out of a possible twelve seats, polled 32.3 per cent of the total provincial vote and won four seats.

The 1977 general election proved to be a decisive turning point in the evolution of Sri Lankan ethnic politics. For the first time in Sri Lankan parliamentary history a Tamil political party—TULF—emerged as the principal opposition in parliament. Thus the TULF secured the important position of Leader of the Opposition for its leader, A. Amirthalingam. The significance of this lay in the fact that, contrary to what had happened in the past, when the opposition was dominated by a southern party, this time the TULF placed Tamil grievances on top of the opposition parliamentary agenda and made them more central to the national political debate.

After the 1977 general election also the TULF continued to negotiate with the government.[24] The establishment of the District Development Councils (DDC) was the chief outcome of these negotiations.[25]

However, the DDCs failed to satisfy Tamil aspirations, especially that of the militant youth. In the aftermath of the July 1983 violence the TULF departed from parliament due to its refusal to abide by the sixth amendment to the Constitution that required all MPs to swear allegiance to a united Sri Lanka. In effect, the traditional Tamil political leadership lost its formal position in the polity. The militants who increasingly controlled the ground in the north and east with the help of arms filled the leadership vacuum.

II: Internationalisation

After 1977, and especially after 1983, there was an external development in the Sri Lankan ethnic conflict that parallelled domestic developments—that is, it got increasingly internationalised, which (as events were to prove subsequently) was decisive in charting the future course of the conflict. There have been several factors responsible for the internationalisation of Sri Lanka's ethnic conflict. For analytical clarity a distinction will be made between the Indian involvement and the involvement of the rest of the world.

India

The first important factor that led to Indian involvement in Sri Lanka's ethnic conflict was the presence of Indian and 'stateless' plantation Tamils in Sri Lanka. India had been negotiating with Sri Lanka for over forty years to solve the problem of plantation Tamils of Indian origin.[26] The issue was apparently settled through an agreement reached between the two governments in 1964 and 1974. Under the settlement India promised to take 600,000 and Sri Lanka 375,000 plus the respective natural increases in each group. It was not implemented in full over the designated fifteen year (1964–79) period. As a result there remained about 100,000 stateless Tamils who should have applied for Indian citizenship but failed to do so. Moreover, the repatriation of those who acquired Indian citizenship also fell behind schedule. Thus, when ethnic violence broke out against the Tamils in July 1983, the Indian government immediately expressed 'concern' over the safety of its citizens in Sri Lanka. This was compounded by the flow of Tamil refugees from Sri Lanka to India, which, according to one estimate, was over 129,000 by the beginning of 1986.[27]

Secondly, Tamil Nadu—which is home to 50 million Tamils—played an increasingly important role in the Indian involvement. It was known from about the late 1970s that Tamil militants used Tamil Nadu as a base for their activities with the help of rival political factions there.[28] Secessionist activity in India included not only political propaganda from Madras but also fund raising, military training, arms procurement for military and terrorist activity and the planning and execution of terrorist attacks. For example, in July 1984 bombs meant for Air Lanka planes in Colombo exploded prematurely in Madras airport killing thirteen people and injuring many more. Congress (I) the party that was in power in Delhi did not want to antagonise Tamil Nadu by discouraging such activity. Indeed, as spelt out below, Delhi had other reasons not only to encourage but even to arm the Sri Lankan Tamil groups.

The third major factor that drew the Indians into the conflict concerns India's perception of itself as the South Asian regional 'super power' and the expectation that Sri Lanka should conduct its affairs in a manner that would not undermine India's own security and interests.[29] In such a context Sri Lanka's pro-Western and especially pro-US foreign policy actions—e.g. establishment of a Voice of America (VOA) transmission facility, visits by US naval ships, etc.—were perceived as being detrimental to India's interests. Here again, the conflict itself has only served to compound matters. Given Indian hostility, the Sri Lankan government had to rely even more on sources such as China, Pakistan, South Africa, Israel and ex-Special Task Force (STF) training personnel from Britain to strengthen its military capability. India strongly disapproved of such links. Indeed, the Indian perception appeared to be that Sri Lanka's military force should essentially be limited to a token 'ceremonial' army and that the Indian military umbrella would cover Sri Lanka's security needs, if any. Thus even the modest build-up of Sri Lanka's military capability was disconcerting to that country for two reasons. First, although by itself Sri Lanka was a military nonentity, India was worried by the possible development of a Sri Lanka–Pakistan–China axis, especially if the latter were to build up its naval strength in the Indian Ocean at some future date. Secondly, there is always a theoretical possibility, however remote it may be, that the United States might get more involved militarily in Sri Lanka.

Fourthly, there was also an economic factor that lay behind the Indian concern. The liberal economy ushered in by the Jayewardene administration in 1977 stood in direct contrast to the planned Indian model of development. It was a well known fact that following import liberalisation in 1977, Sri Lanka became a significant source of supply of imported manufactured consumer goods, especially durables to India.

Indians came in large numbers to Colombo to buy duty-free goods. This was eventually curtailed by the Indian authorities cutting the foreign exchange allowance for Indian visitors to Sri Lanka. Although hard to quantify, it is believed that smuggling of such goods to India also increased after 1977. In the longer term, having a thriving free market economy so close to its own border would perhaps have made India uncomfortable.

West

The internationalisation of the Sri Lankan conflict outside India, primarily in the West, was aided by several factors. The major factor was ethnic violence of July 1983 and the subsequent civil war, which helped to focus attention on Sri Lanka.

A second factor was the successful publicity campaign of Tamil groups publicising their cause abroad to get international support and sympathy. In this they were helped by several factors. One was the existence of an educated and relatively prosperous Tamil diaspora in the West, who for a long time had been committed to the Tamil cause. Secondly, the leader of the TULF, A. Amirthalingam, who was also the leader of the official parliamentary opposition from 1977 to 1983, used his official status to great advantage to explain the Tamil case abroad, especially to foreign governments.[30]

Thirdly, human rights violations by the Sri Lankan troops and the enactment of laws (for example, the Prevention of Terrorism Act) that were anathema to Western liberal opinion had prompted human rights advocacy groups (such as Amnesty International) and even certain governments (such as Norway) to take an international stand against Sri Lanka. Tamil international propaganda, extensive coverage of Sri Lankan events by the international news media and the general Western sympathy for the 'underdog', all helped to build up international public opinion generally unfavourably to the Sinhalese and the Sri Lankan government. The large and growing influx of Tamil refugees to Western Europe, North America and Australia after 1983 further strengthened the negative image of Sri Lanka and also heightened the concern of the governments of these countries to seek a solution to the ethnic problem to stop the refugee inflow.

Fourthly, several aspects of military operations of the Tamil secessionist groups also helped the internationalisation process. One was their military training activities with other similar groups such as the PLO. Another was the raising of funds for arms by these groups through the smuggling of narcotics, which attracted a great deal of international concern.[31] In addition, certain acts of Tamil terrorism in Sri Lanka that involved foreigners—kidnapping an American couple, the Allens, and an English journalist, Mrs Willis, in Jaffna and the bombing of an Air Lanka plane in May 1986—also served to internationalise the issue.

Fifthly, the Sri Lankan government and Sinhalese expatriate groups conducted counter-propoganda abroad to create a favourable image of the country. This was particularly important because the government had to retain the goodwill of the aid donors on whom it depended for funds.

Finally and most importantly, two factors combined to provide India with a specific opportunity to intervene directly in the Sri Lankan conflict: one was the situation that developed in the north-east following the July 1983 communal violence; the other was the recognition—despite diplomatic protestation from Colombo—by the Western powers, most notably the United States and the Soviet Union (but not China and the other South Asian countries), that Sri Lanka must settle the conflict with India's assistance. This, in effect, diplomatically legitimised Indian intervention in Sri Lanka.

III. Developments after July 1983

The Tamil militants were fragmented into several groups. Many were mutually antagonistic for reasons of ideology, regional affinities, caste and competition for leadership and power. The LTTE (Tamil Tigers), the group that eventually emerged as the most powerful militarily, gradually established its dominance in the north, especially in the Jaffna peninsula. Sri Lankan military operations in Tamil areas that aggravated the sense of Tamil grievance and the antagonism among the Tamil community caused by the July 1983 ethnic violence enormously helped the LTTE to tighten its grip on the north. From early 1985 the Sri Lankan troops in the Jaffna peninsula were forced to confine themselves to barracks and to get their supplies by air. The LTTE effectively ruled Jaffna and ran a sort of civil administration of their own.

In the east the Sri Lankan government still had a considerable measure of control. The troops were mobile and the best that the Tamil militants could do was to resort to hit and run guerrilla tactics. The LTTE had no significant base in the east, where the most powerful group was the Eelam People's Revolutionary Front (EPRLF).

Indian intervention

Between 1983 and 1987 the Jayewardene administration concentrated on building up the strength of its military forces.[32] By early 1987 the government felt sufficiently confident to launch a major attack on LTTE positions in the Jaffna peninsula. In May government troops initiated a major campaign in the eastern (Vadamarachchi) division of the peninsula. President Jayewardene publicly declared that it would be a 'fight to the finish'. Within about two weeks of launching the attack the Sri Lankan forces overcame LTTE resistance and were on their way to taking Jaffna town. It was at this point that India directly intervened. The Indians first tried to send supplies to Jaffna in a flotilla of fishing boats but it was turned back by the Sri Lankan navy. However, within twenty-four hours the Indians reacted to this snub with an air drop of supplies by the Indian air force, which violated Sri Lankan air space. The real purpose of the Indian action was to publicly signal that Colombo would not be permitted to vanquish the Tamil separatists militarily. Indeed, it is now known that the Indian High Commissioner (Ambassador) in Sri Lanka informed the Colombo government that India would intervene militarily if the Sri Lankan offensive in the north continued. Thus, an ethnic dispute that started as a purely domestic quarrel was converted into an international dispute involving Sri Lanka's powerful neighbour.

Once Colombo realised that India stood in the way of a possible military victory over the separatists, it decided to seek a negotiated settlement. Direct negotiations between Sri Lanka and the Tamil separatists held in 1985 in Thimphu with India acting as an intermediary had failed largely because both sides were unwilling to shift from their respective initial negotiating positions. So it was that in July 1987 India and Sri Lanka came to a direct agreement, signing the Indo–Lanka Peace Accord. The separatist groups were not signatories to the Accord. India was supposed to have obtained their informal consent to the Accord's terms that were underwritten by India. This, however, proved to be too optimistic an expectation.

Peace Accord

The Peace Accord had two basic components to it. One was a set of clauses that essentially protected Indian regional security interests. In essence Sri Lanka promised not to take any steps that would be prejudicial to India's security.[33] The second set of clauses attempted to provide a framework for the settlement of the ethnic conflict. The Accord, *inter alia*,

(1) affirmed that Sri Lanka was a multi-ethnic and multi-lingual state;
(2) committed the Sri Lankan government to the establishment of a system of provincial councils with devolved powers;
(3) temporarily combined the northern and eastern provinces into one administrative unit (an arrangement that could be made permanent if approved by a referendum in the east);
(4) stipulated that both sides should cease hostilities within forty-eight hours of the agreement being signed and that the separatists should surrender their weapons within seventy-two hours.

Simultaneously with the signing about 6,000 Indian troops (IPKF) were brought to Sri Lanka to assist the Sri Lankan government to collect arms from the militants. The Accord and the arrival of the Indian troops, especially, were bitterly resented by many, probably the majority, of the Sinhalese. The government faced strong criticism from the parliamentary opposition and even from within its own ranks. More importantly, the militant Sinhalese nationalist group the Jathika Vimukthi Peramuna (National Liberation Front—JVP) launched a massive and bloody campaign against the government and others in the south who supported the Accord. Work stoppages and boycotts of classes by school children and university students instigated by the JVP caused serious disruption to the life of the community and especially to the economy. The official figure for JVP killings of its opponents and counter-killings by government vigilantes and security forces between July 1987 and December 1989 totalled over 6,000. But unofficial estimates put the number very much higher.

With the sole exception of the LTTE, the Tamil population warmly welcomed the Accord and the IPKF. The LTTE, whose leader—V. Prabhakaran—was unhappy with the terms of the Accord, refused to hand over all its weapons. The relationship between the LTTE and the IPKF quickly turned to one of open hostility. Thus in October 1987 the Indian troops, which within two months had increased to over 40,000, fought a major battle with the LTTE for the control of the Jaffna peninsula. The Indians won the battle but both sides, as well as civilians, suffered heavy casualties. The LTTE withdrew to the jungles of Vavunia to the south of the peninsula and continued to engage the Indians in a guerrilla war that cost the lives of over 1,250 Indian soldiers and nearly 700 LTTE fighters. The original token force of 6,000 eventually rose to over 60,000 and stayed in the north-east for over two and a half years. In time, not only the Sinhalese but also many Tamils came to view it as an army of occupation.

In principle, two theories can be advanced to explain the failure of the

Indians to completely subdue the LTTE militarily. One is that the Indian army was incompetent against a comparatively small but highly motivated and disciplined guerrilla force that was operating in home territory. The other is that the Indians did not want to completely destroy the LTTE and strengthen the hand of Colombo. Some element of the former could have influenced the outcome. However, the latter is the more plausible explanation. The northern jungles of Sri Lanka are not quite impenetrable. Indian army intelligence was aware of the hide-outs of the LTTE leadership and contacted them when necessary. Thus the Indian decision not to liquidate the LTTE was probably a calculated one.

The Sri Lankan government fulfilled its commitments in the Accord by making Tamil an official language, by establishing Provincial Councils (PC), and by temporarily amalgamating the northern and eastern provinces. The elections to the north-east PC held in November 1988 were boycotted by the LTTE. The EPRLF, which now enjoyed Indian patronage, was returned to power in a moderate poll. The referendum in the east to decide whether the north-east link should be made permanent ought to have been held by the end of 1988 at the latest. That, however, was postponed several times and it eventually became unclear whether it ever would be held.

President Ranasinghe Premadasa, who succeeded President Jayewardene, in January 1989 demanded the quick withdrawal of the Indian troops, at the latest by the end of July in that year. India ignored the demand and set its own deadline—end of December—that it then chose not to keep. The new Indian Prime Minister, V.P. Singh, elected to office in December 1989 set a new deadline, end of March 1990, which was kept.

The LTTE, which began to talk to Premadasa from early in 1989, joined Colombo in demanding the Indian withdrawal. Colombo has agreed to an LTTE demand for fresh elections to the north-east PC. The Indians trained and armed a new force—Tamil National Army (TNA)—that supported the EPRLF. Fighting broke out between the TNA and the LTTE in almost every area from which the Indians withdrew. In every instance the LTTE easily won. Indeed it is difficult to see the survival of any opposition to the Tigers. They have ruthlessly destroyed by violent means every group that opposed it including the leadership of the old Tamil parliamentary party Tamil United Liberation Front (TULF).

IV: The aftermath of the Indian intervention

Four major questions arise in the aftermath of the Indian intervention. First, has secession been permanently removed from the agenda as a solution to the ethnic problem in Sri Lanka? Secondly, how decisive was the Indian intervention of July 1987 in influencing the direction in which the conflict has evolved? Thirdly, what are the implications of the events of the past decade for the integration process of the Sri Lankan post-secessionist state of the 1990s and beyond? Fourthly, what possible lessons can we learn from the Sri Lankan experience about contemporary Third World secessionist movements and especially about the role of external involvements in such movements?

End of secession?

Wilson has argued that Tamil secession in Sri Lanka reached the point of no return some time ago and that it would only be a matter of time before *de facto* Eelam becomes *de jure* Eelam.[34] This argument, however, ignores two factors that have stood against Tamils achieving a separate state in Sri Lanka. One is the decisive role of India in the Sri Lankan conflict and the other is the relative strength of the modern state that secessionist movements have to confront. Both these make a separate Tamil state in Sri Lanka less probable.

It is now accepted without dispute that but for India's direct military assistance, Sri Lanka's Tamil separatist groups would not have been in a position to mount a serious challenge to the Sri Lankan security forces. It is also equally true that in signing the Peace Accord India signalled to the Tamils that it would not help them to establish a separate state. For some time now it has been evident that it would not be in India's best long-term interest to divide Sri Lanka and create a Tamil state in the north. For one thing, it would encourage separatists in the Punjab, Kashmir, Tamil Nadu and elsewhere, which might lead to the Balkanisation of India. The division of Sri Lanka would also mean the creation of an anti-Indian Sinhalese state in southern Sri Lanka, which will be prejudicial to India's security.

Given the lack of support from India for a separate Tamil state it is unlikely that the Tamil guerrilla groups would be able to overcome the military strength of the Sri Lankan state by themselves. Thus while both the Indian and the Sri Lankan state had to concede partial victories to the Tamil guerrilla forces neither was compelled to suffer a total defeat. The collaboration between the Indian and Sri Lankan states revealed a mutual interest for self-preservation that overrode the principle of self-determination of an ethnic group.

The above arguments, however, do not imply a return to the pre-secessionist state. The PC system wil institutionalise Tamil separatism short of secession. The major challenge then will be to develop an integrated Sri Lankan polity to fit the new reality.

Integration

The events of the past decade have several implications for the integration process of the post-secessionist Sri Lankan state. The Colombo government and the Sinhalese leadership have come to appreciate the truth, however unpalatable that may be to some sections of the Sinhalese public, that the only way to end the costly civil war[35] and preserve the territorial integrity of Sri Lanka is through a devolved system of government that is acceptable to the Tamils and essentially endorsed by India. While the Indo–Lanka Peace Accord failed in many respects, its provision for the creation of PC will remain as its lasting contribution to the Sri Lankan polity.

Given the painful events of the last decade, Sri Lanka will have to relaunch her national integration process to create a stable polity. Some of the key elements of that process will be the following. First, the Sri Lankan polity is now in the process of redefining its identity at the individual, group and national levels. At the individual level, as a result of the ethnic polarisation that took place in the last decade, the average citizen is more conscious than ever before of his or her ethnic identity. This ethnic consciousness is now reinforced by the creation of the north-east PC with ethnic regional boundaries and by aspects of public policy that use ethnic quotas for the distribution of state land, government jobs and other economic resources.

This heightened ethnic consciousness at the individual level has in turn helped to sharpen group ethnic differences and, in some instances, helped to overcome intra-ethnic division. The rise of Muslim ethnic consciousness and militancy, which has led to the creation of a Muslim political party (Sri Lanka Muslim Congress) and the demand for a separate Muslim regional administration in the east, are examples of the former. The lessening of the traditional Jaffna (northern) and Batticaloa (eastern) Tamil division is an example of the latter. In general, the Sri Lankan polity at the sub-national level will have ethno-centric focal points for the foreseeable future.

At the national level the Sri Lankan government reaffirmed through the Peace Accord that the state was 'multi-ethnic' and 'multi-lingual' and that 'each ethnic group has a distinct cultural and a linguistic identity which have to be carefully nurtured'. This, in effect, says that Sri

Lanka's national identity is a 'multi-cultural' identity as opposed to, say, a Sinhala-Buddhist or Tamil-Hindu identity.

Secondly, partly as a result of the conflict and partly as a result of the passage of time Sri Lanka is now witnessing the birth of a new political leadership. One of the most distinctive features of this new leadership is that for the first time in Sri Lanka's post-Independence history, it is without anybody who was in politics at the time of the transfer of power from the British over forty years ago. On the Sinhalese side the departure of J. R. Jayewardene and the old guard of his party, the UNP, from the political scene at the end of 1988 marked that change. On the Tamil side, largely as a result of the conflict, almost the entire traditional leadership has been replaced by a new set, who have acquired power through the militant separatist movement. The bloody ethnic conflict of the 1980s is a testimony to the failure of the old political leadership to build an integrated Sri Lanka. The challenge facing the new leadership is to succeed where the old elite failed in creating a stable polity within a multi-ethnic framework.

The process of integration of the post-secessionist Sri Lankan state will depend on three main factors, namely centre–province relations, the international environment but, especially, Indo–Sri Lanka relations and the economy. The PCs have provided a basic framework for devolution. However, the key issue of power sharing between the centre and the provinces remains largely unresolved. There are many reasons for this. One is the difficulties that any country would have to face when attempting to reform a strong centralised administration with a one hundred and fifty year old history. Secondly, in a resource-poor country it is difficult to create quickly a new resource base for a new layer of administration. Thirdly, there is political opposition to PC, especially from Mrs Sirima Bandaranaike's Sri Lanka Freedom Party (SLFP), the principal opposition party. Fourthly, and perhaps most importantly, notwithstanding the commitment of the ruling UNP to devolution, neither the ministers nor the bureaucrats are very keen to give up control over subjects that were formerly under their purview. For example, an attempt on the part of some PCs to take over the running of the state-owned bus services—an ideal activity for devolution—has been resisted by the central government.

The District Development Councils (DDC), established in 1981 to devolve power, were ineffective largely because of inadequate funding. The Sri Lankan tax base is almost exclusively under the control of the central government. Therefore Sri Lanka's local authorities and regional administrations have to rely largely on central government grants for funds. In the case of DDC, a shortage of funds was not the only reason that held back the central government from providing more grants. The absence of a strong political commitment to make the system succeed also was an important factor. By 1990 there seemed to be a more genuine commitment to devolution in Colombo. The government allocated Rs 13.5 billion (about 20 per cent of the total central budget) to the PCs for 1990. This was a sizeable amount and a very substantial increase over the Rs 1.5 billion allocated in 1989. However, a significant portion of the 1990 sum is foreign aid earmarked for rehabilitation work in the north-east. As that source dries up the centre is certain to face strong pressure to allocate additional funds to the north-east.

Given the events of the 1980s, the integration process of the Sri Lankan polity can no longer be divorced from the international political and economic environment. Politically, Sri Lanka will have to take into account, as implied in the Peace Accord, more than ever before the 'Indian factor', not only in the conduct of its foreign policy but also in its conduct of inter-ethnic relations.

Economically, Sri Lanka's sagging economy has to be revived for integration to succeed. Economic prosperity will help to ease the ethnic competition for resources. Sri Lanka's future economic prosperity, however, will only partly depend on internal factors. It will also depend on the international economic environment, especially on aid and capital flows and on continuing access to western markets.

V: Conclusions

The Sri Lankan separatist movement illuminates three general propositions raised in theories of ethnic conflict. One is the strength and limitations of external actors in shaping such conflicts. For a third party that got involved in a contemporary separatist problem in a foreign country, India undoubtedly was in one of the strongest positions. Sri Lanka was weak economically, militarily and diplomatically. International sympathy was largely for the Tamil minority on whose behalf the Indians claimed they intervened. The superpowers had no direct interest in the conflict and approved of India's role as 'honest broker'. The proximity of Sri Lanka to India gave the former an enormous strategic advantage. The world at large also ignored the double standards that India adopted in dealing with ethnic conflicts. India has always been quick to protest at the slightest sign of external interference in its own ethnic problems in the Punjab, Assam, Kashmir and elsewhere. But with total impunity it helped the Tamils to develop a separatist movement with a strong military wing that waged a bloody and destructive war in Sri Lanka. On the positive side, India used its military power and the influence it had over the separatists to extract major political concessions from the Sri Lankan government for the Tamils. But India did not approve of secession largely for reasons of self-interest. In that sense it was India that decided whether Sri Lanka's territorial integrity should remain inviolate or not. However, India failed to make all the Tamil groups completely subservient to its own interests. Sri Lankan Tamil nationalism, it appears, had its own local roots with a strong sense of independence. Thus, the LTTE was not prepared to do India's bidding. The Indian experience in Sri Lanka reinforces yet again, as happened in Vietnam with the French and the Americans and in Afghanistan with the Soviets, the limits of the power of external forces in conflict with nationalism.

Secondly, the Sri Lankan case suggests yet again that notwithstanding Bangladesh the odds are largely against secessionists who wish to redraw existing political boundaries to create new states. For various reasons the international community generally disapproves of this as a method of solving ethnic conflicts. As the Sri Lankan case and recent events in the Soviet Union, Philippines, Sudan and elsewhere illustrate, the preferred solution is devolution, a subject which is bound to occupy the centre stage in national integration processes in the 1990s in many ethnically divided societies.

Thirdly, the Sri Lankan study clearly shows the dynamic nature of separatist movements. Under such conditions it is not easy to develop a model that can predict future events with much confidence. However, what is clear is that such a model of ethnic conflict can be made more realistic by incorporating into it the external factors that interact with internal factors.

Notes

1. John R. Wood, 'Secession: A Comparative Analytical Framework', *Canadian Journal of Political Science*, vol. 14, no. 1 (March 1981), p. 109.
2. K.M. de Silva, *Managing Ethnic Tensions in Multi-Ethnic Societies: Sri Lanka 1880–1985*, Lanham, Md, University Press of America, 1986, pp. 103–5.
3. Ibid., pp. 181–2.
4. Ibid., pp. 259–61.
5. Ibid., S.J. Tambiah, *Ethnic Fratricide and the Dismantling of Democracy*,

London, I.B. Tauris, 1986. For a brief account, see C.R. de Silva, 'The Sinhalese–Tamil Rift in Sri Lanka', in A. Jeyaratnam Wilson and Dennis Dalton, eds, *The States of South Asia: Problems of National Integration*, London, Hurst, 1982, pp. 155–74; A. Jeyaratnam Wilson's 'Sri Lanka and its Future: Sinhalese Versus Tamils' in the same volume (pp. 295–312) gives a historical account that is particularly sympathetic to the Tamil viewpoint.

6. See, for example, Wood, 'Secession', op. cit.; and James N. Rosenau, ed., *International Aspects of Civil Strife*, Princeton, N.J., Princeton University Press, 1964.
7. See Harry Eckstein, 'Introduction: Toward the Theoretical Study of War' in Harry Eckstein, ed., *Internal War*, Glencoe, Ill., The Free Press, 1964, pp. 1–32.
8. Wood, 'Secession', op. cit., p. 133.
9. See S.W. R. de A. Samarasinghe, 'The Indian Tamil Plantation Workers in Sri Lanka: Welfare and Integration' in K.M. de Silva *et al.*, eds, *Ethnic Conflict in Buddhist Societies: Sri Lanka, Thailand and Burma*, London, Pinter Publishers: Boulder, Westview Press, 1988, pp. 156–71.
10. Gananath Obeyesekere, 'Political Violence and the Future of Democracy in Sri Lanka', *Internationales Asien Forum*, vol. 15, nos. 1/2, 1984, pp. 39–60.
11. K.M. de Silva, *Managing Ethnic Tensions*, op. cit., pp. 29–37 and pp. 196–206; Kumari Jayawardena, 'Ethnic Consciousness in Sri Lanka: Continuity and Change' in Committee for Rational Development, *Sri Lanka — The Ethnic Conflict: Myths, Realities and Perspectives*, New Delhi, Navrang, 1984, pp. 115–73.
12. K.M. de Silva, 'Rhetoric and Reality: The Politics of Language Policy in Sri Lanka, 1940–1986', Seminar on Ethnicity and Human Rights, Columbia University, New York, 1986 (mimeo).
13. N. Satyendra, 'Language in the New Constitution', *Ceylon Daily News*, 4 October 1978. Satyendra is a prominent Tamil lawyer not associated with the government.
14. C.R. de Silva, 'Sinhala–Tamil Relations and Education in Sri Lanka: The University Admissions Issue — the First Phase, 1971–7', pp. 125–46; and K.M. de Silva, 'University Admissions and Ethnic Tension in Sri Lanka: 1977–82', both in Robert B. Goldmann and A. Jeyaratnam Wilson, eds, *From Independence to Statehood: Managing Ethnic Conflict in Five African and Asian States*, Pinter Publishers, London, 1984, pp. 97–110.
15. There is another more controversial factor. I refer to the widely-held belief among the Sinhalese of alleged favoritism shown by Tamil examiners towards fellow Tamils. (The University admissions test is held in the Sinhalese and Tamil languages.) An official committee that once enquired into this in regard to mathematics examination could not find any evidence to substantiate this allegation. However, such allegations have been made in respect of other instances also (see for example, *Diabolical Conspiracy*, undated pamphlet published by Karandeniye Wimalajothi Nayaka Maha Sthavira). In any event, what is relevant to the conflict is not so much the objective truth or otherwise of this allegation so much as the perception that people have about the issue.
16. It is on official record at the University Grants Commission that Tamil MPs in these areas strongly supported the quota system.

17. See S.W.R. de A. Samarasinghe, 'Ethnic Representation in Central Government Employment and Sinhala–Tamil Relations in Sri Lanka: 1948–81' in Goldmann and Wilson, *From Independence to Statehood*, op. cit., pp. 173–84.
18. *Census of Public and Corporations Sector Employment: 1980, Sri Lanka*, Department of Census and Statistics, Colombo.
19. G.H. Peiris, 'An Appraisal of the concept of a Traditional Homeland', paper presented at the National Workshop on the Economic Dimensions of Ethnic Conflict in Sri Lanka, International Centre for Ethnic Studies, Kandy, 1985 (mimeo); K.M. de Silva, 'Traditional Homelands of the Tamils of Sri Lanka: A Historical Appraisal', ICES, Kandy, 1987.
20. See Wilson in Wilson and Dalton, *The States of South Asia*, op. cit. and K.M. de Silva, *Managing Ethnic Tensions*, op. cit.
21. This viewpoint is articulated most frequently in the popular Sinhalese language press which has a powerful influence on Sinhalese public opinion. For an English version of this viewpoint relating to the homeland issue see Gamini Iriyagolla, *Tamil Claims to Land: Fact and fiction*, Institute of Public Affairs, Colombo, 1985. The government itself has published several pamphlets—e.g. Ministry of State, Sri Lanka, *The Truth about Discrimination against the Tamils*, Colombo, 1983—seeking to demonstrate that the Tamils are not discriminated against. A more balanced view of these issues can be found in C.H.S. Jayewardene and H. Jayewardene, *Tea For Two: Ethnic Violence in Sri Lanka*, Crimcare, Ottawa, 1984.
22. Especially since 1983 there has been a large number of publications that present this Tamil perspective. For a somewhat extreme version, see Satchi Ponnambalam, *Sri Lanka: The National Question and the Tamil Liberation Struggle*, Zed Books, London, 1983. For a more balanced version see Tambiah, *Ethnic Fratricide*, op. cit., or Wilson in Wilson and Dalton, *The States of South Asia*, op. cit.
23. See K.M. de Silva, *Managing Ethnic Tensions*, op. cit., pp. 403–6 for the text.
24. Wilson in Wilson and Dalton, *The States of South Asia*, op. cit., pp. 309–11.
25. K.M. de Silva, *Managing Ethnic Tensions*, op. cit., pp. 313–18.
26. S.U. Kodikara, *Indo–Ceylon Relations Since Independence*, Colombo, 1965.
27. S. Guy de Fontgalland, *Sri Lankans in Exile*, Madras, Cerro Publications, 1986, p. 83.
28. Both the Western press (e.g. *The Sunday Times*, London, 1 April 1984) as well as the Indian press (e.g. *India Today*, 31 March 1984, pp. 88–94) reported on this from time to time.
29. See text of speech delivered by J.N. Dixit, Indian High Commissioner to Sri Lanka (1982–88) at the Indian Defence Institute, *Island International*, Colombo, 24 January 1990.
30. Wilson in Wilson and Dalton, *The States of South Asia*, op. cit., p. 308.
31. See, for example, *The Guardian Weekly*, (Manchester, England) 11 August 1985.
32. Government expenditure on the armed forces rose from Rs 560 million (US$52.2 million) or 1.3 per cent of the GDP in 1979 to Rs 13 billion (US$428 million) or 7.3 per cent of the GDP in 1987.
33. Ralph Premdas and S.W.R. de A. Samarasinghe, 'Sri Lanka's Ethnic

Conflict: The Indo–Lanka Peace Accord', *Asian Survey*, vol. 28, no. 6 (June 1988), pp. 676–90.

34. A. Jeyaratnam Wilson, *Break-up of Sri Lanka: Tamil–Sinhalese Conflict*, London, Hurst, 1988.
35. Lee Ann Ross and Tilak Samaranayake, 'The Economic Impact of the Recent Ethnic Disturbances in Sri Lanka', *Asian Survey*, vol. 26, no. 11 (November 1986), pp. 1240–55.

4 THE MORO SECESSIONIST MOVEMENT IN THE PHILIPPINES

Samuel K. Tan

The Moros of the Southern Philippines are engaged in a struggle for an autonomous government in a separate territory. Believing that they are a different people with a unique history and values, they assert that, by the fact of their uniqueness as a nation, they have the right to self-determination. The Moros have sought their objectives for many centuries having endured deprivation, exploitation, and oppression under several alien regimes. In seeking their right to determine their own destiny, the Moros have designed several strategies and have experienced many types of accommodation with their dominant cultures. In this chapter, I begin by discussing the Moros and their values and traditions. From here, I proceed to discuss the evolution of a Moro consciousness over the years of contact with the outside world. Throughout their history, Moro ethnic identity has shifted, picking up Islam along the way and adapting to the challenges of change. The Moro quest has been beleaguered by internal dissension, at times with different factions defining their own tactics, objectives and allies. What is clear, however, is that the Moros want to govern themselves as a separate 'nation' either as part of the Philippines or as an independent entity.

The Moros in tradition and history

For about six centuries from the introduction of Islam around 1280 AD to the present, the Moro has acquired an image that integrates two contrasting perceptions of the Moro personality. Derived from oral and written sources, the imagery aids understanding of the attitudes, values and behaviour of the Moros in relation to themselves, their community and others. From the rich source of oral literature, the Moros are presented in an image of native humanity with the natural instinct to recreate a little of Mother Nature in poetic, musical and artistic expressions. The image varies from one ethnic group to another and adds complexity to the Moro mind and personality.

In ethnic literature, which has been preserved to the present, the Moro moves from one value configuration to another and yet something common runs through the diversity. The Tausug *parangsabil*, an ethno-epic of beauty, glorifies the exploits of a unique individual called the *sabilallah*, from the Arabic which means one who dies for the faith.[1] In the epic, the Moro emerges as a hero seeking death as the only means towards the highest self-fulfilment. His passion to kill those enemies who are not Muslims brings social and spiritual merit. The *darangan*, an epic of sublime passion, is an embodiment of Maranao and Maguindanao imagery.[2] The Moro image in this epic is seen in the hero Bantugan, whose anti-Spanish or anti-colonial struggle is glorified as a mark of heroism and culture.

From the oral literature of the three major groups (Tausug, Maranao and Maguindanao), the Moro image expresses dedicated courage that is indifferent to death. In fact, the oral traditions present the positive image of the Moro as a lover of freedom and a hater of all forms of foreign intrusion and bondage. And yet, there are other equally important types: the man who tends his farm; the woman who patiently grinds the cassava for staple food; the fisherman who paddles his *vinta* to sea; and the artist who sings the *luguh* and the *lolo*, who dances the *pangalay* or *singkl* with colour and grace, and who carves with his knife and stylus *ukkil* (*okir*) or *gulis* designs on his boats, utensils and weapons. The various images of the many Moro personalities simultaneously portray the Moro as a lover of peace, a humanist interested in creativity and a person sensitive to the rhythm of nature and the universe.

This is the Moros' historic image. External influences have distorted it, unjustly to the Moros. But the Moro pride in colonial history has been preserved by the life-giving inspiration of their Islamic roots. The thirteenth century, probably about 1280 AD, marked the beginnings of Islam in the Philippines.[3] A new consciousness was superimposed on the Moro mind in beginning to appreciate what Islam could offer. As the Moros embraced the faith, they at once felt part of a larger world, the *darul islam* which the *ummah* conceptually created. It is anchored on the belief that he who believes in Islam, especially the Five Pillars, becomes a part of a universal body of believers bound only by common spiritual ties. This is expressed forcefully in the *shahada*, the First Pillar: 'There is no God but Allah and Muhammad is his messenger'. At once the Moro consciousness transcended the boundaries of ethnicity and geography and imparted a sense of community otherwise absent in the pre-Islamic societies.

With this new Islamic consciousness and community, the Moros found new meaning in their activities and struggles.[4] But they were not willing to abandon the old ethnic culture entirely. Instead, they blended the two elements and created a folk-Islamic tradition. Their lives revolved around this cultural synthesis. Thus, the new world view of the Moros tied their roots to their environment, while it also provided them with a window to a wider world of new realities.

In their daily life, the Moros were fishermen, farmers and traders, active in the internal trade of the Philippines, particularly between Mindanao-Sulu and Visayas, Mindoro and Manila and in the external trade between Brunei and the Philippines. In their economic activities, the Moros developed seafaring values that made the sea literally their playground and boats their creative and imaginative focus. Thus, they produced remarkable boats and rafts such as the *sappit, kumpit, peland, sakayan, biggung, balanghay, parau, carakoa*, etc., each for their own purposes.[5] They became expert navigators, mastering the currents, the wind and other forces of nature without the benefit of scientific instruments. But they also developed a mystical relation with their environment, attributing to nature a certain supernatural intelligence which they could not really understand. Consequently, by their own creative imagination, they formulated rituals and formulas to neutralize nature's outrages such as the storm, thunder and lightning. The *tawal* and *duwaa* were rituals frequently used to calm the sea, to tame the storm and to salute the thunder. Thus the seafaring life of the Moros developed in them not only a fatalistic attitude to life, but a courage hardened by constant encounter with natural dangers. Brinkmanship became a source of excitement, and risk-taking in the hazards of trade helped to shape the Moro character in a way that has left its mark on the Filipino psyche and Western historiography.[6]

It was at this point in the fifteenth century, when the synthesis of culture had strengthened the *ummah*, that a new political institution entered Moro history. The 'Sultanate', as it was known, emerged formally in 1450 when 'Sheriful Hashim' or Abu Bakr founded the Sulu Sultanate, the first in Philippine history. Then, early in the sixteenth century, about 1511, Sherif Kabungsuan established the Maguindanao Sultanate in Maguindanao, the modern-day Catobato City on the mainland of Mindanao.

This political structure enlarged the Moros' political vision and sense of authority beyond the narrow confines of the datuship or the rajaship. The Moro datu or rajah and his subjects were now subject to the higher authority of the Sultan, whom they readily accepted because he carried a divine mandate under Islam as the 'shadow of God'. This was one of the most important contributions of Islam to the Moro mind. While, therefore, the Moros were zealous of their liberty and individuality, they also acknowledged a higher authority they were willing to obey. This new divine authority, through faith in God, enhanced their freedom and identity. The Sultan's authority was a complement to what they had because it provided them with commitment beyond themselves. In a sense, they found a greater sense of security in a system that unified the independent and often conflicting local chieftaincies into a common loyalty. A new Moro personality that blended their individuality with the *ummat sin nabi* (follower of the Prophet) would confront the challenge of colonialism, taxing the energy and imagination of the Occidental mind.[7]

The Moro in colonial history: 1565–1946[8]

In 1565 the first major challenge to the Moro began. The last Spanish expedition under Miguel Lopez de Legaspi finally succeeded in establishing a Spanish presence in Cebu, where Rajah Tupas and his subjects accepted Spanish rule and were converted to Christianity. It was from this initial inroad that Spain began the conquest of the Moros. Following the conquest of Manila, the Spaniards began to prohibit the lucrative Brunei–Manila trade for economic reasons as well as political strategy, which led to the conquest of Mindanao and Sulu, the homes of the Moro sultanates. So the Moros now had to face Spanish invasions of their homeland, beginning with the expedition under Francisco Sande in 1576 consisting of forty ships, 400 Spaniards, 1,000 Filipinos, and 300 Borneans. This was followed in 1578 by another expedition to Jolo under Captain Esteban de Figueroa and two more in 1579 to Mindanao, Sulu and Borneo under Gabriel de Rivera and Juan de Arce Sardonil. To the Moros whether datu, warrior or serf, the Spanish operations were efforts not only to destroy their economic foundations, but also their political and cultural future in the archipelago.

The Moros responded by retaliatory raids right into the heart of Spanish rule, sparing no villages or community. For the Moros, the period from the Figueroa expedition in 1578 to that of Urbiztondo in 1850 was marked by their successful attacks on the Colonial State. Spanish records of the seventeenth, eighteenth and nineteenth centuries preserved what the Spaniards referred to as *piraterias mohametanas* (Moro piracies). Spoils of raids, especially captives, occupied the imagination of Spanish writers, chroniclers and reporters.

While they spared no effort to destroy their enemy, the Spanish or Christian *kafir*, the Moros were pragmatic traders seeking opportunities to profit from their activities. By the turn of the eighteenth century they had added a new motive for their raids on the Visayas and Luzon, that of the lucrative returns from the slave trade in South-east Asia, as well as the need for farm hands and auxiliary helpers in their own homeland. In this way they combined war and vengeance into the practical realities of commerce and trade. Captives of all sorts were taken; the able-bodied for the farms and labour markets; marriageable women for the slave markets in Batavia (Jakarta) where Chinese, European and native buyers were ready to bid for concubines or domestic slaves; the weak, old and infirm for the human sacrifices of Bornean tribal rituals; and children for adoption in Moro households where they would be culturally integrated as Moros.

But the Moros could only enjoy the luxuries of their values of pride, courage and freedom as long as their mastery of the sea and their homeland remained undisturbed. The moment that reality was changed, as it was by the 1850s, the Moros' character and image also began to change. The introduction of steamboats and gunboats in the last half of the century effectively eliminated Moro control of the sea and ultimately destroyed the Moro fleet. Consequently, the Moro raids on the Christian areas, while still conducted, became increasingly counter-productive. Renewed Spanish invasions of Moroland stopped the Moro raids and forced them to defend their homeland. The destruction of Moro villages, farms and boats crippled their capacity to retaliate. A sense of helplessness filled their consciousness, and their dependence on supernatural powers and charms increased tremendously.

Before long, the Moros found themselves transformed by frustration and anger into fanatical fighters willing to die at any moment for their cause and their faith. By the late nineteenth century, especially after the spoiling campaigns of José Malcampo in 1876, the Moro had become the *sabilallah*, whom the Spaniards called *juramentado* (mentally deranged). It was this image of the Moro as a person seeking nothing but death that dominated the perception of those outside his society, especially the Christian community whose losses from the *sabilallah* were numerous and ghastly. It was this image that was most feared, that subsequently formed the continuing thread in Philippino literature and history in regard to the Moros. It also provided the basis of Christian prejudices against the Moros.

By the turn of the twentieth century, when a new colonial power, the Americans, replaced Spanish rule, the Moros' notoriety was well established. The peaceful trader had become the scourge of the sea preying on vessels flying the colonial emblem. The former lover of nature and natural artist had been changed into a ferocious attacker of Hispanism and Christianity. Even the gentle and passionate Moro women had assumed the warlike posture of their men. But this new image of savagery was not altogether the creation of the Moro. It was largely the imaginative work of the colonial writers, whose interpretation of Moro history and culture had gone unchallenged because the Moros had ignored the development of an intellectual tradition. It was their failure to develop this intellectual tradition that enabled colonialism and neo-colonialism to preserve the prejudice against them and that created the greatest obstacle to Moro aspirations.

So it was that the United States, which succeeded Spain in 1898 as colonial ruler, confronted for the first time the Moro 'savage' as the early American writers described him, putting him on the same level as the North American Indians. What mattered to the Moros, as exemplified by the resistance of Datu Ali in Cotabato (1903–5), Panglima Hassan in Sulu (1903–5), Datu Tungul, Datu Gamour and Datu Ampuanagus in Lanao (1902–3), was the preservation of their homeland and the 'ancient liberties' they dearly cherished.[9] They had already lost their fleet and his economic position in the South-east Asian trade to the Spaniards. Their Islamic faith was under constant threat from neighbouring Spanish missions. But instead of softening, the Moros had become hardened by conflict and had sworn forever before Allah and their mothers' graves to resist every foreign intruder in their homeland. Their fanatical defence of their freedom and independence was the only thing that kept them alive.

When the United States tried to enforce its will in the Muslim South from 1899 on, the Moros resisted fiercely. The Moros lost many lives in the Lanao campaigns from 1899 to 1903, in the operations against Datu Ali from 1903 to 1905, in the Bud Dajo Massacre (1905) and the Bud Bagsak battle (1913), the last decisive conflict. After 1913, the Moros were compelled nominally to accept American rule.

The Japanese invasion of the Philippines in 1941 and the subsequent establishment of a Japanese presence in Moroland were accompanied by unparalleled atrocities which brought about a Moro–Christian united front under American leadership against the 'yellow peril'. Many Moros joined the USAFFE and other anti-Japanese organisations until the enemy was finally ousted in 1945. The Moros contributed their share of sacrifice and the common experiences of the war gave both Moros and Christians reasons to live co-operatively together. But the aims of the earlier Moro independence movements had not been forgotten. Therefore, when the United States proclaimed on 4 July 1946 the independence of the Philippines and transferred sovereignty to the Christian Filipinos, the Moros were faced with a great dilemma: would they now accept a subordinate role under the Christian Filipinos whom they had once regarded with suspicion and misgivings? Would they now abandon their struggle for independence for a prospect that was still ambiguous?

The Moros and Filipino rule after 1946

Like their Filipino Christian counterparts, the Moros were seeking a way to adapt to post-war independence which was more symbolic than real. American economic and military privileges in the post-war Philippines neutralised the gains of Filipino nationalism. The fervour of secessionist agitations from 1946 to 1968 was subdued, often diluted and neutralised by government pre-emptive concessions to traditional leaders. But the growing neglect of the substantive part of Moro societies, especially the improvement of socio-economic conditions, eventually provided the more idealistic Moro youths and professional people with the reason for organising the secessionist movement along traditional patterns.[10]

The 1968 proclamation by Governor Udtong Metalam of Cotabato, a traditional Maguindanao leader, of a Mindanao Independence Movement (MIM) caught the government by surprise. It stressed the need to establish an Islamic State in Mindanao as the only answer to Moro aspirations. Matalam was persuaded by the government to reconsider, and the initiative passed to younger Moros, who organized themselves into the Moro National Liberation Front. Nuruladji Misuari, head of the MNLF, epitomised these new Moro liberationists, the alternative leadership to the traditional form which included Rashid Lucman, who organized the Moro youth in favour of secession in 1969. Lucman later revealed that he parted ways with Misuari because of the latter's ideological leanings.[11] In effect, Misuari's ideology was distinct from that of the traditional leadership.

What was Misuari ideology? It was a synthesis of Islam and Marxism springing from Misuari's own personal and professional experiences. Misuari was born in Cabingaan, Sulu, an isolated island inhabited by Tausug-Samals. Nur, as he is popularly known among colleagues, or 'Professor', to the general Moro public, does not come from the traditional elite.[12] His humble origin forced him to rely on his own resources for his education. But it was actually his years at the University of the Philippines, the State University famous for its role as a breeding ground of all kinds of radicalism, that shaped his mind.

Thus, Moro liberationists, exemplified by Misuari, became modern and formidable foes, no longer circumscribed by the limitations of traditional concepts and strategies which had contributed to the failure of their predecessors.[13] As modern freedom fighters, they could appreciate both the confrontational approach of their forebears and the evasive, elusive, guerrilla strategy of a contemporary people's war. They could see the practicality of the struggle to achieve victory at the least cost. The Moro leadership had learned to value the liberationist concept of a people's war, which recognises above all else the collective interest of the people rather than the personal self-fulfilment of the individual. Whereas before, the Moros would not run away from combat even when confronted by an overwhelming number of opponents, now the Moro liberationists regard discreet retreat or evasion as an equal act of heroism. And yet they are ready to die to achieve the highest collective good. Consequently, they have endeavoured to acquire expertise in the use of modern weaponry, technology and propaganda, including the subtle use of media for their own purposes. They have also come to value the establishment of ties with other movements. In short, the Moros have joined the international ranks of liberationist fighters in the Third World and have acquired international stature. It is this new and international dimension of the Moro struggle that has made Filipino rule more difficult than ever. It is what has made the Moro insurgency, as the Philippine government calls the Moro struggle, potentially explosive.

The Moros today

Today, the Moros no longer stand at the crossroads of history as they did immediately after World War II. They have definitely taken the road to independence, a revolutionary aim that has made secession the choice of the Moro people. The less extreme alternative of internal autonomy, which was agreed upon by the Philippine government and the Moro representatives in the Tripoli Agreement of 1976, was an accommodative measure to allow serious reflection by both parties on Moro–Filipino relations.

Misuari had himself expressed opposition to the internal autonomy provision of the Constitution before the 2 February plebiscite. But the government ignored his demand to suspend that particular provision until after peace talks had been concluded. In effect, the ratification of the Constitution proscribed Moro independence, which was no longer negotiable. This has, therefore, created for the Moro struggle a problem not so much of objectives but of strategy. The Moro National Liberation Front (MNLF) had publicly shown in words and deed that it had taken internal autonomy as a basis for peace talks. This had placed the Misuari MNLF faction on the same negotiating premise as the MNLF Reformist under Dimas Pundato and Macapanton Abbas, and the Muslim Islamic Liberation Front (MILF) under Ustadz Hashim Salamat. It is noteworthy that the three factions represented the three major Moro groups, Tausug, Maranao and Maguindanao respectively.

Moro factionalism has been exploited by certain interests to the detriment of Moro aspirations. Also it has been used by the Moro factions to obtain substantial concessions from the government. But the government, both under the Marcos and the Aquino administrations, has followed the unitary approach to the Moro problem. Marcos concluded the Tripoli Agreement in 1976 with the MNLF under Misuari. The break up of the Moro movement into three has not persuaded the Aquino leadership to discontinue the unitary approach. The factional character of the movement has made it quite difficult for the government to bring about an acceptable solution, thus keeping the problem in a highly fluid state. Moro factionalism has also reduced the armed threat to Philippine security.

Two concepts relevant to the Bangsamoro struggle were declared by Misuari in 1980.[14] These are *gaosbaugbug* and *kaadilan*. The first consists of two specific ideas combined into a whole: *gaos* which means 'ability' or 'capacity' and *baugbug* which means 'commitment', or 'conviction'. By combining the two ideas as a native ideological concept, Misuari has introduced into the MNLF struggle the primacy of the 'capacity to commit' to a cause. On what this commitment is anchored is provided by the second idea expressed in *kaadilan*, which refers to 'destiny', similar in implication to the messianic expectation of the 'Datu Adil'. This second concept, which was declared by Misuari in 1983, refers to the antithesis of all forms of injustices to the Moro people and, therefore, anticipates the ideal state of political economic, social and cultural liberation. This is equivalent, in a sense, to the Utopian future that in the MNLF ideological dissertation is beyond the narrow interests or aims of the state and society. Taken together, *gaosbaugbug* and *kaadilan* form the indigenous ideology of the MNLF, a theoretical attempt to derive a guiding principle from the roots of culture in a folk-Islamic tradition. In short, the Moro today has become a real nationalist who has finally found a real 'nation', a community of people distinct from the Filipino. Undoubtedly the Filipinos oppose this ideology, believing that a Filipino nation had already been formed by history by the turn of the century and confirmed by international treaties. It is precisely this kind of argument that gives much credibility to the Bangsamoro claim for their own nation with its distinct history and culture.

As nationalists, the Moros consider the legitimacy of their community no longer debatable. It is only the strategy to get the Philippine government to accept this reality that interests him. It is this search for the best method that occupies his energies and mind. This sense of nationhood increases steadily as the government fails to satisfy Moro aspirations. How to satisfy Moro claims to self-determination has been the main thrust of both informal and formal talks since the Tripoli Agreement of 1976. What the latest Moro proposal for peace implies in specific terms is the autonomous region enjoying the freedom to have the government it wants and to have its own security force, educational system, economic system, taxation and cultural development programmes in accordance with Moro concepts. What it concedes is merely nominal and ceremonial relations with the Philippine state to show a semblance of national sovereignty. This possibility drastically reverses the system of governance that has kept the country under a very strong central government. As pragmatic secessionists, the Moros are interested in attaining the substance of independence and relegate the form to a subsequent struggle. By this approach, the retrieval of ancient liberties and historic rights can be achieved without bloodshed, and the energies of the modern Moros can be devoted to long-term plans envisioned by the Moro armed struggle. In effect, the fundamental aim of Moro secessionism, however divided their leadership maybe, is recovery of historical losses to colonialism and modern progress, namely: political dominance in the Southern Philippines, the historic homeland of the Moro people; recognition of the Moros as a distinct national entity; a just share of national resources; and security of the Islamic faith from external institutional threat. These four specific goals are the ingredients that fuel the Moro armed struggle.

Undoubtedly, the goals of Moro secessionism are realizable within the context of the 1986 Constitution. There are sufficient provisions (particularly Article X, Section 14–21 on the autonomous regions) providing for a federal system which seems to be the only way of reconciling realistically the imperatives of Filipino national sovereignty and Moro claims for self-determination.

Notes

1. The *parangsabil* of 'Abdula and Putli Isara', sung by Indian Anura of Jolo, Sulu, is a Tausug ethno-epic of 182 quatrains. See Jovita V. Castro *et al*, *Anthology of Asian Literatures*, Quezon City, APO Production Unit, 1985, pp. 219–99. This metrical romance tells of the exploits of a hero and heroine whose fate is determined by the *sabilallah* value of Moro society.
2. The *darangan* is a Moro epic that portrays the heroism of Bantugan as he takes his chance in battle against the Spaniards. See 'Maharadia Lawana' by Juan R. Francisco, *Asian Studies*, vol. 8, no. 2 (1969), pp. 186–249.
3. See Cesar A. Majul, *The Muslims in the Philippines*, Quezon City, Philippines University Press, 1973, p. 60.
4. The nature of Moro consciousness is briefly dealt with in Samuel K. Tan, 'Historical Perspective and Problems of Muslim Autonomy: Some Policy Implications', a paper presented at the First National Scientific Conference on Muslim Autonomy, University of the Philippines, Los Banos, September 1986. A more detailed discussion of historical consciousness is found in Chapter 10 of Tan's *The Filipino Muslim Armed Struggle, 1900–1972*, Makati, Filipinas Foundation, 1978.
5. The different types of Moro craft are treated in Chapter III of Tan's *Decolonization and Filipino Muslim Identity*, PCSS Policy Monograph Series, Number 5, The President's Center for Special Studies, Manila, 1985.
6. For an insight into a specific area of Moro art and the mind behind it, see Mamutua Saber and D.G. Orellana, *Maranao Folk Art: Survey of Forms, Designs, and Meanings*, Marawi City, Mindanao State University, 1973.
7. The political synthesis created by the Islamic and native blend through the Sultanate and datuship or rajaship is treated by Michael O. Mastura in 'The Maguindanao Core Lineage and the Dumatus', *Notre Dame Journal*, vol. 7, no. 2 (1977), pp. 9–24.
8. For an adequate treatment of the Moro response to Spanish colonialism, see Najeeb M. Saleeby, *The History of Sulu* (Manila: Filipinina Book Guild, Inc., 1963) provides good data on the Tausong sector of Moro society. But Majul's *The Muslims in the Philippines*, Quezon City, University of the Philippines Press, 1973, gives a more comprehensive discussion of the three major Moro groups (Tausug, Maguindanao and Maranao). Also James F. Warren gives valuable data for understanding Moro character and institutions in his 'Trade, Raid, Slave: The Socio-economic Patterns of the Sulu zone, 1770–1898', a dissertation submitted for a doctoral degree to the Australian National University in 1975. Chapter VIII on the Iranuns, chapter IX on the Balanguingi, Chapter X on slave markets, and Chapters XI and XII on slavery in the Sulu Sultanate and captive respectively, are particularly useful. For a contemporary observation on secessionism in relation to Mindanao as a whole, see T.S. George, *The Mindanao Revolt*, New York, Oxford University Press, 1980.
9. The Moro armed struggle during the American regime is treated by several

authors among whom are: Samuel K. Tan, *Sulu Under American Military Rule, 1899–1917*, Quezon City, University of the Philippines, 1967, and *The Filippino Muslim Armed Struggle, 1900–1972*, Makari, Filippinas Foundation, 1977; Ralph Thomas, 'Muslim But Filipinos: The Integration of Philippine Muslims, 1917–1946', a doctoral dissertation submitted to the University of Pennsylvania, 1971; and Peter G. Gowing, *Mandate Over Moroland*, Quezon City, University of the Philippines, 1977.

10. The alternative to independence was brought out in 1969 by Alunan C. Glang in his *Muslim Secession or Integration*, Quezon City, R.P. Garcia, 1969.
11. A confidential memorandum from Rashid Lucman to Mr Chasl Tethi Tevetoglu, Assistant Secretary General, Islamic Secretariat of the Islamic Conference of Foreign Ministers, handwritten and undated. The fourteen-page xerox copy of the memo shows every indication that the Late Sultan Lucman of Lanao wrote his sentiments and recommended that the Conference send a delegation to the Philippines and consult with seven Muslim leaders: Senator Ahmad D. Alonto, Justice Mama D. Bursran, Mrs Suraida A. Tamano, Mayor Amikadra Abubakar, Atty. Michael Mastura, Datu Abdul Yahiya, and Atty. Findausi Abbas.
12. The author personally knew Nur Misuari as a colleague at the then College of Arts and Science, University of the Philippines. In October 1979 the author had the opportunity to see and talk with Nur Misuari during the international conference on the Green Book at Bengazi, Libya. The MNLF Leader, after exchanging pleasantries, strongly affirmed the need to continue the armed struggle.
13. The ideas, concepts and strategies of Misuari are best expressed in several papers which carried his by-line. The most important are: 'The Final Struggle of the Moro People' (1973), 'Appeal to the Islamic World for Support of the Moro people in the Southern Philippines' (1975), 'Setback to Peace Initiative in South Philippines' (1977), 'A Note on the Flight of Muslims in the Philippines' (no date), 'Speech Before the 11th Islamic Conference' (Pakistan, 1980), 'The Bangsamoro Revolution' (1981), and 'The Danger of Future Accommodation, the Imperative For a New Political Strategy of the Bangsamoro Problem' (1984).
14. For a statement of these concepts, see Misuari's 'MNLF Guidelines: For Political Cadres and Military Commanders', *Selected Documents for the Conference on the Tripoli Agreement September 12–13, 1985 of the Philippines*, Law Complex, University of the Philippines, Diliman, Quezon City, 1985, p. 145.

5 BANGLADESH: THE FIRST SUCCESSFUL SECESSIONIST MOVEMENT IN THE THIRD WORLD

Harun-or-Rashid

In the process of nation-building, newly independent Third World countries face secessionist challenges from their minority communities. While secessionist movements are many, successful ones are rare. Forces for separation are both internal and external. Though external assistance from a superior power may be important for success, as in the case of India's role in Bangladesh's independence, the internal factors create the objective conditions for its conception, growth, rise and maturity. The aim of this chapter is to examine the internal dynamics of the Bengali secessionist movement.

Bangladesh (former East Pakistan) presents a unique case where the majority Bengalis fought a war of liberation against the minority West Pakistanis to form a separate state. Earlier the Bengalis had played an indispensable role in Pakistan's struggle for independence (1947) from British rule. Bangladesh's emergence as a sovereign state through the break-up of Pakistan raises many questions: why did the Bengalis, who extended their total support for the Pakistan ideal in the 1940s, break up the same Pakistan in 1971? Was the attempt to make Urdu, a language alien to the Bengalis, the only state language of Pakistan, a mistaken Pakistani policy? Why did the power elite of Pakistan fail to respond to the political demands of East Pakistan for majority rule and autonomy? How far did the differing social structures of the two regions of Pakistan inhibit their permanent unity? Did the strategy of economic development and nation-building followed by the power elite of Pakistan compound the problem of political accommodation between West Pakistan and East Pakistan? Was the emergence of Bangladesh inevitable? This chapter examines these questions which point to the disintegration of Pakistan and the emergence of Bangladesh.

A Bengali view of Pakistan

The socio-economic setting of Bengal was different from that of other provinces in India. Though at the beginning of the twentieth century the

Bengali Muslims emerged as the majority community of the province, most lived in poverty. Their appalling backwardness relative to most Hindus extended over all important aspects of life—administrative, social, educational and economic; in trade and commerce, in agriculture, in the professions and services. In Bengal's peasant economic structure, while the large majority of cultivators comprised the bulk of the Muslim community, the *zamindars* (landlords) and *mahajans* (money-lenders) were mainly but not exclusively Hindus. The interests of the backward Bengali Muslim community were in conflict not only with those of the minority Hindu community, but also with those of the non-Bengali Muslims, particularly the privileged minority Muslims of Uttar Pradesh (UP) who were at the helm of the All-India Muslim League and the Pakistan movement. With the gradual betterment of the Bengali Muslim community and with measures towards self-government by the British, the Bengal Muslim peasantry and sections of the petty bourgeoisie supported the League, the platform of the Muslim middle class and landed oligarchy, and its Pakistan ideal, i.e. partition of India and the creation of a separate homeland for Muslims.[1] They wanted to emancipate themselves from exploitation by the *zamindars* and *mahajans*. In other words, their immediate aim was to get rid of Hindu domination. However, the ideal of a leading section of the Bengali Muslims, headed by Fazlul Huq, H. S. Suhrawardey and Abul Hashim, was completely different from Jinnah's for a single united Pakistan. In 1944, the Bengali Muslims developed the ideal of an independent Eastern Pakistan in Bihar based on the 1940 Lahore Resolution, which they understood to recognise sub-national variations of the north-east and north-western parts of India as it then was.[2] This section of the leadership was proud of its language and culture, remaining alive throughout the League and the Pakistan movement to the distinct identity and interests of the Bengali Muslims compared with the non-Bengali Muslims outside Bengal. The abortive move by H. S. Suhrawardy, the last chief Minister of undivided Bengal, for a united, independent and sovereign Bengal,[3] preceding the 1947 partition, brought the Bengali Muslims into Jinnah's Pakistan.

Internal colonialism

In spite of the formidable role of the Bengalis in the achievement of Pakistan and their numbers (the Bengalis constituted 54 per cent of the total population of Pakistan), they came under the domination of the non-Bengali Urdu-speaking Muslims in the new state. This was inevitable, since the Bengali Muslims did not have effective representation in the leadership of the League, now the party in power, in the pre-Pakistan period.[4] Thus, the capital of the state and the headquarters of the defence forces—army, navy and air, could be safely seated in West Pakistan as the non-Bengali power elite decided. The number of non-Bengali businessmen grew in Dhaka. Administrators and soldiers arrived from West Pakistan. All key posts in the East Pakistan Secretariat down to the sub-divisional level were occupied by Urdu-speaking Muslims.[5] It was true that there was a historical reason for the imbalance between the Bengalis and the West Pakistanis in their share in the civil and military bureaucracy,[6] but the discriminatory policies pursued by the central government from the start were detectable which continued till the disintegration of Pakistan (see Table 5.1). A feeling of

Table 5.1 Pakistan: East-West shares in the higher administration and military command, Pre-1971

	East		West		Total	
	No	%	No.	%	No.	%
1955						
Secretary	–	0.0	19	100.0	19	100.0
Joint Secretary	3	7.3	38	92.7	41	100.0
Secretary	10	7.5	123	92.5	133	100.0
Under Secretary	38	6.9	510	93.1	548	100.0
Army	14	1.5	894	98.5	908	100.0
Navy	7	1.2	593	98.8	600	100.0
Air Force	60	8.6	640	91.4	700	100.0
1963						
Army		5.0		95.0		100.0
Navy		5.0		95.0		100.0
Air Force		17.0		83.0		100.0
1969–70						
Secretaries	3*	15.0	17	85.0	20	100.0
Army Generals	1†	2.9	34	97.1	35	100.0

*Acting
†Major General

Sources: 1955 and 1963 from Rounaq Jahan, *Pakistan: Failure in National Integration*, Dhaka, University Press, 1972, pp. 25–6 and p. 62; 1969–70 from Talukder Maniruzzaman, *The Bangladesh Revolution and Its Aftermath*, Dhaka, Bangladesh Books International, 1980, p. 10.

becoming 'a colony of western Pakistan' grew rapidly among the Bengalis,[7] exacerbated by the cultural-linguistic policy of the ruling elite. Despite the fact that the Bengalis comprised the majority of Pakistan's population, and not even 1 per cent of the Bengalis spoke Urdu, the Pakistani ruling elite made the declaration that 'the state language of Pakistan was Urdu and no other language'.

Economically, East Pakistan was exploited by the western wing on the classical colonial pattern. East Pakistan was the largest producer of jute—'the Golden Fibre'—in the world, which accounted for a large portion in Pakistan's foreign exchange earnings. It also produced other exportable items such as tea and leather. Most of the traders and exporters of these products were West Pakistanis. They purchased these goods cheaply in local currency while they earned foreign exchange through exports. In turn, these profits were invested in the industrial and commercial sectors in the west. The peasants of East Pakistan were deprived of a fair price for agricultural products and regionally, East Pakistan was reduced to a 'bazaar' (market) for West Pakistani manufactured goods. No effective steps were taken for import substitution in East Pakistan. There was diversion of capital from East Pakistan to the West though the former had a surplus in international trade. The foreign trade balance from 1948–9 to 1966–7 showed that East Bengal's cumulative surplus amounted to 4,878.7 million rupees. Yet during these nineteen years East Bengal had a deficit trade balance of 5,712.1 million rupees with West Pakistan.[8] In development expenditures under the Second (1960–5) and Third (1965–70) Five Year Plan, while the share of the East was 31 per cent and 36 per cent respectively the share of the West was 69 per cent and 64 per cent respectively.[9] Thus the Bengalis, who fought for the achievement of Pakistan's independence, soon came to discover that 'they had emerged, thanks to Pakistan, from a position of subordination to Bengali Hindus—only to find themselves in a new kind of subordination of Karachi and Lahore'.[10]

It can be seen that the people of the two wings of Pakistan had different ethnicity, history, tradition, language, and culture, precedents and practices, and social stratification. The main problem of nation-building in Pakistan was the creation of the common Pakistani nationhood integrating the Bengali sub-national category. Although Jinnah's Two Nations theory was presented as the ideological basis of Pakistan and 'Pakistani nationhood', for the Bengali Muslims it had a different meaning. They considered the Two Nations theory as a strategic framework to forge unity among the divergent Indian Muslims in their fight for self-determintion against the common enemy—the Hindus or Congress. The only points of unity between the Bengali and non-Bengali Muslims were a common religion and a shared fear of Hindu domination in a United India.[11] Even so, during the League/Pakistan movement, there was the occasional manifestation of sub-national sentiments among the Bengali Muslims leading them into conflict with the non-Bengali Urdu Muslims, though it remained low-key when compared to the fear of Hindu domination. With the removal of that fear, the other underlying controversy, language, came to the fore. Pakistan was suffused with the language controversy from its very inception.

In politics, a party may play a significant role in integrating regional, ethnic and linguistic centrifugal forces while developing a common point of unity in programme and ideology. Although the Pakistani ruling elites inherited the Muslim League, they did not attempt to transform it from a nationalist movement into a viable national party by adopting a pragmatic socio-economic programme with organisational networks in both wings down to the lowest level of society. Rather, they favoured reducing the League to a Sarkari Dal (government party) whose only aim was to support government policy and whose survival became solely dependent on government backing. This was essentially because of the colonial character of the Pakistani ruling regimes, who believed that the civil-military bureaucracies, and not the party, were instrumental in ruling the country. Indeed, in the given socio-economic setting of Pakistan, coupled with its geography, the founding of a national party representing inter-regional interests seemed to be a difficult task. Pakistan came into being as a geographical absurdity with two wings separated by more than one thousand miles of Indian territory. It seemed to be a 'double country',[12] making mass mobility difficult and hindering socio-economic interactions. Geography inhibited the idea of a single country in the minds of the people belonging to both wings. The Islamic bond of unity was not effective enough to hold the two separate parts together. It required something tangible if it were to remain united.

The Bengalis' demand and the centre's responses

As will be seen below, in the Pakistani polity the demands of the Bengalis and the responses made to them by the centre did not lead to accommodation but confrontation. The language controversy came first. Although the Bengalis' demanded that their language be made one of the state languages of Pakistan along with Urdu, the Pakistani ruling elites did not agree until they were forced to do so by the blood of the Bengali language martyrs in February 1952. While Bengali was given recognition as one of the state languages of Pakistan in the 1956 Constitution, slogans and symbols were already created which set fire to the imagination of every patriotic Bengali. From the rising middle class among the Bengalis and educated youths, the language issue received the attention and vigour of a crusade, not simply because the Bengalis are 'intensely attached to and proud of their language,[13] but also because their material advancement (jobs, etc.) was closely connected with it.

The question of representation was another important subject involving conflicts between the two wings of Pakistan. While the political, commercial, industrial, military, bureaucratic and cultural leadership was in the hands of West Pakistanis, the Bengalis were favoured only by numbers. In order to turn their numbers into political power, the Bengalis persistently opted for a parliamentary form of government based on the principle of 'one man, one vote'. Mainly as a result of this debate, the making of the Constitution was delayed for nine years, strengthening the grip of central civil-military bureaucratic control.

The West Pakistani power-elite arbitrarily established parity in representation in the National Assembly (Parliament) between the two wings to curb the political power of the Bengalis. They also unified the four regional provinces in the west into 'one unit' in 1955. After the crushing defeat of the Muslim League in the 1954 elections in East Pakistan at the hand of the United Front,[14] although the Bengali counter-elites formed a ministry in the province under Fazlul Huq (the veteran Bengali leader), the ministry was dismissed within fifty-six days of its assumption of power by the centre. In late 1956, when H. S. Suhrawardy formed an Awami League-Republican coalition ministry at the centre, which was followed by the installation of an Awami League-led government in East Pakistan, the aspirant middle-class Bengali began to feel a sense of participation in the Pakistani polity. For the first time, an equal number of ministers were taken from East Pakistan for the Central Ministry. Certain steps were undertaken to redress the disparities between the two wings of the country. However, Suhrawardy was unable to stay in power for more than a year, mainly because of the hostility of West Pakistani civil-military bureaucracies and commercial interests.[15] The abrupt dismissal of the United Front ministry and the fall of Suhrawardy's coalition only exacerbated anti-West Pakistan feelings among Bengalis. The military take-over under General Ayub

Khan in 1958 formalised the political dominance of the civil-military bureaucracies, meaning total control by the West which lasted till the disintegration of Pakistan. Although Ayub attempted civilianisation of his regime in presenting a new Constitution to the country in 1962, it did not suggest any change in the bureaucratic nature of the regime with a regional bias and in the pattern of relationship between the two wings. Ayub's attempt to counterbalance the urban elites by elevating his 80,000 Basic Democrats to social and political positions and giving them leadership only served to alienate the counter-elites in East Pakistan, hardening their mood against West Pakistani domination.[16] Finally, the Bengali claim to the right to decide policy matters involving the relationship between the two wings of Pakistan, as expressed in the landslide victory of the Awami League in East Pakistan in the 1970 general elections, evoked a wild military response from General Yahya Khan's military junta in March 1971.[17] In fact, the resort to a 'military solution' of the political dilemma to escape from internal colonialism had become unavoidable.[18]

The demand for regional autonomy was another bone of contention in the Centre–province relations in Pakistan. The initial demand of the Bengalis for regional autonomy was directed towards established majority rule in Pakistan, a popular government in the province and cultural autonomy. The central government all along stood for a strong centre, trying to give the impression that this alone could hold the two wings of Pakistan together.[19] Meanwhile, political realism demanded the adoption of a 'unity in diversity' approach, and certainly not centralisation or unitarism, if Pakistan were to remain united. In other words, in Pakistan a strong centre with concentration of powers meant a weak bond of unity between its two wings. The domination by West Pakistani political elites, civil-military bureaucracies and commercial interests or, in a word, the perpetuation of West Pakistani colonial rule required the centralisation of power in the name of a strong centre and so-called national integration.

In the absence of competitive democracy, lack of a sense of participation among the Bengali petty-bourgeoisie, and the colonial pattern of exploitation of East Pakistan by the West, the Ayub period (September 1958 to March 1969) contributed largely to radicalise the Bengali demand for autonomy.[20] In fact, Ayub's 'decade of development' may be termed a 'decade of mounting frustration' among the Bengalis. The Awami League's six-point programme (1966)[21] came as the Charter of Rights and Self-preservation for the Bengalis after the fashion of the Lahore Resolution (1940), arousing the same amount of enthusiasm among them as the Pakistani cry for independence did in the 1940s. Even so, within a shorter time (five years) than the Lahore Resolution (seven years), the ideal of the six-point formula had been crystallized. Striking at the roots of internal colonialism in the most articulate way, the programme took everybody by surprise, causing a revolution in the mind of the Bengalis. While in the pre-Pakistan days the Bengali Muslims were united against the Hindu domination, this time the Bengalis—both Muslims and Hindus—united against the domination by West Pakistan. The Awami League emerged as the embodiment of the Bengali nationalist movement.

The differing social structures and the question of unity

Pakistan began with a basic social imbalance between its two wings. This was the outcome of a long historical process including deliberate policies. Further, the migration that occurred following the 1947 partition had a bearing on the different social formation of both parts of Pakistan. During the British colonial rule, the Muslims from the west received preferential treatment in recruitment to the army and civil bureaucracy and this continued in the post-Pakistan period. They also owned land. The Hindus who occupied influential positions among the commercial and professional men left for India at independence. Meanwhile, a group of Muslim entrepreneurs and trading people from minority provinces in India migrated to Pakistan and settled in the west, the land to which they were for long culturally attached, and where they found very congenial infra-structures and the political support.

The eastern wing had a different experience. As seen above, the Bengali Muslims were essentially a peasant community. Most Hindus owned and controlled land. With the partition of India, which further entailed Bengal's partition, most Hindu *zamindars* (some of whom were already absentee landlords in Calcutta) migrated to West Bengal, now in India. The flight of the Hindu *zamindars* was complete following the passing of the East Bengal Tenancy Acquisition Act in 1950 which abolished the *zamindari* system. These two events caused a power vacuum in the East Bengal society and this soon came to be filled by the *jotedars* (i.e. rich peasants) among Muslims.[22] Because of Pakistani internal colonialism and the absence of state patronage, they were unable to turn themselves into industrialists. Their sons were sent to colleges and universities for higher education, where they became involved in student politics. At the end of their student life, they began their career as professionals, college and university teachers, government employees, etc.

Thus, while the civil-military bureaucracy, the commercial-industrial gentry and the landed oligarchy, who also composed the power elite of Pakistan, constituted the dominant social forces in the west, the professionals and other petty bourgeoisie comprised the dominant forces in the East, with the peasantry and the working men commanding the large majority of the population at the lowest level of Bengali society.[23] In a study of the occupational background of the members of the Central and Provincial Assemblies in Pakistan during the period from 1947 to 1958, it was found that while 68 per cent of the members in East Bengal were drawn from professional groups, a similar percentage of members in West Pakistan were landlords.[24]

It can be seen that there was virtually no integrative structures covering both wings of Pakistan. The situation was further aggravated by the geographical incontiguity. The dominant social structures of the Pakistani polity were regionally based (coming from the west). The conflict between the Bengali and the West Pakistani power elite was the result of their conflicting socio-economic and political interests emanating from the uneven social structures of the two wings and it could not be resolved within the existing social order.[25] In the given situation, the adoption of the growth-oriented economy pursued by the Ayub regime only contributed to widening the disparity between the two wings.

Conclusion

Some scholars, like W. H. Morris-Jones, K. B. Sayeed, Rounaq Jahan and G. W. Choudhury, say that Pakistan might have been saved if the rulers had not resorted to the 'military solution'.[26] This thesis, however, is untenable. It was not a matter of choice on the part of the Pakistani rulers; rather it was the only course of action they could have adopted in their attempt to 'safeguard' the existing relationship between the two parts of Pakistan.

As far as the unity of the country was concerned, things could not have been improved even if power were transferred to the Awami League on its victory in the 1970 elections. The Awami League was also a regionally-based party. It is true that a transfer of power to it would have meant the coming into power of the aspirant Bengali petty bourgeoisie. However, they might have soon come into conflict at the state level with the (West) Pakistani power elites who were not in a position to allow any effective sharing of power by the rival Bengali petty bourgeoisie because of their own need for monopoly of the state power for self-aggrandisement. Thus, a political crisis and showdown would have been inevitable.

In fact, the differing social structures, the regionally-based nature of the power elite of the state, the abnormal geography and the strategy of economic growth and development of the capitalist economy as adopted by the Pakistani rulers ruined the prospect of permanent integration of the two wings of Pakistan. All these have been proved totally uncongenial to the growth of an integrated national political party, a pervading ideology as a common basis of nationhood. While nation-building requires the development of one overall political culture, in the case of Pakistan there was nothing like a national political culture. Rather the conflict between its two wings involved the conflict between their differing political cultures. In view of this condition, it can be held that the disintegration of Pakistan and, thus, the emergence of Bangladesh was inevitable. The short-sighted West Pakistani leadership only accelerated the process.

Notes

1. For example, in the 1946 elections, which were virtually a referendum for the Muslim League on the issue of Pakistan, the League achieved the most astounding of its victories in Bengal capturing 114 seats (94.21 per cent) out of 121 with 87 per cent of the Muslim votes cast, being able to form a government on its own. Meanwhile, the League was able to capture only 17 seats (47.2 per cent) out of 36 in the NWFP securing 50.20 per cent of the votes cast and it secured 74 per cent of the votes in the Punjab. It also initially failed to form a government in Sind and the Punjab. For details, see Harun-or-Rashid, 'Problems of Organisation, Policies and Mobilization in the Development of the Bengal Provincial Muslim League, 1936–1947', PhD Thesis, University of London, 1983; also see Talukder Maniruzzaman, *The Bangladesh Revolution and its Aftermath*, Dhaka, Bangladesh Books International, 1980, p. 4.
2. For details, see Harun-or-Rashid, 'Problems of Organisation' op cit., pp. 216–32.
3. Ibid., pp. 307–70.
4. Ibid., pp. 279–82; also see Maniruzzaman, *The Bangladesh Revolution*, op. cit., p. 5.
5. Talukder Maniruzzaman, *Radical Politics and the Emergence of Bangladesh*, Dhaka, Bangladesh Books International, 1975, p. 32.
6. *Indian Statutory Commission Vol. 1, Survey*, London, HMSO, 1930, pp. 96–7; Talukder Maniruzzaman, *Group Interest and Political Changes: Studies*

of Pakistan and Bangladesh, New Delhi, South Asian Publishers, 1982, p. 5.
7. Begum Shaista Ikramullah's speech in *Constituent Assembly of Pakistan Debates*, II, No. 1 (24 February 1948), p. 7.
8. Maniruzzaman, *The Bangladesh Revolution*, op. cit., p. 1. Further, over 80 per cent of all foreign aid obtained during the period 1947–70 was utilised in West Pakistan. Over two-thirds of all imports over the same period went to the West.
9. Rounaq Jahan, *Pakistan: Failure in National Integration*, Dhaka, University Press, 1977, p. 13.
10. W.H. Morris-Jones, 'Pakistan Post-Mortem and the Roots of Bangladesh', *Political Quarterly*, vol. 18 (April–June 1972), pp. 187–200.
11. Abdul Hashim, *In Restrospection*, Dhaka, Mowla Brothers, 1974, p. 23; also see Hashim's speech in *Star of India*, 2 February 1945, p. 2; Suhrawardy's interview with the correspondent of *Hindu*, quoted in *Star of India*, 17 September 1946, p. 3; also M.S. Rajan, 'Bangladesh and After', *Pacific Affairs*, vol. 45, no. 2 (1972), p. 191.
12. Richard Weeks, *Pakistan: Birth and Growth of Muslim Nation*, Princeton, NJ, Van Nostrand, 1964, p. 3.
13. Jahan, *Pakistan*, op. cit., p. 85.
14. While the Muslim league won only nine seats (about 27 per cent of votes) out of 237 Muslim seats, the United Front obtained as many as 223 seats with nearly 64 per cent of the votes polled.
15. See K.B. Sayeed, *The Political System of Pakistan*, Boston, Houghton Mifflin, 1967, pp. 192–3; also K.B. Sayeed, *Politics in Pakistan: The Nature and Direction of Change*, New York, Praeger, 1980, pp. 45–6.
16. See Talukder Maniruzzaman, 'Crises in Political Development and the Collapse of the Ayub Regime in Pakistan', *Journal of Developing Areas*, vol. 5 (1971), pp. 221–38; also see Jahan, *Pakistan*, op. cit., pp. 109–26.
17. In a National Assembly of 300 members the Awami League captured 160 seats out of 162 allocated to East Bengal.
18. See Asaf Hussain, 'Ethnicity, National Identity and Praetorianism: The Case of Pakistan', *Asian Survey*, vol. 16, no. 10 (1976), pp. 918–30.
19. See Mohammad Ayub Khan, *Friends, Not Masters*, London, Oxford University Press, 1967, p. 192; also see the view of the leading West Pakistani political parties on the strong centre in Zillur R. Khan and A.T.R. Rahman, *Autonomy and Constitution Making: The Case of Bangladesh*, Dhaka, Green Book House, 1973, pp. 83–162.
20. For details, see Maniruzzaman, *Radical Politics*, op. cit., pp. 30–7; also see Jahan, *Pakistan*, op. cit., pp. 143–77.
21. See the six-point programme in Maniruzzaman, *Radical Politics*, op. cit., p. 36.
22. See Ram Krishna Mukkherjee, 'The Social Background of Bangladesh', in Kathleen Gough and Hari P. Sharma, eds, *Imperialism and Revolution in South Asia*, New York, Monthly Review Press, 1973, pp. 399–418.
23. For details, see Hamza Alavi, 'The State in Post-Colonial Societies: Pakistan and Bangladesh'; and Feroz Ahmed, 'The Structural Matrix of the Struggle in Bangladesh'; both in Gough and Sharma, eds, *Imperialism and Revolution*, op. cit., pp. 145–73 and 419–44 respectively.
24. Maniruzzaman, 'Crises in Political Development', op. cit., p. 227.

25. See Hamza Alavi, 'Bangladesh and the Crisis of Pakistan'; and Tariq Ali, 'Explosion in South Asia'; both in Gough and Sharma, eds, *Imperialism and Revolution*, op. cit., pp. 289–317 and 449–65 respectively.
26. See W.H. Morris-Jones, 'Pakistan Post Mortem' op. cit.; K.B. Sayeed, *Politics in Pakistan*, op. cit., pp. 66–9; Rounaq Jahan, *Bangladesh Politics: Problems and Issues*, Dhaka, University Press, 1980, pp. 26–48; G.W. Choudhury, 'The Last Days of United Pakistan — A Personal Account', *International Affairs*, vol. 94, no. 2 (1973), pp. 229–38.

6 THE KAREN REBELLION IN BURMA

Ronald D. Renard

Background

Burmese often urge that one of the failings of the British when they governed Burma* was that they ruled by the principle of divide and conquer. The Burmese mean that the British gave minorities, such as Karens, Kachins and Shans, advantages over the Burman majority. For example, although Burmans were not recruited, generally, into the armed forces, special inducements were used to attract Karens and Kachins into these forces. According to Burmans, this was to keep them weak and the British in power: one of the results being the outbreak of many ethnic rebellions after Burmese independence in 1948, the most serious of them by the Karens.

Similarly, many British colonialists criticised the traditional government of Burmese kings as one of divide and conquer. By this the British meant that the Burmese rulers had broken down the Burmese population into small discrete groups who were kept from banding together in their own interest. According to the British, one result was that the Burmese have not progressed to the full extent possible.

Both contentions are only partly valid, however, since the British and Burmese did not use these terms to denote the same thing. Burmese kings certainly wanted to keep minorities weak but they well understood that their neighbours in traditional Burma shared what Edmund Leach called a ritual language and did not attempt to separate the ethnic groups within the kingdom of Burma (Leach 1964: 279). The British, however, believed that these groups were unassimilable and kept Karens apart from Burmans, who in turn were kept distant from Kachins, and so on. Although this may have impeded Burmese nationalism (one of this policy's purposes), the generally Anglophile minorities seemed to support British rule and the strengthening of their respective positions.

One trend characterising British rule was the breaking down of Burma's ethnic fabric into distinct threads. Believing the laws of progress and development universal and immutable, the British assumed that once they had studied the ethnic groups in Burma they could rule, say, the Karens and Burmans, as separate entities. The British failed to comprehend the 'and' connecting Burmans and Karens just as they misunderstood the unity of Shan–Kachin life. This gap in understanding made their entire effort suspect. One result has been the Karen rebellion which started in 1948 and now shows little sign of ending, partly due to this newly imparted sense of ethnicity.

The Karens

One of the first groups the British encountered when they came to the Tenasserim in the early eighteenth century were the Karens. They were well-versed in swidden cultivation (farming by frequently shifting, slash-and-burn methods), and grew a considerable amount of the produce sold in the local markets. In 1826, a British official recorded that 'The Karians . . . are the wandering races, who prefer the independence of the woods to the restriction of towns . . . The Karians supply the markets with ivory, wax, honey, sesame oil, cardamoms and other articles' (Blundell to Sudden Board 1839: 186). Hill Karens also worked teak, for which they were assessed for 10 per cent tax which was generally remitted after paying 5 per cent to the local officials. The Burmans taxed upland Karens 15 rupees per family per year, by which is meant per longhouse, and lowland Karens, who grew rice were taxed 18 rupees per yoke of buffaloes per year (Wilson 1827: xiv). Burma Delta Karens made canoes which they sold for what the British said was a very low price. A British account notes that the Karens are 'sober and industrious, of peaceable disposition, but not devoid of courage. They have no religion, nor law, peculiar to themselves, and encourage the Burman priests to settle amongst them to educate their children' (Wilson 1827: xlvi).

Accounts such as this represent the first solid evidence we have of Karens. Old inscriptions in the Pagan refer to groups of Cakraw and Plaw that may well be the Sgaw and Pwo sub-groups of the Karen but this has not been proved. Similarly, the Karens have many old stories, but they too have not been confirmed by independent sources.

The effect of this official attention on the Karens, besides the general policy of separating Karens from neighbouring groups, helped in developing a separate Karen identity. This trend was aided by thousands of Karens, mostly Sgaws, becoming Christians.

In 1828, the American Baptist missionary, Adoniram Judson, converted one of his servants, Ko Tha Byu, whom Judson had bought out of slavery. Instrumental in the conversion were similarities between

Karen tales and Old Testament stories, as well as the likeness of the name of the Karen god, Ywa, with the Hebrew Yahweh. The personalities of Judson and other missionaries, including Ko Tha Byu, also contributed to evangelist success. Perhaps more significant was that many Karens identified the Caucasian missionaries as their long-lost younger brothers bearing the golden book of Ywa, which a legendary Karen ancestor had carelessly lost, thus forfeiting the chance to be an advanced people. This convinced many Karens that Christianity was appropriate to them and conversions to the new faith grew rapidly. As a result, but also because many Karens saw Christianity as a means of escaping their traditional lot, thousands converted to Christianity. Quite a few Karens became so inspired that they set out to convert other Karens, and even Kachins—whom Karens at first had considered as their brethren. Most Karens remained rural farmers but some began moving into cities. From this start, Christianity among the Karens in Burma grew rapidly; the Bible was translated, education was provided to many Karens and a Karen script was devised. Similarities between Old Testament stories and Karen legends, such as of a world-wide flood, and a lack of knowledge that such stories are found in almost all folklores of the world led missionaries to believe that Karens were one of the lost tribes of Israel.

Although the main proponent of this notion, the American Baptist missionary, Francis Mason, later changed his mind, thinking instead that Karens learned such accounts from Jews in China, many Karens began reinterpreting their history. Some Karen-language accounts then had Karens coming from the Middle East or other unlikely scenarios.

In so doing, many Karens began adopting a new sense of identity. From non-ethnic self-identification, rooted in (and well described by Leach) their own socio-cultural role *vis-à-vis* neighbouring groups, a new definition of Karen emerged in the mid-1800s. They began taking up instead the traditional Western concept of an ethnic group—a racially distinct group of people with a set of shared customs and ancestry. Similarly, they began to see the Burmans ethnically. Instead of the considerable assimilation of Burman and Karen which occurred in the traditional Burma, these new definitions, based on shared ancestry within each group, severely impeded assimilation.

Although not understanding that as a part of this process, Karen self-identity was changing in nature, the Burmans were irritated by it. Accustomed to thinking of themselves as the elite Buddhist city-dwellers and of Karens as the less auspicious non-Buddhist lower-status forest dwellers, some Burmans feared a fifth column. One official objected;

> This is the way you do it . . . is it? You come and fight us and get away part of our country, and now you wish to turn away the hearts of the poor ignorant Karens . . . If you gave these books [religious literature] to the Burmese who know too much to be carried away with their nonsense it would be no matter; but what do the poor ignorant Karens know? [Carpenter 1883; p. 27]

Regardless of Burman objections, when Karens became Christians and new opportunities opened up, they received a modern education. With the new Karen scripts, a Karen literature began and, for the first time known, certain Karens began producing written records.

As Karens in Burma became better educated they wanted to know more about their roots, and many Karens sought to unite the various (traditionally disunited) Karen groups into a more compact unit. Towards this end, in 1881, a group of Karens, mainly Christians, formed the Karen National Association (KNA), the title coming from the phrase, *Daw k'lu*, the whole race. The purpose of this association was to give Karens a national platform on which all Karens could unite.

The KNA became militarily active after the Third Anglo-Burmese War of 1884–6 when many Burmans took revenge on Karens whom they accused of being British lackeys. Through the KNA, Karens procured British arms enabling them to resist most Burman retaliation that continued for a number of years after the end of the war. A Baptist missionary noted, 'I never saw the Karens so anxious for a fight . . . This will put virility into our Christianity' (Smeaton 1920: 13–16). This encouraged many Karens to seek a state of their own. By 1887, a British sympathizer of the Karens, D. M. Smeaton, asked 'Why should we not try—if only as a political experiment—to give the Karens a chance of growing as a nation . . .?' (San C. Po 1928: p. 8).

Karens, as a part of their developing nationalism, often tried to prove they were distinct from the Burmans; for instance San C. Po wrote that Karens were closer to the 'Tai Chinese'. Contrarily, Burmans, who were also influenced by Western ideas of race and ethnic group, tried to prove that Karens and Burmans had the same ancestry.

As Karen nationalism grew, it often conflicted with Burman nationalists, who about thirty years after the Third Anglo-Burmese War, had begun to call for a say in local rule. When young Burman patriots were called for home rule at the end of World War I, the Karens presented a memorial to the Viceroy Lord Chelmsford and Edwin Montagu, Secretary of State for India, important figures on the Joint Committee on Indian Constitutional Reform, saying that 'we, the Karens of Burma, are sensible that the country is not yet in a fit state for self-government' (San C. Po 1928: p. 66). A decade later, the well-known Karen Sir San C. Po suggested a national alliance of the four principal ethnic groups to be the most promising method for ruling Burma. Comparing Karens to the residents of 'Gallant little Wales', Sir San C. Po was convinced that both the Karen and the Welsh had a 'peculiar genius, and . . . special gifts' to offer the majority (San C. Po 1928: 80). He hoped for a semi-autonomous Karen area, comprising Tenasserim District, something anathema to the Burman nationalists.

Burman–Karen conflicts were sometimes impossible for the British to control. British favours to Karens, whom they found to be reliable soldiers, irritated the Burmans, who had for centuries considered themselves superior. When the British allowed Karens to overshadow Burmans in the British army, the martially-proud Burmans became upset. When the Karen police captured the rebel hero, Saya San, in 1932, the Burmans were outraged. This displeasure evoked sympathy among the British, one of whom wrote, 'If I were the Karens and could not get communal representation, I would emigrate to Siam, where I would fare no worse and might fare better' (quoted in San C. Po 1928: 8).

These changes occurred mainly among Karen Christians, not extending to many Karen sub-groups. Many such Karens—perhaps even a majority—instead of developing a new identity began assimilating into Burman life (Lewis 1924). These Karens, more Pwo than Sgaw, began speaking Burmese, becoming Buddhist, and adopting other aspects of Burman culture, things those in the KNA downplayed or denied. Lewis also noted that Christian Karens 'will be the last to succumb to Burmanization if they ever do' (Lewis 1924: p. 163).

Although there was less antagonism between these assimilating Karens and Burmans than between Christian Karens and Burmans, problems of Karen involvement in national life was growing. With communal strife between Karens sympathetic to the KNA and Burman nationalists during World War II, the division between these two groups of Karens was further accentuated, with all Karens suffering. Relations between the two extremes degenerated so that after the War, the fate of Karens was a major topic in the negotiations leading to independence. By this time, Karens held many high government posts, such as Commander-in-Chief of the Armed Forces (General Smith Dun), and communal Karen–national Burmese–British talks became important to the fate of the new country.

From negotiations to conflict

Although Karens and Burmans had clashed under British rule, there were no major confrontations until after the British were forced to evacuate Burma at the onset of World War II. According to Dorothy Hess Guyot, who studied Karen–Burman conflicts during the War, the removal of the British from Burma 'so wracked the prevailing role system as to create new and conflicting definitions of ethnic self for both Burmans and Karens'. This set the stage for the communal warfare that occurred in the Burma Delta (Guyot 1978: 195). The worst fighting took place in Myaungmya between Burmans, Karens and Indians, with hundreds if not thousands of fatalities resulting in the first half of 1942. Following July 1942, the Japanese were able to bring about a halt to most hostilities and little warfare occurred for the rest of the war. However, the distrust brought about during 1942 was to impede Burman–Karen accord after the war.

Further impeding good Karen relations with the Burman was the loyalty of many Karens to their former British overlords, which expressed itself during the war by attacks on the Japanese and their installations. Burman nationalists often found such activities inexcusable in the light of the fact that they believed the British to be the greater enemy.

Both factors contributed to a mass meeting of Karens in Rangoon in October 1945 at which it was agreed to press for a separate Karen state including Tenasserim. After an unfavourable British response a Karen delegation under Saw Ba U Gyi went to London in August 1946 to push either for a Karen State, operating under British protection and having a seaport, or for a Karen State in a Federation of Frontier Area States apart from Burma but in the British Commonwealth. Although this proposal got a positive response from some opposition conservatives, the Labour government was not interested in it and so the delegation returned to Burma empty-handed.

The Frontier Areas Committee of Enquiry, which in 1947 investigated Burma's minority, examined the problem of communal fighting during the war. A Karen National statement made before this Committee noted ominously:

> The Karens of this area firmly claim that their right of self-determintion be recognized by the concession of a separate Colony for the Karens. If the British fail to honor this great responsibility of theirs, the Karens should not be blamed if they think of other alternatives to achieve their legitimate objectives. [FACE, quoted in Cady 1960: 550]

Although not all Karens agreed with this statement, it clearly represented the thinking of a significant portion of the Karens, mostly Sgaw and Christians. When the Burmese leader Aung San travelled to London in 1947 to discuss the details of independence without any non-Burmans, the Karen National Union refused to participate in the April 1947 elections for the Constituent Assembly. Many Assembly seats set aside for Karens then went to members of the Karen Youth Organisation, a group set up by Aung San during World War II, and more sympathetic to national unity. Since they were more favourable to staying within the soon to be established Union of Burma they did not press for an independent Karen state.

When (following Aung San's assassination in July 1947) the Constituent Assembly presented its draft of a Constitution, it included a provision for the future establishment of a Karen state including Karenni, Salween District and some adjacent areas to be decided upon by a Special Commission. In the meantime, Salween District and some adjacent areas were to be called 'Kawthulay' and run under the Karen Council and the Minister of Karen Affairs.

Karen separatists, objecting strongly, rejected the Constitution. None the less, on 17 October 1947 U Nu and Clement Attlee signed a treaty formally recognising Burmese independence to begin on 4 January 1948. Karens, under Saw Ba U Gyi, were crestfallen that the British would agree to the treaty in spite of strong Karen reservations to it. As a result, Saw Ba U Gyi began actively planning for revolt, hoping to establish a Karen-Mon state including all of Tenasserim, Salween State and some adjacent territory. Unfortunately, for the Karen cause, however, large portions of the area they claimed were occupied by Burmans and others neither Mon nor Karen.

Karens found it possible to work with Mons and, although aware that Karens and Mons differed ethnically, pointed to a history of Mon–Karen co-operation. 'Mon and Karen rule of the Karens in the old kingdom of Hanthawaddy must have been adequate', remarked an ageing Karen from the Burman Delta, 'since the elders say nothing about it'. In 1948, in a plea to the British government, Saw Ba U Gyi and others wrote, 'The Mons and Karens, traditionally brothers and sisters having always had the highest regard for each other, firmly believe that their destinies are identical and their fates linked' (Saw Ba U Gyi 1948).

As Karens (and Mon) activists prepared for revolt, skirmishes were fought and the Karen National Defence Organization (KNDO) twice occupied Moulmein briefly as well as other nearby cities. To reduce tensions, U Nu set up the Regional Autonomy Enquiry Commission to satisfy 'legitimate aspirations of the Mons, Karens, and Arakanese nationals' (quoted in Cady 1960: 591).

At this time, the KNU leadership together with Mon nationalists, demanded on 13 November 1948 that the government set up an independent Karen–Mon state to include all Tenasserim and Irrawaddy division plus adjacent Karen and Mon areas, not counting Rangoon. This ultimatum was a demand no national government could agree to; agreeing to it would rend the very fabric from which the Union of Burma was cut. The same factors, however, that brought about this demand also led eventually to revolts by almost all of Burma's other minorities; the Shans, Kachins, Kayah, Arakanese, Chin, Pa-O and Wa all have rebel groups in the field opposing the Burman government. The changes in ethnic identity, Burman nationalist attitudes towards minority groups and previous links with the British, all factors in the Karen rebellion, led also to many other minority revolts.

Before the KNU ultimatum could be rejected, other developments took the initiative out of the hands of official negotiators. At the Kwa Cheh church, Palauk Township, Mergui District, Burmese troops killed 30–40 Karen worshippers on Christmas Eve in an apparently unprovoked attack (*The Karen Revolution*, p. 10). According to Karens this incident catalysed the Karen rebellion which began a few weeks later. It is strange, though, that works like Cady's *History of Modern Burma* and U Nu's autobiography ignore this incident.

From this point, a confusing number of attacks, ambushes, counter-attacks, and alleged atrocities began to occur that involved many more than just nationalist, Christian Karens. Although in the forefront of the move towards rebellion, not all Christian Karens fought while many animist and Buddhist Karens did. U Nu tried hard to preclude a rebellion, meeting often with San C. Po, Saw Ba U Gyi and other Karen leaders. U Nu's enemies took the opportunity to attack him over such meetings as being pro-Karen, calling him 'Karen Nu' and referring to his large jaw, considered by many Burmans to be characteristic of Karens (U Nu 1975: pp. 171–2).

The position of Saw Ba U Gyi regarding outright rebellion is difficult to assess. Certainly he gave speeches, such as at the Karen National Club on 9 October 1948, in which he urged that 'The Karens and Burmans should join hands and ask those Burmans who are taking refuge . . . to return to their homes' (Union of Burma 1949: p. 51). As President of the Karen National Union he fought for a separate Karen state. Whether this struggle was to be violent or peaceful is difficult to assess; Saw Ba U Gyi himself may well not have been sure.

All this was to no avail. In mid-January 1949, the KNU's fighting arm, the Karen National Defence Organisation (KNDO) began disarming government officials just seven miles out of Rangoon; Burmese troops attacked them. On 31 January 1949, the KNDO took Insein and the rebellion was in full swing. The Karens took the initial edge since many soldiers and officers went over to the rebellion, taking weapons with them. Fighting broke out in Bassein and then at Toungoo with Karens even launching an air raid on Maymyo in the Shan States.

The general plan of the Karens was to have the various forces converge on Rangoon. Columns from Prome, Toungoo, Bassein and Insein all set out for the capital. The first three were checked by military units that remained loyal to the national government. The contingent from Insein, however, was not defeated on the battlefield. Burmans often say that Karens are easily duped and gullible—*tahseima manabu* (not sophisticated). Although generalizations such as this are rarely true, in this case gullibility did here undermine the Karens. Upon getting to within ten miles from Rangoon, the Karen contingent from Insein halted for talks proposed by the Burmese. Karen leaders, who had ordered their troops not to advance until they returned, were escorted into the capital where they were subsequently detained. The Burmese hastily threw up barricades sufficient to blunt the Karen onslaught when the troops left behind finally decided they had been duped and attacked. The position of General Smith Dun became untenable. Although committed to the national government, he also sympathised with the Karen rebels. Eventually he went on leave before taking an early retirement. He was succeeded by his second in command, General Ne Win. Unable to capture Rangoon, the KNDO eventually was forced to retreat. The national government derived considerable advantages by holding the main port of the country and its continued presence in the capital also gave the national government political legitimacy. Thus, even though the Karens did occupy strategic towns, such as Mandalay, the government maintained enough stability to survive.

The Karens received little overseas support. Conservative elements in Britain remained sympathetic to the Karens, believing Prime Minister Attlee's treaty unfair to the Karens. British agents did aid the Karens and encouraged the rebels to set up a Mon–Karen state. However, the Labour government was unenthusiastic and the Burmese discovery of this plot ended all chances of official British aid reaching the KNDO (Seagrave 1984, pp. 65–6). Even Conservative efforts to remove the British military mission from Burma, to make it see that the British were not anti-Karen, failed (Cady 1960: 595–6). There was much dissatisfaction with the Karen demands for incorporation into the proposed Karen State areas in which Karens were only a minority constituent. Occasional Karen excesses also hurt Karen efforts to attract overseas help.

Survival occurred in spite of other rebellions that broke out at the same time. Other rebellions were by the People's Volunteer Organization (PVO) including remnants of anti-Japanese guerrilla units, a Pa-O (Taungthu) group in the Southern Shan States, some Kachins in the Northern Shan States, Red Flag Communists ('Trotskyites'), White Flag Communists ('Stalinists'), and other smaller groups.

None the less, by 1949 government forces had retaken Mandalay, Maymyo, Insein and Thaton as well as carrying the fight to the Shan States, Karenni and Pegu State. In 1950, the government seemed secure and the long struggle between Karen guerrillas on the western border of Burma and the government began. In August 1950 the Burmese dealt a serious blow to Karen leadership by ambushing and killing Saw Ba U Gyi and some close associates (Prani Sirithon 1985: 494).

In early 1950, the KNDO controlled large sections of the Irrawaddy delta, and much territory east of the Sittang River and south through Tenasserim. U Nu felt confident enough in July 1950 to offer amnesty but very few KNDO rebels were interested. The following year, U Nu allowed the Rangoon Police Department to reinstate ninety-one Karen policemen suspended when the rebellion broke out. Efforts to help loyal Karens continued and some loyal army officers were allowed back into the armed services (Silverstein 1980: 217–18).

U Nu encouraged Karen loyalty through political means as well, his main step being the establishment of Karen State—the old Salween State—in 1952. The United Karen League (UKL) was established outside of Karen State to succeed the Karen Youth Organisation. Inside Karen State, a rival group, the United Karen Organisation (UKO), was set up. These two parties contested power over Karen affairs in the Union of Burma until 1956, at which time the UKL dissolved itself. When, on 9 March 1956, the UKO merged with the national party, the Anti-Fascist People's Freedom League, with Dr Saw Hla Tun as the leader, the government had an alternative, the KNDO, for leadership in Karen affairs (Silverstein 1980: 218–19).

The working out of this arrangement represents the efforts of the national government to bring Karens into the national whole. As Taylor has shown (1982, 1983, for example), Burma has always been multi-ethnic, but national needs require that minorities be brought into some kind of working arrangement. Thus, aspects of the minorities' cultures must be given up in return for national unity. With the Karens, however, where there is a high degree of longstanding personal antagonism, these efforts, even when legitimate—like requiring control over local education—are often denounced as unjust or worse.

However, these efforts have won the loyalty of many Karens in non-rebel areas. Various offers of amnesty have been largely ignored but a few Karens always do give up. Furthermore, the area in which the Karen rebels are active has shrunk almost continually since 1949. As noted above, many Karens were already assimilating into Burmese life at the beginning of the twentieth century; this process, as far as is known, has continued to the present. Although no pertinent statistics are available, by 1960 probably more than half the Karens in Burma were essentially loyal to the central government. At present, the amount is quite likely more than this.

Nothing during the rule of the Ne Win has changed the stalemate existing since the 1950s. Except for a few government strongholds, Karens control the Thai border with Burma from just north of Victoria Point up to the boundary with Kayah State. The government attacks in every dry season with some success; the troops withdraw at the onset of the rains and the Karens recoup what they had lost. In some places, as in the Burma Delta, assimilation has proceeded so far that many Karens are difficult to differentiate from those of other groups.

There are even Karens, such as one met by Professor Charles Keyes of The University of Washington, Seattle, on a recent trip to Burma, who contended that the Karens attacked in the Christmas Eve massacre must have been at least partly responsible for what happened (interview with Keyes, 1985). Regardless of how much Karen rebels argue to the contrary, there are many such Karens in Burma, a sign that government policies towards amalgamation and assimilation are meeting with some success. Unfortunately, there is at present no way to learn significantly more about this phenomenon.

However, the presence of a force hostile to the central government controlling most of Burma's eastern border for over thirty years has profoundly affected life in Burma. As the most active rebellion in Burma, the Karen revolt has destabilised Burmese life by, firstly, diverting so much government military attention that other rebellions can flourish and, secondly, restricting government access to a considerable portion of territory with many resources, such as Burma's main teak forests, as well as tin, wolframite and lead mines. Furthermore, the Karens have managed to restrict official government trade with Thailand to a trickle. The rebels have used these advantages to prolong the war in spite of being outnumbered and perhaps without even considerable support from the Karens of Burma.

The enduring rebellion

Although understanding of the Karens in Burma is poor, it is possible to know the state of affairs in Karen-held Kawthoolei. A stream of reporters, government officials and even tourist trekkers have visited Karen rebel camps from Thailand for at least two decades. This also surely serves to allow politicised accounts of Karens elsewhere in Burma to dominate public opinion in Thailand.

Imbued with Western notions of what denotes an ethnic group, and on record as saying that the Karen rebellion is motivated for racial reasons (Hulme 1981: p. 4), the rebels have very clear ideas about their identity. According to a Karen rebel publication, *Karens and Communism* (n.d.: 1), Karens have eight characteristics:

(1) the knowledge that there is God, the Divine Being;
(2) High moral and ethical standards;
(3) honesty;
(4) simple, quiet and peaceful living;
(5) hospitality;
(6) language;
(7) national costumes;
(8) aptitude for music.

Whether these are true is not so important as the realization that these Karens have internalized Western notions of ethnicity and have set out to make themselves in the image of their own definition. According to one Karen army veteran, 'The Karens and Mons have been fighting the Burmese since God created the universe' (Hail 1980: 28). In so doing they have created serious obstacles to ever reaching a conclusion to their war with the Burmese government.

Were these Karens to characterize the Burmese, probably the list would include craftiness, duplicity, selfishness and other negative qualities. By setting themselves and the Burmese (characterized by Burman aspects) up as unique races, traditional means of inter-group dealings previously popular in Burma cannot be used. The result of this definition, a relic of the British influence, has impeded resolution of the fighting. Instead, Western-style negotiations are resorted to, with the result that the Burmese demand surrender, the Karens refuse, and the conflict continues. Stubbornness and determination might well be added to the list of Karen and Burman characteristics.

During decades of life on the Burma–Thai border, Karens have come to dominate the cross-border trade. For a variety of reasons, not the least of which is the Karen rebellion itself, the Burmese economy is not flourishing. To compensate for deficiencies in local production, a black market has emerged by which considerable amounts of goods come from Thailand to Burma through Karen areas. One prominent market in Rangoon is known informally as *yodhaya ya zei* (the Thailand market) because that is where most of the goods on it originate.

The Karens assess a tax, usually 5 per cent on all goods crossing their areas. Thai exports through Karen areas into Burma include modern consumer goods like cameras and tape recorders and necessities such as soap and batteries. Even calendars, freely distributed in Thailand, are sold to the Burmese. It is hard to imagine how Burma could survive without this trade; one estimate has over 80 per cent of Burma's consumer goods entering the country illegally, and mostly through Karen areas (Wolf 1983: p. 4). Although Burma's government finds the black market troublesome, it recognises Burma's need for it. Particularly following unrest in Rangoon in 1974, the government has not pressed too hard to curtail this trade. The demonetisation of all large Burmese bank notes in 1987 may mark a change in this policy.

Goods entering Thailand are perhaps even more lucrative. These include so much teak that in 1984 the *Bangkok Post* estimated that sixty-five Karen saw-mills were kept busy in this lumber trade, involving not only Thailand but also Malaysia and Singapore (Subin and Pichai 1984: p. 9). In 1986, the Thai government encountered difficulties when one minister tried to rationalise this trade by opening it to bids by Bangkok companies. Additionally, much jade and other precious stones cross the border as do thousands of cattle each year. Almost half a million US dollars realized from this trade are deposited in northern Thai banks.

The millions of dollars annual income from this trade primarily supports Karen troops and buys them weapons. This trade takes many forms. Former Thai Prime Minister, M. R. Kukrit Pramoj, recalled that during his time in power around 1975, he helped negotiate a deal by which Thai fishing boats entering Burmese waters would pay the Burmese government 30 per cent of the profit. However, in a few months the Burmese requested a halt to this trade since the Thai fishing boats were carrying weapons to Karens in Tenasserim (BBC 1984–5). Karen rebels are also said to have sea links with traders in Malaysia and

Singapore, the means by which some teak reaches those countries.

One item not traded by the Karens or allowed through their area is drugs. Heroin carriers, if caught, are liable to be executed; one such case occurred in about 1983. Some drugs do trickle through but much less than through areas to the north, in Shan State.

For many years this situation existed almost routinely. Except for the annual Burmese probes into Karen areas, the rebels were left essentially alone. The Thai government unofficially appreciated having a Karen buffer zone between them and the opium gangs and the Communist groups active in Burma's hinterlands.

Similarly, the Karens caused the Burmese government little overt damage through actual attacks. This changed somewhat in 1983. Perhaps eager to hurt the Burmese directly and to bring the Karens on to the world stage again, the Karen National Union kidnapped Jacques Bossu, a French engineer working at a Burmese cement plant near Pa-an, the capital of Karen State, and his wife. The couple were held for thirty-eight days while the KNU threatened to put them on trial unless the French government responded. Although no response was received, the KNU president, General Bo Mya, freed the couple in November 1983.

The Burmese, humiliated by their inability to rescue the couple, launched one of the heaviest attacks on the Karens ever. Determined to take the major Karen trading centre, Wang Kha, just north of Mae Sot on the Thai-Burma border, the Burmese attacked *en masse* in the first months of 1984. Thousands of refugees fled into Thailand, the black market trade was briefly halted, and the fighting raged for months before the Burmese captured their objectives.

The situation has stabilised. Some Burmese troops have withdrawn but the Burmese control Wang Kha and some nearby crossing points. The Karens still, apparently, are able to ship large amounts of teak into Thailand and continue to collect much duty on cross-border shipments. Thailand has reassessed its unofficial policy towards using the Karens as a buffer, but no decision has been made because the Karen–Burma situation has remained unresolved.

The Karen rebellion, thus, continues as a major irritant to the Burmese, allowing other problems in Burma to go uncorrected. Were there no Karen rebellion, the Burmese could perhaps put down many of its other insurgencies. Then, with access to many natural resources steps could be taken to upgrade the country's very low standard of living. However, so long as the Karens remain able to resist the Burmese government, and there is no sign of the Karens relenting, the conflict is unlikely to be resolved. Since the Burmese government seems unable to increase incentives enough to talk sufficient number of rebels fighting against the government out of the jungle, all signs point to Karens carrying the fighting into the twenty-first century.

The only apparent beneficiary to this are Thais. Thai traders profit from exchanging the goods entering Burma; Thai manufacturers profit from making goods that are sold into Burma; Thai banks profit from Karen deposits; rural Thais benefit by development projects, such as in opium replacement, that otherwise would be directed at Burma, being carried out in Thailand; and the Thai government seems pleased that a weak country borders Thailand to the west and reduces the chance of serious conflict there. For these reasons, it is hardly surprising that when Burmese troops pursue Karens near the Thai border, Thai Rangers and Border Patrol Police ensure that the Burmese do not cross over into Thailand and gain a strategic advantage over the Karen camps with their unprotected backs to the Thai border. From the Thai point of view, the Karen rebellion has many advantages, few disadvantages, and could well be prolonged indefinitely.

*In 1989 the government officially changed the name of the country to Myanmar.

References

Blundell, E.A. (1929), 'E.A. Blundell to Sec. to the Sudden Board of Ft. William, December 9, 1839', *Selected Correspondence of Letters issued from and received in the Office of the Commissioner Tenasserim Division for the Years* 1825–26 to 1842–43, Rangoon.

British Broadcasting Corporation, 1984–5. 'Cadres and Kings', radio series on South-east Asia.

Cady, John F. (1960), *A History of Modern Burma*, Ithaca, NY, Cornell University.

Carpenter, C.H. (1883), *Self-Support, Illustrated in the History of the Bassein Karen Mission from 1840 to 1880*, Boston, Rand, Avery.

Guyot, Dorothy Hess (1978), 'Communal conflict in the Burma Delta', in Ruth T. McVey, ed., *Southeast Asia Transitions*, New Haven, Yale University, pp. 191–234.

Hail, John (1980), 'A Blow to the Heartland', *Far Eastern Economic Review*, 9 May 1980, pp. 38–9.

Hulme, David (1981), 'The Karen Tribes', *Asia Magazine*, 1 March, pp. 3–6.

The Karen Revolution, n.d., Singapore, Sam Art.

Leach, Edmund R. (1964), *Political Systems of Highland Burma*, Boston, Beacon (first published about 1954).

Lewis, James Lee (1924), 'The Burmanization of the Karen Peoples of Burma', Master's Thesis, University of Chicago Divinity School.

Nu, U (1975), *U Nu: Saturday's Son*, New Haven, Conn., Yale University Press.

Prani Sirithon (1985), *Nua Khwaen Daen Siam* (Beyond the Borders of Siam), Chiang Mai, Chang Phuak.

San C. Po (1928), *Burma and the Karens*, London, Elliot Stock.

Saw Ba U Gyi *et al.* (1948), 'Annex "A" to the Minutes of the Third Meeting of the Karen Affairs sub-committee', 13 November (typescript).

Saw Moo Troo (ca. 1980), 'The Karens and Communism' in Saw Moo Troo and Mike Rolley, *The Karens and Communism*: *Karens Fight for Peace*, n.p.

Seagrave, Sterling (1984), 'A 35-Year Struggle for Independence: Karen Rebels in Burma', *Soldier of Fortune*, April.

Silverstein, Josef (1980), *Burmese Politics: The Dilemma of National Unity*, New Brunswick, NJ, Rutgers University.

Smeaton, Donald (1920), *The Loyal Karens of Burma*, London, Kegan Paul, Trench, Trubner.

Snow, John (1983), 'The Forgotten War', *Asia Magazine*, 4 December, pp. 3, 5–8.

Subin Khuenkaew and Pichai Chuensuksawadi (1984), 'Reappraisal due on Thai policy towards Karens', *Bangkok Post*, 2 May, p. 4.

Taylor, Robert H. (1982), 'Perceptions of Ethnicity in the Politics of Burma', *Southeast Asian Journal of Social Science*, vol. 10, no. 1, pp. 7–22.

—— (1983), *An Underdeveloped State: The Study of Modern Burma's Politics*, Melbourne, Monash University Centre of Southeast Asian Studies Working Paper No. 28.

Union of Burma (1949), *Burma and the Insurrections*, Rangoon, Government of the Union of Burma Publication.

Wilson, H.H. (1827), *Documents Illustrative of the Burmese War with an Introductory Sketch of Events of the War and an Appendix*, Calcutta.

Wolf, Jim (1983), 'Asia's civilized insurgents', *Bangkok Post*, 9 November, p. 5.

7 HMONG ASPIRATIONS FOR A SEPARATE STATE IN LAOS: THE EFFECTS OF THE INDO-CHINA WAR

George M. Scott Jr

This chapter will focus upon the Hmong tribal people's desire for an independent state in north-central Laos during the 1960s and upon the effects that the Indo-China War had on this desire. It should be stated at the outset that this desire never reached the stage of an organised separatist movement in the true sense of the term, although had the war ended differently, this movement might have begun; rather, it remained for the most part as a wish embedded in religious terms—specifically as a 'messianic impulse'—that was given new life and meaning by the war but was also abruptly extinguished by its results. After exploring background material on Hmong history and culture, particularly as it relates to the Hmong desire for secession, we will proceed to analyse this recent impulse, as well as how the war both facilitated and hindered it.

Background

Since their arrival into Laos from China during the mid-nineteenth century, the Hmong remained for the most part a mountain tribal people whose economy was based mainly on subsistence, swidden horticulture (shifting, slash-and-burn methods); whose political organization was coterminous with their patrilineal descent system and was centralized only at the local, village level; whose world view was largely determined by their animistic belief system; and whose language was unwritten.

Although there is disagreement about the ultimate origins and earliest movements of the Hmong,[1] there is no doubt that they were well established as a distinct ethnic group in west-central China over 2,000 years ago, as this is when they were first mentioned in the Chinese classics (Ruey 1962: 181). From that point on their history is one of conflict with the politically dominant and numerically superior Han-Chinese people, who pushed the Hmong further south over the centuries, engaging them in a series of military campaigns in a continuing attempt to pacify and subjugate them.[2] The Hmong resisted this attempted subjugation vigorously and even managed to win a few major battles, but ultimately they had to give way in the face of overwhelming Chinese military superiority. Those who admitted defeat were gradually Sinicised, but those who fled before the victorious Chinese armies remained fiercely and stubbornly independent. This slow, gradual, southward movement eventually brought the Hmong into northern Indo-China around 150 years ago.

Although historians such as Ruey (1962) focus on this pressure from the Han-Chinese as the sole causal factor for the Hmong's (as well as other similar ethnic groups') southward migration into Indo-China, anthropologists such as Geddes (1976) and Cooper (1978a, 1978b) adduce an additional reason: namely, their commitment to opium poppy cultivation. This reliance on opium as a cash crop, which dates back at least 300 years to their previous land in southern China, had kept the Hmong confined to the highest elevations of the South-east Asian mountains, between 3,000 and 4,000 feet, where the opium poppy grows best, and most importantly for this chapter, where the Hmong could easily maintain their political autonomy from the lowland-controlled state. In addition to its relatively high, stable selling price and its portability, a feature of the opium poppy that makes it attractive as a crop is that it can be grown successively on the same plot of land for up to about twenty years.

The Hmong took full advantage of this feature, filling as much land with the crop as possible, to the point that there was seldom enough land left over for fallowing, had they desired to use this method. Some land, of course, also had to be set aside for rice, a crop that has to be fallowed or rotated at least every other year to ensure optimal yield. This the Hmong would do—if land were sufficient also to support the desired yield of opium, which it seldom was.

Thus, once the Hmong had committed their economy to the cash crop of opium, they severely limited their alternative reliance on rice as a subsistence crop, and, as a result, they sealed their fate as perpetual migrants. For once the opium harvest began to decline, which in some areas would occur in as early as ten years, there was no alternative but to abandon the village and move on.

Although most of the so-called 'hill tribes' of northern Laos grew the opium poppy as a cash crop, the Hmong relied on it to a much greater extent than did the others. Thus, all of these opium-growers were migrants, shifting themselves rather than their crops; but among migrants, the Hmong were gypsies. Geddes has compared the migratory way of life of the Hmong to the behaviour of a species of rapacious mountain birds: the flock swoops down and forages ravenously until the food is totally exhausted and then flies off in search of new sustenance (1976: 88). This comparison seems appropriate, considering that the Hmong's basic life orientation was towards *speculation* rather than assuredness, towards *exploitation* rather than conservation, towards *pioneering* rather than permanent settlement, and towards the *accumulation of wealth* rather than mere subsistence. Whether these attitudes led the Hmong to choose opium cultivation as the mainstay of their economy or whether opium cultivation led them to develop these attitudes is a moot point as far as this chapter is concerned, but once they were both established they became mutually reinforcing and together made the Hmong the most frequent and widest ranging migrants of the mountains of mainland South-east Asia, as well as the wealthiest and the most likely to want to retain their accustomed way of life. Moreover, they were both central components of the traditional Hmong ethnic identity, as well as crucial determinants of the Hmong's desire for political autonomy.

Hmong ethnic identity

As is the case with any ethnic group anywhere, the traditional Hmong identity was not a fixed and static concept, but changed according to the situation in which they found themselves, which, in turn, was mainly determined by the ethnicity of the others involved.[3] Thus, when interacting with, or even just thinking of, members of the various other ethnic groups[4] with whom they shared the northern highlands in Laos, the Hmong considered themselves to be socially and racially superior, tougher physically, sharper mentally, more determined and clever economically, more advanced technologically and morally purer. Indeed, they had defeated some of these peoples in inter-ethnic warfare at various times over the past two centuries and recently had occasionally employed some of them as wage-labourers (paid in opium and other goods) in their fields, while pointing with pride to the fact that a Hmong had never worked in a similar, demeaning capacity for any of the others.

Thus, the Hmong claimed for their own the highest reaches of the Northern Indo-Chinese mountains, which were largely unpopulated; and when they did find a desirable piece of mountain-top land inhabited, they simply swept the inhabitants out of the way (which was the source of most of the inter-ethnic strife mentioned above). Their traditional self-conception *vis-à-vis* the other mountain groups, then, was akin to 'the tough new guys on the block'. In other words, not only did they live at the highest elevations in the mountains,[5] they considered themselves to be uppermost in the local racial and socio-cultural scale as well.

Their ethnic identity *vis-à-vis* the lowland Lao, however, was more complicated. As long as they were *thinking* of themselves in relation to the Lao, they could maintain their self-conceived superiority, specifically that their harder life in the mountains made them both tougher and morally purer than the soft and decadent lowlanders, who had had it too easy for too long.But when in the actual presence of a Lao person, and especially persons, the Hmong would not only behave deferentially and fearfully, but would also conceive of themselves in the same way that the Lao did—as culturally inferior and simple-minded 'country bumpkins'.

As long as they remained isolated from any but piecemeal contact with lowland Lao culture, as well as with the Lao themselves, the Hmong could maintain their grudging superiority, both literally and figuratively looking down on the lowlanders from above. But when they came into more continuous contact with the Lao and their culture, they could no longer ignore the technological, economic and political superiority, as well as the simple numerical dominance, of these people. Their self-conception as simple-minded and culturally primitive hill folk was thus reinforced at the expense of the other component of their traditional ethnic identity—that of the pride of a fiercely independent and resilient people whose more difficult existence had made them racially and culturally superior to the corrupt, decadent lowlanders. But while this negative change in identity affected the majority of the Hmong in the towns and 'modernised' provinces, the few who were better educated and who had made a more successful economic adjustment to lowland society actually had the traditionally positive component of their ethnicity reinforced. For these few Hmong, then, any bigoted or otherwise discriminatory treatment on the part of the Lao would have the opposite effect of arousing their ethnic pride.[6] It was from among this group that the rational leadership for the 'secessionist' movement was drawn. But for the majority of the Hmong thus affected, the response to this challenge took the form of a passive desire for an 'otherworldly' solution to their dilemma.

The messianic desire for a separate state

Until their southward migration brought them into contact with the dominant Lao population, then, the Hmong desire for political autonomy as such was subordinated in the face of the reality in which they lived: they had no need to desire something that they already possessed.[7] They, in other words, were their own political masters. The need to change this *de facto* autonomy into a *de jure* autonomy was not felt until the Lao began to threaten the former by extending their national control into the Hmong areas. This control was expressed in the form of building roads, creating district village councils, establishing schools and, most of all, of applying the national legal system to traditional Hmong society. The Hmong in these 'border' areas began to find that they were no longer free to cut down and burn hardwood trees, grow and sell opium, and punish their own wrongdoers, with impunity. These were all matters in which the Lao national government took a keen interest: it wanted the trees for its fledgling timber industry; under pressure from the US government, it wanted to stop opium production within its borders; and, as a sovereign state, it wanted to have sole jurisdiction over all legal matters among its population. And, above all, it wanted to bring the Hmong, as well as all of the other ethnic minorities living in the northern mountains, into the national, politico-economic mainstream. They were of little use as contributors to the national economy as long as they remained isolated, and autonomous, in the mountains.

The Lao government effort to integrate the Hmong and the others into the national mainstream existed more as a threat than as a reality; it simply lacked the resources to effectively implement such a far-reaching programme, especially when it was having to devote an increasing amount of attention to the mounting Communist insurgency. But in the few isolated areas where at least part of this programme was begun, it had a chilling effect on the Hmong involved: today the government simply was asking them to send their children to Lao schools; who knows what it would be asking tomorrow—perhaps for them to stop cutting down trees so they could plant their crops in their traditional fashion, and maybe to stop growing opium. And the day after, it might even ask them to move out of their mountains all together. The threat was thus to the core of the traditional Hmong identity and lifestyle—to the proud sense of tribal autonomy—and the result was to rekindle the traditional messianic dream of a final, secure freedom. This messianic desire surrounded a traditional Hmong legend (Marks 1973: 932) concerning the existence of Hmong 'king' centuries ago in China who had, at least for a time, successfully opposed the Han-Chinese army sent by the emperor to subdue him, but who was finally defeated and captured. Just before his execution, he vowed one day to 'return to bring final liberation and freedom' to his people. It was thus this king whose promised return the newly threatened Hmong in Laos eagerly awaited.

The effects of the Indo-China war on the Hmong desire for secession

While the majority of the Hmong population had remained isolated from the more Western-like society of the Lao lowland towns, they nevertheless were affected by another form of Western influence— namely, the Indo-China War, which at first added fuel to this messianic desire for autonomy, but in the end extinguished it all together. Rather than providing them with their final, hoped-for freedom, in other words, the war had the main effect of disrupting their traditional culture and society, traumatising their lives, and ending their hope for a separate Hmong state all together.

Hmong guerrilla troops, who had gained recognition as dependable and effective jungle fighters during the earlier French Indo-Chinese and Lao Civil Wars, became during the years US involvement (1960–74) the military mainstay and first line of defence of the Royal Lao Army against the Communist forces. Trained and equipped by the US Central Intelligence Agency (CIA) and the US Army Special Forces, supported by US air power, and led by the capable and experienced General Vang Pao, these Hmong troops, known as the 'Armée Clandestine', fought both the Pathet Lao guerrilla and North Vietnamese regular forces to a virtual standstill during this period in their mountain homeland, centred on the Plain of Jars, of northern Laos (Adams and McCoy 1970; Castle 1979; Dommen 1971; and Toye 1968). This loyalty to the US Indo-China War effort cost the Hmong dearly: they suffered over 30,000 casualties out of a total population estimated at 300,000 (Vang 1979). Not only was their traditional family structure undermined accordingly, but continual relocation as strategy dictated disrupted the economic and political infrastructure of traditional village life as well.

Hugo Adolf Bernatzik, an early German ethnographer who worked in Indo-China, wrote of the Hmong's 'indomitable desire for freedom' and of their 'aversion to being ruled by members of other peoples' (1970: 625), and added a warning to would-be 'colonisers': 'Their urge for independence, their fearlessness bordering on defiance of death, their glowing love for freedom, which had been strengthened through thousands of years of fighting against powerful oppressors and has given them the reputation of feared warriors, will perhaps make difficulties for the colonizer' (1970: 674).

This reputation of belligerence of course made the Hmong attractive as political and military allies to both the Royal Lao and the Communist sides at the outset of the Indo-China War, but it was also recognized that their equally strong sense of ethnic pride and political autonomy would make the control of Hmong troops problematic and their loyalty to the 'larger' cause suspect (Dommen 1971: 75; Toye 1968: 195). In fact, ever apprehensive of the Hmong's loyalty, the Royal Lao Government in the early 1960s banned the printing of any material in the Hmong language,[8] fearing that the possession of their own written language might become the catalyst for the already strong in-group sentiments of the Hmong (Barney 1967: 292–3). Hence, to ensure Hmong allegiance to the larger 'cause', each side had to convince their Hmong allies that defeat would bring a complete end to their tribal freedom (Dommen 1971; Toye 1968), while victory would bring, or, more apropriately, *might* bring, an autonomous Hmong state (Branfman 1970: 252; Department of the Army 1970: 654).[9]

Both sides in the war thus played upon the traditional Hmong messianic theme as a way of securing their allegiance to the 'cause'. The Hmong, at least those on the side of the Lao government, responded by reformulating their messianic myth in terms of both the war and the Christianity the missionaries had increasingly been propagating among them: Jesus Christ, clad in camouflage army fatigues and driving an army jeep, would soon appear among them not only to lead them to victory over the Communist forces, but to help them depose all local Lao government officials and take over Vientiane, the national capital, as well (Halpern and Kunstadter 1967: 242). The Communists for their part, used the Hmong messianic theme as the basis for their propaganda message that there is a reincarnated Hmong (Meo) king living in Peking ('Meo' Tse-tung) who has ordered all Hmong to join him in Peking and all lesser leaders to adopt the Communist system (Marks 1973: 932).[10]

Another major effect of the war was on Vang Pao's rise to prominence as a military leader in Laos and later as a de facto political leader to his fellow refugees both in Thailand and abroad.[11] Having served with distinction with the French forces in their war against the Communists during the early 1950s, he was immediately selected by the Royal Lao Government and its US military allies to be the leader of the Hmong guerrilla troops that were put into action against the resurgent Pathet Lao forces a few years later. He quickly rose in rank from lieutenant-colonel to major-general and commanded great respect from his own people and his American advisers alike, if not from his supposed Lao 'allies' in the government and army, who tended to resent the forceful self-confidence of this 'primitive hillbilly'. While he has been variously described by American observers as a 'despotic warlord' who became wealthy from dealing in opium (McCoy *et al.* 1972: 268), as the 'one honest general over there' (Castle 1979: 131), and as a 'clever and courageous leader, with a deep concern for his people' (Castle 1979: 54), one fact remains certain: he was, and still is, above all, a *charismatic* leader, as evidenced by the reverential devotion shown to him by his followers.[12]

Although reportedly Vang Pao never himself claimed to be the Hmong messiah, the returned king, he was not averse to having his followers think of him as such. One thing is clear, however: he definitely did aspire to the leadership of the new Hmong state, which was promised him by his CIA allies, when their victory was complete. He even went as far as naming his 'cabinet' and designing a flag for this new nation.[13]

Conclusion

The aftermath of the war

While the war gave initial impetus to this Hmong dream of a separate state, its final outcome proved to have quite the opposite effect. US support for the Royal Lao Government was withdrawn in 1974, effectively ending any Hmong aspirations for secession associated with this support. When the Communists took control of the national government soon thereafter, those Hmong who had actively served in the 'Armée Clandestine' or who were not yet under the control of the Pathet Lao were immediately placed in extreme jeopardy. The Communist forces initiated a programme of reprisal that was variously described, at best, as one of forced relocation into lowland 're-education' camps and, at worst, as one of genocide (*Los Angeles Times* 1970; McBeth 1970; Pringle 1979; US Congress, House 1979; Vang 1979). At this point, the Hmong began to flee their homeland by the tens of thousands travelling southward mainly on foot, often over hundreds of miles on jungle trails, and then over the Mekong by boat or other means of flotation into northern Thailand, where they were placed in temporary refugee camps to await eventual permanent resettlement abroad, primarily in the United States, but also in France and Canada.[14] These Hmong thus lost any hope of returning to Laos, not to mention of any separate Hmong state.

But what of their brethren who allied themselves with the victorious Communist cause? Apparently, they have not fared much better; far short of achieving the promised separate homeland, they too have been placed into re-education camps, to ensure their continuing allegiance, as well as their integration into the 'new order' of lowland Lao society, which has no place for potentially rebellious mountain tribal people.[15] In other words, the Communist Lao regime wants them out of their traditional mountain homeland, knowing all too well that to allow them to stay there would be to help keep their hope for an autonomous state alive.

Thus, whether still in Laos or abroad, the Hmong have lost their traditional way of life in the mountains and thereby their long-cherished goal for final political autonomy as well. But while the realistic chances of achieving such a goal have been irretrievably lost, the dream of somehow one day returning to Laos and reclaiming their mountain homeland lives go on whenever old Hmong men sit and talk about the past and make plans for the future. The younger generation, for their part, view these aspirations simply as idle talk of old men; for the younger Hmong, this dream of complete political autonomy has faded altogether, to be replaced by a more sober orientation towards the exigencies of adjusting to life in their new land.

Theoretical implications

What are the theoretical implications of the Hmong secessionist-cum-messianic movement? It seems clear from the above presentation that this type of movement fits Premdas's category of extreme external influence[16]—namely, those movements that involve a high degree of external ideological impetus as well as technical assistance. We shall now proceed to elaborate on this type of movement on the basis of the material presented above.

As can be adduced from the above data, this type of secessionist movement most often occurs in societies that are technologically simple, politically decentralised, and non-literate—those, in other words, that lack their own *rational* means to achieve the desired end of secession. Lacking such means, they combine not wholly rational, or at least realistic, internal means deriving from, or at least influenced by, their traditional religious belief system, with similar means whose ideological origin is external. To these non-rational means they add whatever external rational means that either come their way or they are able actively to muster. In such societies, the original ideological impetus for secession may also derive from outside, to be combined with the original internal desire that exists as a reaction to a perceived external threat.

Thus, the Hmong 'secessionist' movement arose from the mounting threat posed to their traditional political autonomy by the dominant Lao, but was given added impetus by the military advisers-cum-manipulators on both sides in the Indo-China War, who sought to gain the allegiance of the Hmong by playing upon this desire. The internal means to achieve this end, however, were clothed in the religious ideology of a messianic movement—the magical return of a mythical 'prophet-king' who would lead his people to their final freedom—and hence were non-rational in nature. Combined with these internal means were the external non-rational ones derived from missionary Christian theology on the one hand and Communist mytho-political ideology on the other. The rational means, namely, the military equipment and training, as well as the proffered future assistance in establishing the separate Hmong 'state', were provided by external forces: the United States on the one side and the Asian Communist bloc on the other.

The outcome of the Hmong 'secessionist' movement, however, points to another important theoretical dimension to the problem—namely, the fact that the *rational* means of this movement were wholly external in origin and derived from political entities whose technopolitical superiority to the Hmong was overwhelming meant that the Hmong themselves had little if any ultimate control over it. They were simply pawns in a game whose rules were determined by modern international political processes of which the Hmong had only a dim understanding and over which they had no effective influence. Hence, the outcome of the movement was determined not by the Hmong themselves but by these external forces, and in this case the outcome was far from what the Hmong had desired.

The question arises here as to the feasibility of the Hmong establishing an independent state even if the outcome of the movement had been different. That is, how were a people who for millennia had been restless, perpetual migrants, who possessed a decentralized political organization commensurate with this type of adaptation, and whose language was not written until relatively recently, going to establish a modern state, which, by definition, must be defined by stable, permanent territorial boundaries and administered by a centralized political structure with an accompanying bureaucracy? According to

Imong refugee informants in San Diego, the vast majority of the Imong were simply not aware of this problem—indeed, few of them ven understood what a state was, especially what its requirements ould be—yet the small group of educated leaders, with Vang Pao at e helm, not only knew what the problem would be, but even went so ar as to think of ways that their people could become more stable. For xample, following the advice of USAID advisers,[17] they decided that hey would try to convince them to adopt the techniques of more isciplined fallowing, crop rotation and the application of chemical ertilisers and pesticides, all of which would significantly reduce the requency and extent of their migrations. But even more importantly, hey assumed that they would have the assistance of whichever world ower on whose side they fought. But as was just stated, the outcome of he war rendered these plans useless and this assumption wrong.

But an unwanted outcome need not always be arrived at in the case of hese messianic-secessionist movements. The Papua New Guinea truggle for independence, which was given original impetus by the arlier messianic 'Cargo Cult' movements, is an example of the opposite ort of outcome. The point to be made here is not that these types of novements are always doomed to failure, or that they will always ucceed, but simply that the secessionists themselves do not have much of hand in determining the outcome, whatever it may be. They are like udderless boats cast adrift in the ocean, which are entirely at the mercy of the whims of wind and water to achieve their desired course. And like uch boats, they sometimes reach port safely, depending on favourable weather, but most often they end dashed upon the rocks.

One thing, however, is certain: if they are to have any hope of success in the modern world, these messianic-secessionist movements *must* have some degree of external rational means. Otherwise, their fate will be that of the Native American 'Ghost Dance' and the African 'Congo Kartelite Cults',[18] whose magical charms did nothing to protect their adherents from the bullets of their white conquerors. With no rational means of their own, they will invariably fall before the inexorable, rational means of their oppressors.

Notes

1. This debate takes the following form. Savina (1930), on the basis of Hmong legend, places their origin in the Pamir Mountains and claims that their earliest migrations took them east and north-east through Turkestan and the Tanu Ola Mountains across Siberia, and then south through Mongolia

and Shensi to Honan (p. 247). Ruey (1962: 180–1) counters this hypothesis arguing that it cannot be accepted because there simply is no substantial historical or archaeological evidence to support it and that it is futile even to speculate on the Hmong's ultimate origins and earliest movements. At any rate, both Savina and Ruey agree that they began their southward migration from China into northern Indo-China, both Laos and Vietnam, around 150 years ago.

2. At that time the Hmong were known either specifically as the 'Miao' or generically as the 'Man' ('barbarians') (Ruey 1962: 182). Later, in Indo-China, they became known as the 'Meo'. Both Miao and Meo, however were names applied to them by outsiders; they prefer Hmong, the name they themselves use.
3. For a treatment of the theoretical development of the concept of situational ethnicity, see Okamura (1981); for empirical applications of this concept, See Nagata (1974) and Berreman (1982).
4. These neighboring ethnic groups included the Yao, Akha, Khmu, Lamet, Muong and Lolo. See Lebar *et al.* (1964) for a brief ethnographic sketch of each.
5. F.M. Savina, the only European to have devoted an entire work to the history of the Hmong (then termed 'Miao'), placed great importance on their mountain existence, which had begun some 4,000 years earlier in China: 'Beaten by the Chinese they had to give way . . . That is how the Miao became mountain men, in spite of themselves, some four thousand years ago, and that is how too they were always able to keep their independence in the middle of other peoples, keeping intact, along with their language and their customs, the ethnic character of the race' (1930: 175; translated and quoted by Geddes 1976: 31).
6. The effect of contact with Westerners was in general to reinforce the Hmong's traditionally positive self-image, since they usually did not treat them as inferiors, as did the Lao. But the effect of contact with missionaries, in particular, was more equivocal, as they considered Christianity to be morally superior to the Buddhism of the Lao, but *also* to the animism of the Hmong.
7. The Hmong were little affected by French colonial policy, which did not effectively penetrate their remote mountain land and thus did not threaten their political autonomy.
8. A Romanised orthography for the Hmong language was developed in the 1950s by a team of missionary-linguists (Barney and Smalley 1953). The details of this orthography (called the 'RPA', or Romanised Popular Alphabet) are to be found in Heimbach (1979). This method of writing was taught to Hmong children only in the few missionary schools; because of the above mentioned fear, it was not used in government schools. Accordingly, far from being literate in this system, relatively few Hmong even knew it existed. Thus the fear of the national government was directed more to the *symbol* of a separate written language than to its actual use.
9. Apparently, this tactic of promising eventual autonomy, according to Hmong refugee informants in San Diego, California, was promulgated primarily by the US CIA operatives, much to the discomfort of Lao military and government officials, who did not want to encourage this feeling in any

way whatsoever. The latters' fears were little assuaged by the formers' assurances that such a thing would never actually happen.

10. Although Marks was referring to the Communist insurgency among the Hmong in northern Thailand, according to Lao Hmong refugee informants in San Diego, this propaganda theme was used in Laos as well, with the added twist that the great 'Hmong king', Meo Tse-tung, would lead his people back to Laos, sweeping aside all Lao government and military officials who tried to oppose him and gain for them their 'promised land'.
11. Another reason for Vang Pao's immense popularity as a politico-military leader was his close alliance and relationship (by marriage) to Touby Lyfong, the most prominent and popular Hmong leader before Vang (see Barney 1967).
12. During this time, Vang Pao also developed through his association with the US military structure and the Royal Lao Army and Government the model for the legal-rational mutual-aid association that he would eventually found in Santa Ana, California, to assist his people with their socio-cultural adjustment to their new receiving society—namely, Lao Family Community, Inc.
13. This information was obtained from Lao Hmong refugee informants in San Diego.
14. This process continued unabated in 1979, when I began my research into the problems of adjustment among the Hmong refugees in San Diego, but within two years it had begun to taper off, as word of the difficulties in adjusting to American society began to reach relatives still in the camps, and today it exists as only a trickle of what it had been at the outset.
15. Information obtained from Hmong informants in San Diego.
16. See this volume, chapter 1, for the full explication of this typology.
17. This is not to say that these advisers actually advocated secession to the Hmong; they simply promoted the following techniques to increase the level of productivity of the Hmong's traditional farming methods, as well as to make their settlements more permanent, thus making their lives easier and, at the same time, conserving the valuable hardwood forests.
18. See La Barre (1972: 307–10) for brief descriptions of these two, as well as other 'fantasy of invulnerability' cults.

References

Adams, Nina S. and Alfred W. McCoy, eds (1970), *Laos: War and Revolution*, New York, Harper and Row.

Barney, G. Linwood (1967), 'The Meo of Xieng Khouang Province, Laos', in P. Kunstadter, ed., *Southeast Asian Tribes, Minorities, and Nations*, Princeton, NJ, Princeton University Press, pp. 271–94.

Barney, G. Linwood and William A. Smalley (1953), 'Third Report on Meo (Miao): Orthography and Grammar' unpublished manuscript.

Bernatzik, Hugo Adolf (1970), *Akha and Miao: Problems of Applied Ethnology in Farther India*, New Haven, Conn., Human Relations Area Files.

Berreman, Gerald (1982), 'Bazaar Behavior: Social Identity and Social Interaction in Urban India, in G. DeVos and L. Romanucci-Ross, eds, *Ethnic*

Identity: Cultural Continuities and Change, Chicago, University of Chicago Press, pp. 71–105.

Branfman, Fred (1970), 'Presidential War in Laos, 1964–1970', in N.S. Adams and A.W. McCoy, eds, *Laos: War and Revolution*, New York, Harper and Row, pp. 213–80.

Castle, Timothy Neil (1979), 'Alliance in a Secret War: The United States and the Hmong of Northeastern Laos', Master's Thesis, San Diego State University.

Cooper, Robert G. (1978a), 'Dynamic Tension: Symbiosis and Contradiction in Hmong Social Relations', in J. Clammer, ed., *The New Economic Anthropology*, London, Macmillan, pp. 138–75.

——(1978b), 'Unity and Division in Hmong Social Categories in Thailand', in P.S.J. Chen and H.D. Evers, eds, *Studies in ASEAN Sociology*, Singapore, Chopmen Enterprises, pp. 297–320.

Department of the Army (1970), *Ethnographic Study Series: Minority Groups in Thailand*, Pamphlet No. 550–107, Washington DC, US Government Printing Office 0–351–606.

Dommen, Arthur (1971), *Conflict in Laos: The Politics of Neutralization*, New York, Praeger.

Geddes, William B. (1976), *Migrants of the Mountains: The Ecology of the Blue Miao (Hmong Njua) of Thailand*, Oxford, Clarendon Press.

Halpern, Joel and Peter Kunstadter (1967), 'Laos: Introduction', in P. Kunstadter, ed., *Southeast Asian Tribes, Minorities, and Nations*, Princeton, NJ, Princeton University Press, p. 233–58.

Heimbach, Ernest E. (1979), *White Hmong-English Dictionary*, Ithaca, NY, Southeast Asia Program, Cornell University.

La Barre, Weston (1972), *The Ghost Dance: The Origins of Religion*, New York, Dell Publishing Co.

Lebar, Frank, Gerald C. Hickey and John K. Musgrave (1964), *Ethnic Groups of Mainland Southeast Asia*, New Haven, Conn., Human Relations Areas Files Press.

Los Angeles Times (1979), 'Signs of poison gas use in Laos described by US', 13 December.

McBeth, John (1979), 'Tracing a gas leak', *Far Eastern Economic Review*, vol. 24, no. 12, August.

McCoy, Alfred W., Cathleen B. Read and Leonard P. Adams II (1972), *The Politics of Heroin and Southeast Asia*, New York, Harper and Row.

Marks, Thomas A. (1973), 'The Meo Hill Tribe Problem in North Thailand', *Asian Survey*, vol. 13, pp. 929–44.

Nagata, Judith (1974), 'What is a Malay? Situational Selection of Ethnic Identity in a Plural Society', *American Ethnologist*, vol. 1, pp. 331–50.

Okamura, Jonathan, Y. (1981), 'Situational Ethnicity', *Ethnic and Racial Studies*, vol. 4, pp. 452–65.

Pringle, James (1979), 'The end of the Hmong', *Newsweek*, 27 August, pp. 34–5.

Ruey, Yih-fu (1962), 'The Miao: Their Origin and Southward Migration', in *International Association of Historians of Asia, Second Biennial Conference Proceedings*, Taipei, Taiwan, International Association of Historians of Asia, pp. 179–90.

Savina, F.M. (1930), *Historie des Miao*, 2nd edn, Hong Kong, Imprimerie de la Société des Missions-Étrangères de Paris.

'oye, Hugh (1968), *Laos: Buffer State or Battleground*, London, Oxford University Press.

Jnited States House of Congress (1979), *Refugees from Indochina: Current Problems and Prospects*, Report Submitted by a Congressional Delegation to Southeast Asia, Committee on Foreign Affairs, Washington DC, US Government Printing Office, 30 April.

'ang, Tou Fu (1979), 'The Hmong of Laos', in *Meeting the Needs of Indochinese Students: Highlights of the Statewide Workshop for Educators of Elementary and Secondary Level Indochinese Students*, Arlington Heights, Il., Bilingual Education Service Center, pp. 10–16.

PART III: AFRICA, THE MIDDLE EAST AND THE PACIFIC ISLANDS

8 THE SOUTHERN SUDANESE SECESSIONIST MOVEMENT

Nandini Raghavan

For two decades the Sudan has been wreaked by a debilitating civil war between the north and south. The preponderantly Islamic people of the north with superior numbers and resources have benefited more from government policy than the non-Islamic tribes of the south. Basic differences of religion and values apart, many complaints of oppression, neglect and exploitation have also been ventilated. Foreign powers have become embroiled, thereby internationalising the dispute. Separatist groups have arisen in the south to assert their unique primordial identity as well as combat discrimination and domination.[1] The guns of the civil war have been silenced periodically to permit negotiations and settlement. Several solutions have been attempted including internal regional autonomy and specific compensatory programmes to offset Southern neglect and underdevelopment. In all of this, trust has been wanting. The Addis Ababa Agreement of 1972 came closest to reconciling the differences between the north and south.[2] This, however, fell apart. The attempt by the northern-dominated government to maintain a unified state faces intense challenges from the south for separation and autonomy. This chapter delves into the bases of the north–south cleavage and discusses attempts at reconciliation and causes of their failure.

The bases of the North–South division

The largest country in Africa, covering over one million square miles, the Sudan occupies a unique position between the Arab and African worlds for geographic and political reasons. Straddling the frontiers between Islamic and non-Islamic Africa, the Sudan has common borders with eight countries; Egypt, Ethiopia, Uganda, Kenya, Zaïre, Chad, Libya and the Central African Republic. The country's location astride these strategic and cultural boundaries cuts across significant ethnic and linguistic units which are important sources in the politics of identification in the Sudan.[3]

At the time of independence in 1956, the January census listed six hundred ethnic groups.[4] Racially the census estimated that there were 39 per cent Arabs, mostly in the north, 20 per cent Nilotics in the south, 6 per cent Beja in the east, 6 per cent Nubiya in the extreme north and 5 per cent Nilo-hamitics in the south. The same census revealed that Arabic was spoken by 51 per cent of the population, Nilotic languages by 18 per cent and northern and central Sudanese languages by 12 per cent.[5] The current (1988) population is 22 million and the estimated annual growth rate is about 2.7 per cent.

The ethnic origin of the people of the Sudan is mixed, and the country is still subject to significant immigration by groups from Nigeria and Chad, such as the Fulani. Arab culture and language predominate in the north and the religion is Islam. The people of the south fall into three main categories: the Nilotes, the Nilo-hamites and the Sudanic group.[6] The Dinka, the Nuer and the Shilluki are the most important sub-groups of the Nilotes. To the south of the Nilotes are the Nilo-hamites, who include the Bari, the Latuka, the Mandari, the Kiki and many others. The Sudanic group includes the Kreisch, the Moru and the Madi. While diversity is one of the fundamental causes of the conflict between the north and the south, it would be too simple to reduce these differences to religion alone.[7] Just as the south is a mixture of various cultures, the north is a product of racial and cultural integration between Arab and indigenous Sudanese races, and although various economic, social and political factors have caused the overplay of the Arab symbol, the product can justifiably be called Sudanese. Further, although the colonial era halted the infiltration of Islam into the south, only 5 per cent of the present south population are Christian.

Sudanese history can be traced back to the second century BC but as a political entity the Sudan came into existence only with the Anglo-Egyptian penetration in the early nineteenth century. Although the Sudan was theoretically the joint responsibility of both the Egyptians and the British under the condominium rule, in practice it was a British colony. By accident of history the future of the north and the south had become interwoven due to the arbitrary boundaries drawn under the condominium rule. The centuries of geographic and historical insulation of the south from the north was reinforced by the policy of separate development of the south undertaken during the condominium rule. This was done by specific political and social measures, including the introduction of Christianity in the south and the cordoning off of the south against the influence and spread of Islam.

The two decades between 1926 and 1946 saw the promulgation of the

Southern Policy which was codified by law and adopted officially by the government in 1930.[8] The policy in the southern Sudan was to build up a series of self-contained racial units with their structure and organization based upon indigenous customs, traditional usage and beliefs.[9] This policy was further reinforced by the teaching of English to the local police; replacement of northern employees by locally recruited ones; restricting entry of Muslims into the south; and internal shuffling of the ethnic tribes.[10] Furthermore, Sunday was introduced as the traditional day of rest instead of Friday as in the north. The Southern Policy thus succeeded in keeping the two sections of the country apart.

However, this policy of isolation was revised drastically with the revival of the struggle against colonial rule. The formation of the Graduates Congress in 1937 was a landmark in the history of Sudanese nationalism. Northern political opinion and the rapid spread of the national movement increased the pressure on the government for a reconsideration of the southern policy. The Southern Policy was then reversed. The new policy acted on the fact that the two regions were inextricably bound together for future development. The distinction in the rates of pay and other conditions of government service, the rules preventing employment of southerners in the north, and attempts at economic separation were revoked. The development of communications between the north and the south ended the era of isolation that had existed between them. After centuries of insulation from the north, the southern Sudan was being drawn out of its cocoon in a hurry, just prior to the dawn of independence. The concept of autonomous regional development advanced by the British administrators was later adopted by the southern politicians as the only solution to the problem of national integration in the Sudan.

The last minute attempts to undo centuries of isolation did not work miracles. The policy of separate administration had left its indelible mark on the future relations between the north and the south ensuring that no feeling of fraternity existed at the time of independence. The British had fostered separate customs and languages, and had introduced Christianity against Islam. British policies accentuated differences between the north and the south reinforcing the stereotypes the two sides held about each other. The British had left a country hastily sewed together, in which mutually hostile communities tried to settle their disputes by resorting to force. It was virtually inevitable that, when the British abdicated, the northerners being the strongest of the two sections of the Sudanese people, should attempt to assimilate the south by force. This in turn made the rise of a southern resistance and separatist movement inevitable.

A catalogue of southern complaints and issues

The Juba conference in 1947 was one of the results of the pressures exerted by the southern politicians and the British Governors for safeguards for the south. However, the Anglo-Egyptian Agreement, of 1953 (which had been concluded without southern participation), annulled Article 100 of the Self-Government Statute, constituting southern safeguards. Instead a provision was made in the Statute giving the south only two ministerial posts. Southern mistrust of the north increased as a result of this. The southerners were also beginning to lose faith in the British. The south therefore began to rely more on direct methods for the attainment of their demands. However, in spite of these tensions between the north and the south, the southerners did participate in the elections held in October 1954. The south was allocated only twenty-two out of ninety-seven seats. The pro-Egyptian National Union Party (NUP) won with an overwhelming majority. The party Chairman, Ismail al Azhari, became the Sudan's first Prime Minister.

Azhari's first major political action was the appointment of the Sudanization Committee in February 1954. The south received only four junior posts in a total of 800 vacancies. The effect of this on the already deteriorating north–south relations at the time of independence was devastating. The 1956 and 1965 governments also failed adequately to understand the situation and the causes of the north–south problem in their country. This created the volatile situation of the south having a permanent minority status. Such a distribution of political power and control over the political apparatus, coupled with the legacy of the native administration in the colonial era, then ensured the persistence of ethnic boundaries and, in fact, even played the role of reinforcing these differences. The north, in the eyes of the southern regions, was displaying its unwillingness to share power.

During the two parliamentary regimes (1956–8 and 1964–9) the struggle in the south was for increasing participation in the political system and for economic development of the southern regions. Further, during the election campaigns, political parties used historical hostilities as a weapon against each other. The National Union Party (NUP), for example, 'levelled charges against the Umma Party and reminded the southerners that they [the Umma Party members] were the descendents of their bitter enemies—the slave traders'.[11] Thus, instead of underplaying hostilities, they were rekindled for political advantage. Attractive undertakings were made: the NUP President had promised that 'not only would priority be given to the southerners in the south but . . . shall be greatly fostered in the north, especially in the higher ranks of the central government services' and that 'there will be District Commissioners, Governors and in general they will have a fourth of the jobs in the Sudan'.[12] None of these promises materialised after the elections were over.

Another major source of conflict between the north and the south was in the education policy and the role of religion in the south, both controlled by the missionaries. In February 1957, the Minister of Education announced that he had decided to take direct responsibility for education in the southern provinces. This action was interpreted by the south as a deliberate attempt on the part of the north to 'Arabize' the southern states. In 1957, for example, the Umma Party and the NUP had issued a joint statement calling for the Sudan to be an Islamic country with the Shari'a (Islamic law) as the source of legislation.[13]

The October Revolution led by General Nimeiri was caused by the government's high-handed dealing of the south.[14] However, this policy was based on the mistaken idea that the problem of the south was a military one. The expulsion of the missionaries and military action against the Anya-nya (the southern separatist forces) only heightened the apprehension and anger in the south.

Economic discrimination and secession

The south itself was divided into three groups: some advocated a decentralized system of government, others demanded a federation and the third called for self-determination on the grounds that mistrust, suspicion and lack of statesmanship on both sides undermined the possibility of a compromise.[15] Although the formation of Southern Sudan Provincial Councils (created as a separate government for the southern regions) was a definite threat to the central government and the country as a whole, southern leaders had not always advocated secession. A situation of open-mindedness for bargaining and negotiations did exist which was never taken up by the northern parties until President Nimeiri hammered out the Addis Ababa Treaty. As Joseph Lagu, one of the most influential leaders in the south had once said:

> I was never a separatist. I never believed in secession of the south from the north. My only aim was to obtain recognition for the southerners . . . I had

> resorted to force because I concluded that the successive governments in Khartoum were not willing to concede the point.[16]

The vast economic disparities between the north and the south were no doubt enhanced by the uneven development that occurred during the colonial period. The state reinforced existing disparities by allocating resources and centralizing infrastructure in these areas. The underdevelopment of the southern regions of the Sudan was a direct result of the fact that the British found it extremely difficult and expensive to develop this area. One of the main difficulties here was that of communications and transport, although the authenticity of this reason has been seriously challenged.[17]

In the eyes of the southerners, the northerners maintained this economic policy only in order to ensure the perpetual domination over the southerners. The initial call for autonomy was soon transformed into a vociferous demand for secession.[18] The situation was further complicated by vast differences in employment opportunities and training available to the southerners. Between independence and 1964, 153 northerners were admitted into the Police College as against seven southerners. A similar inequality was evident in the recruitment and promotion opportunities in the army as well. In 1954 and 1955 together four southerners and sixty-four northerners were commissioned as officers in the army. After independence up to 1965 sixteen southerners and 505 northerners were commissioned. The highest rank that a southerner had held in the army until 1965 was that of a major. By 1965 only two were in active service—most having been dismissed after serving various terms of imprisonment for involvement in the 1955 uprising.[19]

The situation was similar in all other government services as well. In public administration, the reluctance of authorities to appoint southerners had a discouraging effect even on the believers of the union with the north policy. The highest post any southerner could achieve was that of Deputy Commissioner. There were no southerners in the Ministries of Commerce, Industry or Supplies. There was not a single southerner as Permanent Under-Secretary or Director of any Department in Khartoum. The sudden introduction of Arabic as well as the prevalent practice of direct nepotism made the chances of a southerner being appointed even more remote.

As Joseph Garang, a prominent southerner noted: 'Northern intelligence occupied nearly all the posts in the Service. The south has neither the national capital nor the trained intelligence'.[20] Though the level of literacy in the Sudan is generally low, the disparities between the north and the south are undeniable. A United Nations Survey recorded that out of the 190 higher secondary schools in the Sudan, only twelve (or 6.3 per cent) were in the south.[21] There were greater disparities in the health services. A statistical survey revealed that there were more doctors in Khartoum than in the rest of the country put together.[22] The same survey noted that the number of men with at least elementary school education were 24.2 per cent in the north-west, 34.4 per cent in the north-east and 9.2 per cent in the south. The study further noted the absence of any 'large urban' centres in the three southern provinces was another major handicap, not only for industrial development, but also for development of other activities in these parts.[23] Uneven development and unequal access to the economic and political resources of the state have then been responsible for exacerbating the ethnic tensions and provoking sentiments for separation. The southerner felt that he was a victim of 'internal colonialism'. Instead of taking positive action to improve the situation and 'conceding the legitimate interests of the south',[24] Khartoum seemed paralysed under the politics of party infighting. The south engaged the north in battle. The civil war was draining the economy further. The estimate of the amount spent on the war during 1968 was Sudanese £12–20 million per year out of a total annual revenue of Sudanese £98 million.

Decentralisation and conflict resolution

President Nimeiri realized that in spite of the undeniable ethnic differences between the two regions, genuine efforts at the economic development of the south and the devolution of power away from Khartoum could be the answer to Sudan's problem of national unity. This section will look into the specific provisions of the Addis Ababa Agreement that put an end to the civil war in the Sudan and analyse the reasons for the breakdown of the Agreement.

The May 25 revolution was a swift and non-violent one. The Sudanese people watched the army return to the political arena less than five years after its removal by a popular revolt. The President assured the people that his party, unlike all the others, was to be primarily a forum for political consensus, transcending sectarian, regional and ideological loyalties. The Addis Ababa Agreement was the culmination of a whole new political attitude in the Sudan. The most significant institutional change was the implementation of the 1971 People's Local Self-

Government Act that defined the position of the south within a united Sudan. This went a long way in convincing the southerners that the new regime was sincere in its promises.

A conference between the two sides (which ultimately culminated in the Agreement) was held in Addis Ababa. There were five main areas of concern: the question of regional autonomy for the south and guarantees against its misuse; the need to accommodate other religions while ensuring that Islam did not lose ground in the north; the balance between a strong one-party presidential system and the system of accountability. The most important section of the argument was the one assuring and enacting self-government in the southern regions. Politically, the Agreement met the demands of the southern nationalists that the then three southern provinces of Bahr el Gazal, Equatoria and Upper Nile be treated as a single region with the power to act autonomously. It was given a regional assembly and an executive organ known as the High Executive Council (HEC). There was a break-up of subjects under regional jurisdiction (for example, regional bureaucracy and the police) and those under the centre.[25]

Another provision aimed specifically at placating southern nationalist sentiments was that 'Arabic was the official language for the Sudan and English the principal language for the southern Sudan'.[26] The permanent Constitution reinforced this by specifying that although Islam was the religion of the Democratic Republic of the Sudan, Christianity and other African religions would be given equal weight as the religions of a large section of the state. A regional university was started in Juba in 1978, thereby realising a long-standing demand of the south for tertiary education catering to its need for trained manpower.[27]

The Addis Ababa Agreement thus not only ensured that the southerners had autonomy to manage their own affairs but, by constitutionally declaring the equality of all Sudanese, it also created the atmosphere in which the scarce resources of the state could be shared equitably. The main premisses were that politico-economic equality and religious tolerance would help contain the centrifugal tendencies of ethnic and racial cleavages in the Sudan. Having surveyed how equality and religious tolerance were institutionalized in the Agreement, we shall now examine how the gradual erosion of the Agreement since the mid-1970s and its final collapse in 1983 were due to the undermining of these structures.

Organisationally, the system of regional self-government adopted in the south entailed not merely a purely administrative transfer of authority from the centre to the regions, but also the creation of new regional legislative and executive organs.[28] Yet the Agreement was either ambiguous or silent on some of the basic matters connected with the executive and legislative functions of the government. These fundamental differences relating to the nature of the political system and its basic principles had resulted in political confusion and legal ambiguity.

The most glaring discrepancy was executive power. Self-government in the south was based on a parliamentary system with the executive responsible to the legislative body. The latter was also empowered to dismiss the former. In contrast, the national constitution provided for a presidential system in which the executive authority was vested solely in the President of the Republic. The Sudanese Socialist Union (SSU) was to nominate the President of the country and select or approve the candidates for the National Assembly. The very idea of a one-party system was inconsistent with the basic assumptions of parliamentary government. Thus, the intrusion of the SSU in southern politics ran counter to the spirit, if not to the letter, of the Agreement and proved to be destabilising and divisive.

For devolution in the south to succeed, public planning, organization and mobilization of resources were crucial. The constitution of the institutional structures was then a priority requirement for the proper and meaningful exercise of public power in the interest of the people. Regional government in the south faced many obstacles in the building of the proper institutions necessary for devolution of power. In spite of the initial trust the south placed in the Agreement, the period between June 1973 and December 1974 brought to light some of the difficulties in implementing the principles enshrined in the Agreement.

The most important difficulty was the time factor: the period of transition between the cessation of hostilities and the introduction of the first definitive law and the machinery by which it could be made effective. This time lag caused a state of continuous conflict between central and regional ministers over the question of jurisdiction, resulting in the gradual erosion of the Agreement. For example, the central Ministry of Finance and National Economy was unaware of the existence of the law that had transferred certain taxes to the regions and had therefore objected to their collection by the regional government. The Ministry also refused to release the money collected by the central government contrary to such laws.

There was a growing feeling among the southerners that the north as a block was developing a strategy of identifying itself with the central government and thereby controlling the distribution of resources and limiting opportunities for equal participation available to the south. To counteract these fears, President Nimeiri divided the north into five regions. Using the division of the north as an example of making the government more responsible and efficient, President Nimeiri also redivided the south into the original three provinces. This division of the south was viewed by the south as an outright abrogation of the Addis Ababa Agreement. Secondly, the constitutional safeguards which had in the first place gone to allay southern fears were swept away with one stroke of the pen. North–south relations in the Sudan were once again left to the mercy of force.

The deepening division: international and other factors

A political development that had a negative impact on north–south relations in the Sudan was the signing of the economic charter with Egypt. A Charter of Integration with Egypt provided for a ten-year agreement on political and economic integration and close co-operation with regard to foreign policy, security and development. In the southern regions, the charter faced opposition from leaders who feared that increased liaison between Khartoum and Cairo would lead to a diminution of their role. The Charter reintroduced the earlier conviction of the southerners of the possibility of 'Arab' domination over them, and thus had a damaging effect on the spirit of the Agreement. The attempt at Islamization of the country through the introduction of the Shari'a was perhaps the most apparent abrogation of the Agreement. Though the Agreement had embodied specific provisions to ensure the equality of all religions in the Sudan, President Nimeiri announced in September 1983 that the Shari'a would henceforth be the basis of all law in the Sudan. This was met with predictable opposition from the southerners and the resumption of the civil war.

In addition to these socio-political features, failure on the economic front for the country as a whole intensified the struggle for control over scarce resources and accentuated the difficulties in the way of any meaningful devolution to the south. The concentration of the population in the Khartoum province and the central regions has always reflected the concentration of development in these regions and the neglect of the other parts of the country. Written in 1976, the following observations were made by the ILO:

> The southern provinces are the poorest in the Sudan. Per capita income is

> about half that of the national average and perhaps only about one-quarter of that of the more prosperous provinces of [Gezira], Kassala and Khartoum. They are relatively neglected in the provision of public services, and much of the south is cut off from the stream of progress in the rest of the country'.

When the Agreement brought about truce in the civil war, development was revived in the north on a wider scale. So the north was being developed more as a result of the peace in the south. Although projects like the Jonglei canal and undertakings for oil exploration were initiated as being beneficial to the south, many southerners believed that the Jonglei canal merely facilitated the flow of the Nile waters to the north. The site where oil was found increased the dispute over boundaries between the north and the south. Disputes over territory, according to the Agreement, were to be resolved through a referendum. The implications of this provision had remained dormant until the discovery of oil in 1980 at Bentiu. Southerners claimed that Bentiu belonged to the southern regions. The location of the refinery also became a part of this controversy. When it was decided that the refinery would be built in Kosti, in the north, the southerners felt that the oil was being dug from 'southern grounds' and was aiding northern development, while the south remained economically backward in spite of the promises made in the Addis Ababa Agreement.[29]

Conclusion

This chapter has adopted the view that the Addis Ababa Agreement recognised the fact that the organisation and political significance of inter-ethnic relations in the Sudan was generally related to the factors affecting the competition for economic and political resources. For secession to be averted, power-sharing between the centre and the regions is essential. If the ethnic conflict in the Sudan is exclusively racial and religious, a solution that satisfies all parties will not be possible. In this chapter, secession is assumed to be curable by pragmatic remedies such as decentralisation and equitable distribution of economic resources and political powers. In practice, associated symbolic issues may make a dispute unamenable to easy solution.

Notes

1. For primordial factors see C. Geertz, ed., *The Integrative Revolution*,

Glencoe, Ill., The Free Press, 1963, p. 157; for an analytic distinction between primordial and secondary factors, see R. Premdas, 'Secessionist Politics in Papua New Guinea', *Pacific Affairs* (Spring 1977).
2. Nelson Kasfir, 'Sudan's Addis Ababa Treaty: Intra-Organizational Factors in the Politics of Compromise', in *Post-Independence Sudan*, Centre for African Studies, University of Edinburgh, 1980; Mansour Khalid, *Nimeiri and the Politics of Dismay*, London, KPI Publishers, 1985; M.O. Beshir, *The Southern Sudan: The Background to Conflict*, London, Hurst, 1968; M.O. Beshir, *The Southern Sudan: From Conflict to Peace*, London, Hurst, 1975: *Revolution and Nationalism in the Sudan*, London, Barnes and Noble, 1974; Oliver Albino, *The Southern Sudan: A Southern Point of View*, publication for the Institute of Race Relations, Oxford University Press, London, 1970; Paul Ledoucer, 'The Southern Sudan: A Forgotten War and a Lost Peace', *International Journal*, no. 30, Summer (1975), p. 406.
3. M.B. Hamid, *Ethnic Studies Report*, Vol. II, No. 2 (July 1984), p. 53.
4. Quoted in *Peace and Unity in the Sudan*, Ministry of Foreign Affairs, Khartoum University Press, 1973, p. 13.
5. J.A. Allan, 'Sudan: Physical and Social Geography' in *Africa: South of the Sahara, 1984–85*, London, Europa Publications, 1985, p. 787.
6. *Peace and Unity in the Sudan*, op. cit., p. 16.
7. See, for example, F.M. Deng, *Dynamics of National Integration in the Sudan*, Khartoum University Press, 1973, p. 108.
8. *South Documents*, National Records Office, Khartoum, File No. 1/77/433.
9. *Administrative Policies in the Southern Sudan*, National Records Office, Khartoum, File No. BGP/SCR/i.c.i.
10. Letter from J.C. Mathews to H.A. MacMichael, Civil Secretary, 30 April 1930, National Records Office, Khartoum, File No. 1/c/1.
11. J. Garang, 'On Economic and Regional Autonomy', in D.M. Wai, ed., *The Southern Sudan: The Problem of National Integration*, London, Frank Cass, 1973, p. 88.
12. E. O'Ballance, *The Secret War in the Sudan: 1955–72*, Hamden, Conn., Archon Books, 1977, p. 41.
13. M.A. Rahim, 'Sudan: Recent History' in *Africa South of the Sahara, 1984–85*, p. 788.
14. O'Ballance, op. cit., p. 76.
15. *Sudan: A Country Study*, Area Handbook Series, The American University, 1982, passim.
16. F.B. Mahmood, *The Sudanese Bourgeoise*, London, Zed Books: Khartoum University Press, 1984, p. 27.
17. Albino, *The Southern Sudan*, p. 89.
18. See S. McCall and P. Russell, 'Can Secession be Justified?' in D.M. Wai, ed., *The Southern Sudan*, op. cit., p. 110.
19. *Sudan: A Country Study*, op. cit., p. 130.
20. Ibid.
21. *UN Statistical Year Book*, New York, United Nations Publications, 1969, p. 602.
22. *Sudan: A Country Study*, op. cit., p. 130.
23. *Population and Man Power in the Sudan*, A Joint Study by the United Nations and the Government of the Sudan, United Nations, New York, 1964, p. 114.

24. Quoted in D.M. Wai, ed., *The Southern Sudan*, op. cit., p. 167.
25. Khalid, *Nimeiri*, p. 5.
26. Khalid, *Nimeiri*, p. 47; and Raphel Koba Badal, *The Addis Ababa Agreement: 10 Years After—An Assessment*, papers presented to the Conference on North–South Relations since the Addis Ababa Agreement, convened in Khartoum in March 1985, unpublished, p. 1.
27. Andrew W.R. Weiu, *Southern Sudan: Institutional Structure; Power and Inter-governmental Relations: Yesterday and Today*, unpublished paper presented to the Conference on North–South Relations since the Addis Ababa Agreement, Khartoum, 1985, p. 4.
28. See the chapter on decentralisation by Ralph Premdas in this volume.
29. Othwong Dak, *Southern Regions: Decentralization or Recentralization?*, unpublished paper presented to the Conference on North–South Relations in Khartoum, 1985, p. 11.

DECENTRALISATION, DEVELOPMENT AND SECESSION: THE CASE OF PAPUA NEW GUINEA

Ralph R. Premdas

In the light of persistent poverty in the Third World, it has been advocated that states decentralise their governmental machinery to share decision-making with grass-roots units in order to promote development.[1] The arguments for decentralisation are persuasive. Decentralisation brings government closer to the people who will participate as active agents in identifying projects and designing ways for their implementation. Julius Nyerere has remarked that development is not something that is done to people, but rather something that people do for themselves.[2] Development theorists also belabour the point that participation and mobilisation are critical ingredients of successful development strategies. Decentralisation will broaden the base of citizen involvement in decision-making. Most Third World states inherited an administrative structure that was highly centralised and had only sporadic links with the outskirts beyond the capital city and provincial centres.[3] Advocates of decentralisation in pursuit of participation and mobilisation posit that the administrative structure must be radically altered so as to bring a regime closer to the people and make decision-makers accessible and accountable for their actions.[4]

Like so many formulas prescribed for changing the Third World, the decentralisation approach is easier to enunciate than to effectively implement. It seems that the reason in this case is that decentralisation is a very sensitive political issue, which threatens to redistribute the structure of power in the state. To put it differently, to decentralise is not merely to shuffle the cards in a pack, but using a more appropriate metaphor, requires the flattening of a pyramid of power. To decentralise is to reorganise power, to take from some and give to others. It is a zero-sum game. The type of decentralisation addressed here is not the routine devolution of administrative discretion to subordinate and accountable sub-units in the same organisation. Rather, it is a different animal that is quasi-federal in structure in that both decision-making powers and administrative responsibility are redistributed to relatively autonomous regional or provincial bodies. The chances are excellent that in this type of extensive decentralisation, the powers of the central government are not reinforced; instead decentralisation entails the creation of the new centres of power, new political actors and new sources of patronage.[5] The new order may insert a new virile layer of politics with actors at the regional and peripheral areas challenging the power of incumbents at the centre. As such, the call for decentralisation, unless it is mere rhetoric, cannot be treated as a technical exercise, but as a pre-eminent political contest in which the highest stakes of survival are involved.

In this chapter, I examine a case of decentralisation in the Third World from the perspective of a zero-sum power contest. I show that demands from the provinces for extensive decentralisation to promote development could not be granted by merely appealing to rhetorical arguments about the virtues of a system of regional government. Those at the centre who exercised power were not willing to concede parts of their domain unless forced to do so. Consequently, the challengers at the periphery threatened secession if their demands for provincial autonomy were not met. It was only when this threat was made with credibility bringing the new state to the brink of civil war, that the national power holders were willing to make concessions. The case examined here refers to the south-west Pacific state, Papua New Guinea (PNG). In this chapter I do not advocate secession. Instead, I point to the pivotal political power relationships which undergird the proposal for decentralisation. Whether these proposals are advanced in Sri Lanka, Nigeria, Sudan or Canada, decentralisation demands cannot be understood unless the political dimension is spelt out. This chapter also addresses the issue of decentralisation as a strategy for promoting democracy and development. The next two sections trace the evolution of a centralised state apparatus, while the following two sections discuss the impact of decolonisation on a new experiment in decentralisation.

Colonisation, centralisation and development

Rivalry among imperial powers as well as security considerations impelled Australia to acquire the eastern half of the New Guinea island.[6] In full command of 'The Territory of Papua and New Guinea' after World War I, Australia administered the country by direct rule.[7] Partly, this was dictated by the structure of social organisation among the indigenous people. Over 700 language groups existed among a population of nearly a million people, while the topographically chopped-up terrain facilitated their dispersion among numerous small-scale self-contained communities having between fifty and a hundred persons per settlement. This highly atomised habitation structure was matched internally within each community by a system of non-hierarchic decision-making. A veritable democracy persisted; community decisions were arrived at through direct participation and consensus.[8] Taken together, Melanesian social organisation was democratic, meritocratic and decentralised.

Until World War II, Australia was satisfied with maintaining a skeletal staff to assert control over 'The Territory of Papua and New Guinea'. The operational link between governor and villager was basically a double-tier hierarchy, the higher echelon occupied by a patrol officer (a *kiap*) and the low by a selected villager called a village constable in Papua and a *luluai* in New Guinea.[9] Called '*kiap* rule', the inadequately staffed district administrative system was intermittent and restricted mainly to law and order.[10] A poll tax was imposed on adult males to raise revenues for administration as well as being a device to conscript them into plantation indenture service.[11] Alien presence was not extensive, constituted mainly by missionaries, plantation owners and supervisors, government officials and miners. Until World War II, colonial rule was still not overly centralised while the bureaucracy was small.[12] It took the massive upheaval of the war to jolt the system out of its stability, transforming it into a new dynamic order.

World War II simultaneously underlined the strategic value of PNG to Australia as well as pointing to the negligence of the colonial administration in developing an infra-structure of basic facilities in the territories. Japanese forces had established a foothold in Papua and New Guinea from which they threatened Australia. While events would contain Japanese expansion, the lesson learnt would translate into a massive post-war development effort by Australia.[13]

It was envisaged that investment in the territory's development would cultivate the loyalty of the people, a critical component in minimising defence costs as well as fortifying PNG as the first line of defence against a northern enemy.[14] In the post-war period, Australia accepted the United Nations Trusteeship obligation to prepare Papua and New Guinea for eventual independence.[15] This commitment would prove to be a major stimulant to political evolution, for touring UN missions made periodic visits, interviewed indigenous residents, carried out inspections, and disseminated its report to the international community.[16]

Two tiers of government institutions were transferred simultaneously from Australia to PNG. At the national level, the appointed Australian Administrator for PNG was progressively phased out by an elected local legislature. In 1951, the first country-wide Legislative Council was established but out of its 29-person membership, only three nominees were Papua New Guineans. In 1961, a Legislative Council was established this time with one third indigenous membership.[17] Devolution of political powers to national institutions was clearly slow, so that when the famous Foot Mission from the UN arrived in 1963, it delivered a scorching critique of Australian tardiness in involving Papua New Guineans in decision-making.[18] The upshot was the introduction of universal adult suffrage and the establishment of the first fully elected House of Assembly in 1964. The momentum of political advance would accelerate particularly after the 1968 elections when the rudiments of an agitational self-government movement emerged.[19] The rest of the story is well known. After the 1972 general elections, a ministerial system was inaugurated under indigenous control. Internal self-government came in 1974 followed by independence in 1976.[20]

At the grassroots level, elected local councils were initiated. By 1956, only ten councils were established; projected at that rate, it would have taken a century to cover the country.[21] Representing several contiguous villages, each council embraced peoples with diverse dialects and traditions. Most villagers did not understand what councils were about since they were still being told what to do even in regard to the structure and operations of the councils themselves.[22] That apart, the local government operations were caught up in a mire of baffling procedural complexity. In the end, councils were reduced to mere agents serving an increasingly top heavy central government.

The rush towards economic development, emphasising efficiency and control, hampered thc transfer of political powers at all levels of government. The strategy of economic development led directly to centralisation of the public service and specialisation of service delivery systems. One observer noted:

> The policies of 'centralization' in the form of a large and powerful bureaucracy in Canberra, and 'specialization', in the form of multiplied functional departments with their own hierarchies in the Territory, were complementary to each other. The strengthened lines of command, from every specialist officer in the field through his own departmental headquarters in Port Moresby to the Department of Territories and Minister, were calculated to concentrate decision-making in the hands of the Minister and his immediate advisers.[23]

Centralisation and specialisation were continuing unabated. The emphasis on rapid economic development necessitated large infusions of skilled overseas staff. The PNG public service increased from about 1,700 in 1948 and about 18,000 in 1968, a tenfold increase. Nearly all public servants were Australians. It was not until 1955 that a Special Auxiliary Division composed of Papua New Guineans was created. For the most part then, development programmes were executed by expatriate staff concentrated in urban centres. The inclusion of large numbers of PNG personnel at the middle and upper levels of the public service did not take place until the mid-1970s. An uncompromisingly hierarchic administrative structure evolved in the country. New specialist departments proliferated, each responsible independently for their programmes right down to district and village level. The territory's public service effectively became 'an extension of the Australian public service, dominated by Australian values and methods'.[24] A World Bank report confirmed the excessive centralisation recommending against 'the concentration of decision-making in the headquarters at Port Moresby'.[25] But these admonitions could not reverse the trend towards increasing centralisation. Australia had become obsessively pre-occupied with laying down an infrastructure to sustain stability. The defence of Australia's northern flanks required a stable and dependent neighbour when self-determination became effective. The massive infusion of aid and investment was such that at all levels while PNG would benefit economically, it would simultaneously become dependent on Australia for its continued survival. If centralisation was an inevitable concomitant of rapid economic change, then it was also an excellent device for welding the PNG economy and society to Australian umbilical control. Throughout the 1970s, after independence in 1976, PNG was the recipient of a phenomenal $250 to $300 million of foreign aid from Australia.[26] Decolonisation, to be effective, would need to reverse this embrace through diversification and decentralisation.

Political independence, decentralisation and secession

To prepare the country for independence, a Constitutional Planning Committee (CPC) was appointed by the House of Assembly in 1972 to solicit opinions from citizens on the structure of the future government. The CPC report contended that there was 'a widespread discontent with the distribution of power in our country'.[27] It described the PNG government as 'highly centralised' arguing that 'all the decisions are made in Konedobu'.[28] A team of consultants to the CPC confirmed this view stating: 'in our experience of political systems in Asia, Africa, and the Caribbean, we have not come across an administrative system so highly centralised and dominated by its bureaucracy'.[29]

Decolonisation for the CPC required the dismantling of the old system to institute meaningful democracy:

> Power must be returned to the people. Government services should be accessible to them. Decisions should be made by the people to whom the issues at stake are meaningful, easily understood, and relevant. The existing system of government should therefore be re-structured and power should be decentralised, so that the energies and aspirations of our people can play their full part in promoting our country's development.[30]

The CPC recommended a radical restructuring of the politico-administrative system that would closely resemble a federal arrangement.

Although the Somare-led government in 1972 adopted an eight-point programme which in part advocated 'decentralisation of economic activity, planning and government spending',[31] it was not prepared for a sudden radical alteration of the inherited colonial order. The Somare government, the first indigenous regime to be bestowed with full ministerial responsibility, was beset by secessionist threats emanating from Papua and Bougainville.[32] Extensive decentralisation as prescribed by the CPC, it was thought, could encourage the next step towards secession. To Somare, national unity was its first priority.

But a more fundamental cleavage, ideological in nature, separated the government from the CPC. The struggle was between the 'pragmatists' led by Somare and the 'radicals' led by Fr. Momis. In principle, the Somare government acceded to a system of moderated powers for provincial governments, even permitting Bougainville to establish an interim provincial structure. But the issue of devolution was part of a wider conflict, which was enmeshed in divergent programmatic strategies for political and economic development. Provincial government was only one of the conflict issues. The upshot reverberated differently in two arenas of contest. At the legislative level, the Somare government, frustrated with the intransigence of the CPC, threw out the entire provincial government section of the constitutional bill. Hence, when PNG acceded to independence on 16 September 1975, its constitution was devoid of an arrangement for provincial or local government. At the field level, the contest deteriorated into violence bordering on civil war. Somare suspended the Bougainville Interim Provincial government upon which the island declared unilateral independence on 1 September, just two weeks prior to PNG's own independence date. This followed Papua's unilateral declaration of independence six months earlier on 16 March 1975. Suddenly, the first indigenous government of PNG was faced with its dismemberment, a prospect that portended its disintegration. Bougainville, with only 80,000 people out of PNG's 3 million, was the copper-rich island on which US $500 million had been invested to build one of the world's largest and most lucrative mines, yielding a substantial part of the central government's revenue. Papua, less wealthy, contained one-third of the country's population. Should Bougainville and Papua successfully secede, then other ethno-nationalist groups such as the Tolais on the Gazelle Peninsula were bound to follow suit.[33] The central government mobilising its military forces decided to confront the Bougainville secessionists who had already proceeded to destroy airfields on the island. Fortunately, at the last moment, passions were contained and both parties negotiated their differences over a six-month period. The settlement struck called for a restoration of decentralised provincial government not only on Bougainville but throughout PNG.

The reintroduction of provincial government: implementation and performance

The Bougainville incident attests to certain crucial aspects of power which we have attempted to trace out in this chapter. To compel the imperial ruler to relinquish power in PNG, the costs of continued control had to exceed the gains. Through a variety of external and internal pressures, Australia finally acceded to PNG's independence, in the knowledge that an indirect neo-colonial relationship can assure loyalty without incurring the stigma of direct colonial administration. Similarly, the national government, PNG, having inherited sovereign power to run the new nation, was reluctant to relinquish power to its peripheral parts. When the costs of maintaining this stance were shown to exceed the gains by the Bougainville secessionists, the central government was willing to make concessions. But, like the imperial power, the central government had learnt that its control of the purse-strings facilitated an equally effective 'neo-colonial' control of the provincial governments. When decentralization was implemented, each provincial government relied for over 80 per cent of its revenues on the central government.

The resolution of the Bougainville–PNG government confrontation was capped with the passage in Parliament of an Organic Law on Provincial Government in 1977.[34] The dubious connection between decentralisation and secession was set aside; the reverse proposition was accepted, that by according maximum autonomy to regions separatist impulses could be contained.

General elections were held in 1977. Fr. Momis, who had joined the Bougainville secessionists, was re-elected. The new Somare-led government created a Ministry of Decentralisation to which Fr. Momis was appointed minister. With this innovation, the implementation of provincial government dramatically accelerated. A handbook produced by the Ministry of Decentralisation described provincial government as 'a bloodless revolution',[35] for the implementation of provincial government would entail a basic alteration of power relationships throughout the polity. Decentralisation was not to be just a paper re-design of organisational structure. In practice, it promised to disrupt the colonially entrenched sources of power and influence. Some interests were bound to lose, while new power centres would emerge.

The Organic Law prescribed the form of provincial government. First, the structure replicated in its broadest outlines the tripartite division of legislative, executive and judicial powers found in the central government. Each province would have an elected Provincial Assembly of about twenty-four to thirty members, and a Provincial Executive Council (Cabinet) of no more than a third of the members of the Provincial Assembly and a Provincial Premier. Secondly, it related to revenues: the extent of financial autonomy is critical to the meaningful exercise of power by any subordinate unit of government. The Organic Law stipulated the following areas where provincial governments could raise their own revenues by taxation: (1) retail sales tax; (2) taxes on public entertainment charging for admission; (3) fees for licences for mobile traders (other than banks); (4) fees for licences for places where intoxicating liquor is sold; (5) fees for licences to operate gambling, lotteries and games of chance; (6) taxes on land; (7) poll tax; (8) any other tax that could previously be imposed by a Local Government Council.

However, revenues from these sources provided only 5 to 8 per cent of the total budget of a provincial government. The remainder was obtained through a system of conditional, unconditional and derivative grants transferred from the central government to the provincial government. In effect, while substantial powers were transferred, provincial governments lacked the independent means to enable them to carry out these functions. They had to depend on the central government to supply most of their treasury. To that extent then, the central government wielded control over the behaviour of provincial government.

The promise of a liberally decentralised form of provincial government that would permit communities to conduct their own affairs had excited the imagination of the PNG citizenry, especially those who suffered neglect at the grassroots. Change was slow however. Fr. Momis announced that by 1 January 1978 all districts would be accorded provincial government regardless of whether they were prepared for it or not. The overall path of implementation was chaotic. Reports of inefficiency, corruption and abuse became widespread, triggering disillusionment with the decentralisation experiment. Fr. Momis, who at one point announced that 'the debate about whether or not PNG should have provincial government has concluded',[36] was faced with an intense barrage of sceptical observations all pointing to the unviability and costliness of provincial government. The entire debate was reopened; criticisms against provincial government grew. We shall look at these briefly.

It was taken as self-evident that provincial government would facilitate people's participation in decisions affecting their lives. As the process of implementation got under way, it became clear that it did not mean less government but more government. Further, it had led to confusion and alienation because of the exponential explosion in the number of paid politicians, cabinet ministers, premiers and bureaucrats.[37] Because of the sheer size and geographical ruggedness of most provinces, provincial government headquarters for most villagers were still too far away and remote. It could legitimately be argued from this point of view that decentralisation resembled the physical transfer of one centralised system from one location to another.

The proponents of decentralisation had also argued their case on the point that the inherited public service in PNG was inefficient, badly co-ordinated at the district level, costly and destroyed self-reliance. Case studies confirmed these allegations. In decentralisation it was believed that 'provincial leaders and the people would show greater initiative and learn more to rely on their own resources'.[38]

These hypothetical salutary effects came under scrutiny by mid-1980 when most provinces had adopted at least an interim provincial structure with cabinet ministers, premiers and senior bureaucrats. For many local leaders, it was their first exposure to substantial powers and financial resources placed under their control. Abuses in official privileges became extensive leading critics to question the lower cost and efficiency associated with a decentralised system. The leader of the opposition argued that 'our nation now has about 140 cabinet ministers. In one province which hardly has roads, every minister has been given a government car'.[39] By 1986 the provincial governments were costing us US $125 million to $150 million simply to maintain. One can counter-argue that the abuses in the provincial governments were not attributes of decentralisation but foibles of the people who ran them.

Another decentralist argument was that the cause of national unity would be best served by accommodating ethnic and regional diversity. PNG has over 700 linguistic entities; mutual fear and distrust are endemic. In each of PNG's twenty provinces, with the possible exception of East New Britain and Enga, numerous linguistic groups were subsumed. How does one preserve this diversity except by proliferating the number of provinces? Many provincial minorities were demanding their own provinces. The reasons given were that provincial administrative machineries were dominated by one or two ethnic groups, which proceeded to colonize the bureaucracy creating exclusive preserves for jobs of their own *wantoks* (ethnic kinsmen). This practice became widespread. It led to the alienation of provincial minorities, who in turn demanded their own provinces. In this sense, provincial government was a *cause* of national disunity.

Another problem was that of restricted mobility. Although each province was a mosaic of ethnic groups, citizens of a province tended to regard themselves as the only rightful beneficiaries of jobs and other economic opportunities within their provinces. Others were 'foreigners'. Consequently, provincial governments were under popular pressure to expel 'outsiders'. The repercussions were predictable with certain provinces intimidating or expelling 'outsiders', followed by retaliation by other provinces. Clearly, in this case, provincial government had become the precipitator of political instability and national disunity. That point apart, the PNG constitution was seriously infringed, since it accorded each citizen freedom of movement. If eviction were taken to its logical conclusion, not only would this affect the efficient utilisation of skilled civil servants, but it was bound to deepen the economic disparities between provinces. The reasons for this are historical. Not all parts of PNG were colonised at the same time; those regions with resources of one kind or another were developed first, benefiting from an infrastructure of roads, bridges, schools, health centres, electricity, etc. In other places, such as the New Guinea Highlands, the people were not even 'discovered' until the mid-1930s. So if each province were left to utilise only its own skilled resources, the poor provinces would become poorer, while the rich would become richer. A system of provincial government that degenerated into a form of rivalry that restricted the deployment of skilled personnel to offset growing regional imbalances was bound to be a cause of political discontent and disunity. A review of the record on the relationship between provincial government and national unity has left an ambiguous picture. Whether long-run unity would result from the extension of a system of provincial government is a matter for the future to tell.

Notes

1. Henry Maddick, *Democracy, Decentralization and Development*, New Delhi, Asia Publishing House, 1966, ch. 2.
2. See Julius K. Nyerere, *Freedom and Development*, Dar-es-Salaam, 1968.
3. See James W. Fesler, 'French Field Administration: The Beginnings', *Comparative Studies in Society and History*, vol. 5 (October 1962), pp. 76–111; also James W. Fesler, 'Approaches to the Understanding of Decentralization', *Journal of Politics*, vol. 27, (August 1965), no. 3, p. 536.
4. See Ralph R. Premdas and S. Pokawin, eds, *Decentralisation in the Pacific*, Waigani, University of Papua New Guinea Press, 1980.
5. L. White, 'Decentralization', *Encyclopedia of Social Sciences*, New York, Macmillan, 1931, Vol. V, pp. 33–4. For discussions of similar definitions, see J. Fesler, 'Centralization', *International Encyclopedia of Social Sciences*, New York, Macmillan, 1968; Arthur McMahon, *Delegation and Autonomy*, Bombay, Asian Publishing House, 1961; Arthur Maas, ed., *Area and Power*, Glencoe, Ill., The Free Press, 1966, ch. I.
6. Harold Brookfield, *Colonialism, Development and Independence*, Cambridge, Cambridge University Press, 1972; also Robert O'Neill, 'Australia's Future Defence Relations with Papua New Guinea', *Australian Outlook*, vol. 26, no. 2 (1972); O. Harris, 'Australia and an Independent Papua New Guinea', *Spectrum* (October 1973).
7. Lucy Mair, *Australia in New Guinea*, Melbourne University Press, 1970.
8. C. Rowley, *The New Guinea Villager*, Melbourne University Press, 1964.
9. B. Jinks, *New Guinea Government*, Sydney, Angus and Robertson, 1971.
10. H. Nelson, *Papua New Guinea: Black Unity of Black Chaos*, Harmondsworth, Middx, Penguin, 1974.
11. Rowley, *The New Guinea Villager*.
12. Ibid.
13. Cited in R.S. Parker, 'The Growth of Territory Administration', in E.K. Fisk, ed., *New Guinea on the Threshold*, Pittsburg, University of Pittsburg Press, 1966, p. 193.
14. M. Tate, 'Australia and Self-Determination for New Guinea', *Australian Journal of Politics and History*, vol. 17, no. 2 (August 1971).
15. See Ch. XI of UN Charter, 'Declaration Regarding Non-Self Governing Territories', for Australia's obligation to a trust territory.

16. 'Report on New Guinea of the UN Visiting Mission to the Trust Territories of Nauru and New Guinea' in Ian Grosart, ed., *A New Guinea Brief*, Sydney, Australian Institute of Political Science, 1967, pp. 31–8.
17. J.R. Mattes, 'Constitutional Development — A Short History', *New Guinea Quarterly*, vol. 7, no. 2 (June–July 1972).
18. A.L. Epstein, *et al.*, eds., *The Politics of Dependence*, Canberra, ANU Press, 1970.
19. Ralph R. Premdas, 'Papua New Guinea: Internal Problems of Rapid Political Change', *Asian Survey* (December 1975).
20. L. Mair and I. Grosart, 'Local Government', in P. Ryan, ed., *Encylopedia of Papua New Guinea*, Melbourne University Press, 1973, p. 637.
21. See J.R.E. Waddell, 'Local Government Policy in Papua New Guinea from 1949 to 1973', *Australian Journal of Politics and History*, vol. 25 (August 1979), pp. 185–200; see also David Simpson, 'The Administrative and Political Development of Local Government in Papua New Guinea', *Yaql-Ambu* (March 1978), pp. 21–57.
22. Parker, 'The Growth of Territory Administration', p. 187.
23. Rowley, *The New Guinean Villager*.
24. See Parker, op. cit., p. 218.
25. R. Premdas, *Toward a Papua New Guinea Foreign Policy*, Santa Cruz, South Pacific Center, 1977.
26. *CPC Report*, Konedobu, 1975, ch. 10, p. 1.
27. Ibid.
28. W. Tordoff and R.L. Watts, *Report on Central–Provincial Government Relations*, Port Moresby, 1974, ch. 2, p. 2.
29. *CPC Report*, op. cit., ch. 10, p. 1.
30. *8-Point Program*, Port Moresby, 1972.
31. See Ralph R. Premdas, 'Secessionist Politics in Papua New Guinea', *Pacific Affairs* (Spring 1977).
32. Ibid. See also R. Premdas, 'Ethno-nationalism, Copper, and Secession', *Canadian Review of Studies in Nationalism*, vol. 4, no. 2 (Spring 1977).
33. For the groups, see Ron May, 'The Micronationalists', *New Guinea Quarterly*, vol. 10, no. 1 (1975).
34. The reason given for the Organic Law, a form of legislation requiring special majorities to alter it, was to discourage opponents of provincial government from reducing its powers and responsibilities.
35. *Decentralization: A Shared Responsibility*, Port Moresby, 1978, p. 7.
36. John Momis, 'Decentralization and Development', in R. Premdas and S. Pokawin, eds., *Decentralization: The PNG Experiment*, Waigani, University of PNG Press, 1980, p. 16.
37. See I. Okuk, 'Decentralization: A Critique and an Alternative', in Premdas and Pokawin, eds., *Decentralization: The PNG Experiment*, p. 22.
38. Momis, op. cit., p. 13.
39. Okuk, op. cit., p. 24.

10 THE NATIONAL LIBERATION MOVEMENT OF THE KURDS IN THE MIDDLE EAST

Laura Donnadieu Aguado

This chapter examines the secessionist movements of the Kurds since the beginning of this century. United by common ethnic, cultural, linguistic and religious characteristics, the Kurds were artificially divided in 1923 among four different national states: Turkey, Iraq, Iran and Syria. Since then there has been a continuous armed struggle between the military forces of the different countries and the militant Kurds, the former fighting to preserve the integrity of the state and the latter searching for the unification of their communal group within one territory.

Who are the Kurds?

The Kurds are an ancient Middle Eastern people with a history stretching back 3,000 years. They speak a variety of dialects of an Indo-European language and belong to the Muslim religion of the Sunni sect. They claim a distinct ethnic identity, separate from the Iranians, Turks, Arabs and others.[1]

The Kurds live in a territory known as the Kurdistan whose 500,000 sq km includes the vast mountainous area that adjoins Turkey, Iran, Iraq and Syria (see Fig. 10.1). It is considered a region of strategic importance because it is located in the so-called 'Heart of the Middle East' with its enormous wealth in natural resources, mainly oil deposits and mineral resources.[2] Estimates of Kurdish population are extremely variable with the four governments concerned tending to minimise their numbers. However, they are said to be the fourth most numerous people in the Middle East with about 20 million people.[3] Their probable distribution among the different countries is shown in Table 10.1. Except in Syria where they constitute less than 10 per cent of the population, the Kurds account for a quarter to a third in the countries where they reside. There are also Kurds located in the Soviet Union, but they are not discussed here because their situation is very different from that of the other countries.[4] There is also a Kurdish refugee population living in Lebanon, around 70,000, and in several countries of West Europe, around 380,000.[5]

Fig. 10.1 Map of Kurdistan

The traditional social organisation of the Kurds was tribal and semi-nomadic, but this is disappearing as a result of the direct control of their internal affairs by their respective governments. Kurdish society is rural and is based on agriculture (wheat, rice, fruits, cotton and tobacco) and cattle-raising. In general terms the territory of the Kurdistan is economically underdeveloped.[6]

The Kurdistan territory has never been politically distinct, always forming part of different Empires in the Middle East from 650 BC until

Table 10.1: The Kurd Population in the Middle East: 1984

Country	Total population of the country (1982)	Total population of the Kurds in each country (1984)		Percentage of total Kurd population
		No.	%	
Turkey	44,736,957	10,000,000	22.4	50.5
Iran	40,240,000	6,000,000	14.9	30.3
Iraq	13,530,000	3,000,000	22.2	15.2
Syria	9,660,000	800,000	8.3	4.0
		19,800,000		100.0

Source: Christiane Moore, *Les Kurdes aujourd'hui: mouvement national et partis politiques* (1984)

the beginning of the twentieth century (1915).[7] In 1639 the Kurds were partitioned between the Ottoman and Persian Empires and remained there for almost five centuries. During this period, they enjoyed a certain degree of autonomy that allowed them to maintain their distinctive ethnic characteristics. At the beginning of the nineteenth century, however, the Sultans transformed the Empire into a centralized military state provoking a series of Kurdish insurrections intended to strengthen their identity and maintain their territorial autonomy. However, in these uprisings the Kurdian tribesmen did not yet think in terms of a sovereign state.[8]

During the period of European contact with the Ottoman Empire, numerous ethno-nationalist movements emerged (Greeks, Slavs, Arabs, Kurds, etc.).[9] With the eruption of World War I and the break-up of the Ottoman Empire, the Middle East came under the control of the League of Nations, which was in charge of demarcating the boundaries of the new states. Under the principle of self-determination, the Peace Conference of 1918 stipulated that the non-Turkish nationalities of the Ottoman Empire would be 'assured an absolute unmolested opportunity of autonomous development' and specifically decided to give the Kurds the right to create their own independent state — the Kurdistan state.[10] The Serve Treaty created Kurdistan as well as the three Arab States of Hedjaz (Saudi Arabia), Syria and Iraq, a Turkish state and an Armenian state.[11] However, the treaty was not ratified by the Turkish National Assembly which disapproved of the delimitation of boundaries made for their own territory.[12] In 1923, a new treaty was signed (Lausanne Treaty) revoking the right of self-determination for the Kurds and

Armenian people and ratified the creation of Saudi-Arabia, Iraq, Syria and Turkey. Since then, the Kurdish territory remains divided between Turkey, Iran, Iraq and Syria.[13] The Kurds then became a minority in each of these countries.

State policies in Kurdistan

After World War I the new countries of the Middle East were created without any geographic, ethnic or religious cohesion; they were under direct or indirect Western control for almost twenty-five years. The European powers pressured the new Middle Eastern governments to guarantee the protection of their minorities. However, in the face of modernisation and strong nationalistic centralised governments, security and unity were sought by the homogenisation of their people even though the majority of these countries were ethnically heterogeneous.[14] Arab nationalism deteriorated into authoritarianism. Its main objective was the achievement of uniformity and the destruction of diversity offered by minorities.

Under the Persian nationalism of Riza Shah, unification policy was executed by destroying the minority tribal systems.[15] Most of these countries applied different degrees of assimilationist policies—'Turquification, Arabisation or Persianisation'—that sought to destroy minority identities. They prohibited the use of the written and oral Kurdish language, their costumes and traditions, and their organisations and celebrations.[16]

The governments applied discriminatory policies that marginalized the people of Kurdistan. The Kurdish region and population were less developed economically, had a higher illiteracy and infant mortality rate and received a lower than average proportion of each government's budget. Political representation was also limited.[17] Another type of policy applied was the transfer of population in order to alter the ethnic balance of the region. Thousands of Kurds were removed by force from their original land and settled in regions dominated by the majority groups. In addition, the governments concerned created several settlements in Kurdistan of people belonging to the ethnic majority.[18] There has also been massive deportation beyond the national borders. They were settled mainly in Syria and Lebanon, primarily by the Turkish government.

The national liberation movements

Twentieth-century Kurdish separatism began in all four states at the close of World War I. The divided Kurds have not forgotten the historical moment when their right to an independent State was recognised (Serve Treaty). Since then the Kurdish people have undertaken a long struggle for national liberation. Although Kurdish nationalist aspirations and separatist agitation manifested themselves in each nation, the centres of gravity of these national liberation movements have been displaced from one country to another in different historical periods. We can distinguish three periods.

The first centre of gravity was in Turkish Kurdistan from 1925 to 1938. The Turkish leaders promised the creation of the Federal State of Turks and Kurds if the Kurds collaborated in the struggle for Turkish independence. When the Turks got their independence and these promises were not fulfilled, the Kurds launched a series of armed struggles with the aim of secession. The second phase was located in Iranian Kurdistan from 1945 to 1946. This period of struggle was unique since it resulted in an independent Kurdish State. The Kurdish Republic of Mahabad led by qazi Muhammad had an existence of less than a year, when it was eliminated as the Allies left Iran in 1946. The third centre of gravity was located in Iraqi Kurdistan from 1961 to 1975. These struggles were divided into five different internal wars that were interrupted by the changes of government that occurred in Iraq. Mullah Mustafa, after signing the Treaty of Algeria in 1975 between Teheran and Baghdad, subdued by force all demonstrations of discontent in each of these countries.

In general terms, the Kurdish liberation movements have had two main political phases. The first phase, from the nineteenth century up to World War II, was characterised by traditional tribal revolts and a coherent religious system. However, there was a great deal of disunity among the tribes and as much energy was spent fighting among themselves as with their traditional enemies—the Christian Assyrians and Armenians, and the Muslim Azerbaijanis and Turkomen.[19] This fissiparous feature of Kurdish political behaviour played a decisive role in undermining the destiny of the Kurds.

When the new states were created in the Middle East in 1923, there were several Kurdish political organizations with different views of their destiny. One, a radical militant youth group, was aiming for the independence of the Kurdish provinces. The other, led by the President of the Kurdish Association and member of the Ottoman state, Abdul

Padyr, defended the incorporation of the Kurds in the new Turkish Republic. This division weakened the Kurdish movement and allowed the Allies to decide the Kurds' future without them being able to raise a unified protest. This period was the most opportune moment for the liberation of Kurdistan and the establishment of an independent state. None the less, this opportunity was missed by the Kurds because of their political disunity. Once the Kurdish territory was divided, the uprisings that followed took traditional tribal lines, leaving them isolated and fragmented. Tribal loyalty seemed much stronger than an embracing national identity.

The second phase of the liberation movement started after World War II and it was characterised by more unity. There was the growth of a Kurdish town population, a new bourgeois class and an intelligentsia had appeared in whom tribal loyalties were weaker and national political ideas stronger. The penetration of socialist ideologies permitted the creation of 'revolutionary' and progressive cadres and the growth of a Kurdish national spirit, partly in reaction against pan-Arabism. The principal new Kurdish political force was the Kurdish Democratic Party (KDP) born during the Mahabad Republic and spread to other Kurdish regions, swallowing older Kurdish organizations. The KDP fought for the rights of the Kurdish people inside each of the countries where they lived. From the 1940s to the 1970s it was the only significant political party that existed in Kurdistan. This party forged an alliance with some of the left parties that existed in these countries. Even though the KDP had the same nominal title in each of these countries, their objectives and programmes were different. The KDP in Turkey and Syria, created in 1965 and 1957 respectively, were trying to win their national rights in relation to their language and culture. The KDP in Iran (1945) wanted the creation of a federation, like Yugoslavia, where minorities would enjoy a certain degree of autonomy and the Kurd language would be recognized as official. The KDP in Iraq (1946) wanted to liberate Iraq from imperialism, but looked for autonomy of their territory inside an Arab-Kurd State.[20]

The political organisation of the Kurds was modified after 1975, following the defeat of the Kurdish Democratic Party in Iraq. Since then there has been in each of these countries a fragmentation of political parties, each having its own ideology and specific political programme. They differed in aim and composition and often competed for membership. Sometimes this factionalism resulted in open conflicts. Each group maintained its own links with other non-Kurdish political organisations within the country and with other Kurdish political organisations in and outside their own country. Most of them had foreign representation as well. Today there were nine Kurdish political parties in Turkey, the main ones being the Kurdish Workers Party and the Kurdish Socialist Party. In Iran there are three Kurdish political parties; the most important is the Kurdish Democratic Party. In Syria there are seven such political parties, with the Kurdish Democratic Party being the most outstanding. In Iraq there are eight, of which the principal ones are the Kurdish Patriotic Union and the Kurdish Democratic Party. All these organisations are committed to obtaining a certain degree of autonomy in their territory within the boundaries of their countries.

However, these diverse political organisations of the Kurds have detracted from their revolutionary struggle. To begin with, their skills in battle were exploited historically by European governments for mercenary activities. An example of this situation is the collaboration of the Kurdish leader with the Turkish government during the 1920s in the Armenian genocide. This fact has enormously weakened the prestige of the Kurdish people. Kurdish tribes have also participated several times in the repression of other Kurdish people who were struggling for their liberation. Secondly, the Kurdish political organisations inside each of these countries have maintained the tribal structural division, which led to a proliferation of the political parties that were never successfully able to mobilize support for autonomy. Thirdly, there has not been an unified liberation movement of the Kurds that includes the different Kurdish communities of the Middle East in one common and consistent struggle against Iran, Iraq, Turkey and Syria for a Kurdistan settlement. This lack of unity can be explained partly by the national border division that makes collaboration and co-ordination very difficult. Fourthly, political parties of the Kurds have practically given up the claim to self-determination, even though they are conscious of the existence of a linguistic and cultural national unity in 'Kurdistan'. Today there is only one foreign Kurdish party, the Yekbun, established in 1978 in Sweden, that is struggling for a united liberation movement for the whole of Kurdistan through secession. Fifthly, the Kurdish political organisations that had obtained external help were not able to comprehend that often such help came with strings attached. Consequently, these groups were usually manipulated by the foreign countries. Once this was done, they became victims of movements on which they had come to depend economically and militarily.

In the Middle East, there have been many struggles among the different governments for supremacy in the region. A common political strategy used to weaken the neighbouring countries was a contribution to the national liberation movements of the frontier country. This inevitably embroiled the Kurds in a variety of causes which have served as well as backfired on them. The Kurds, for instance, have been both an ally and a foe of the Iranians under the Shah. Most recently, since 1980, with the outbreak of the Iran–Iraq war, once again the new Iranian regime is collaborating with the Kurds of Iraq. They have succeeded in uniting two of the main Kurd political parties (the Kurdish Democratic Party and the Kurdish Patriotic Union) opposed to the Iraqi government. They have continued to supply the rebels with military equipment and the Iranian Revolutionary Guards have participated with the Kurdish guerrillas in attacking Iraqi oil installations (Kirkuk). This new co-operation has helped the Kurdish separatist movement to obtain a certain degree of success. It is said that by June of 1987 they doubled the area under their control (800 square miles). The Iranian government has stated that the Kurds have become 'one of the most important instruments of pressure on Iraq'. It is left to be seen if the Kurdish organisations will once again be out-manôeuvred by their erstwhile allies.

The present situation

To date, the ethnic conflicts between the Kurds and the national governments have continued without reaching a satisfactory solution for either party. The situation of the Kurds in each of these countries remains as follows.

Turkey
After the military coup of September 1980 in Turkey the Kurdish situation was considerably aggravated. The Kurds continue to be reduced to a 'non-legal existence'. Turkish law does not recognize the existence of these people as a distinct ethnic group. They are known as 'mountain Turks'. Most of the Kurdish leaders are in prison. However the Kurdish Turkish guerrillas have continued to launch attacks on the Turkish civilian population as a political strategy to gain international attention and the Turkish government has intensified its commando operations as a retaliation against them.

Iran
With the establishment of the Islamic Republic in spring 1979, a tribal

Kurdish resurgence became widespread around the country in response to the Shiite Persian domination. During the 1980s the new regime continued to apply to the tribals and other minorities, including the Kurds, discriminatory policies and a strong Persian chauvinism. With the help offered to the Iraqi Kurds, the government of Teheran could control its own Kurds for a while. None the less, the Kurdish resistance is being felt to date and it has been repressed ironically by the same revolutionary guards that are helping the Kurdish Iraqis.

Syria

In the 1980s the Ba'athist Syrian government reduced the repression against their Kurd minority. Relations between the two groups have improved considerably. However, the Syrian government has not officially recognised the existence of the Kurds as a national group and the latter have not accepted the policy of Arab-Syrian nationalism. It is known that the Syrian government is supplying the Kurd guerrillas of Iraq with weapons through Iran and it has given sanctuary to the Kurdish Turk rebels in the past few years.

Iraq

The government of Iraq is the only one that has offered constitutional autonomy to the Kurdistan region. It has officially recognised the national right of the Kurds through an autonomous law for Kurdistan in 1979. However, this law of autonomy was not accepted by the main Kurdish political organisations because it did not include the whole region of Kurdistan, and most of the local powers were under the control of the central government. In 1984 Baghdad once again reiterated its offer of local autonomy for Kurdistan. However, the Kurdish rebels seem to have learned not to believe in the government's promises any longer and with Iranian help continue to implement the separatist movement on the northern front. The Iraqi government has launched strong repressive policies such as demolishing villages, assembling their inhabitants in enclosed camps and using chemical weapons.

Conclusions

The basic conditions for the development of a separatist movement are present in the Kurdish reality. Mainly, the Kurds are self-conscious of their ethnic identity (bound by language and customs) that distinguish them from other nationalities of the region (primordial factors).[21] An unequal centre–periphery relationship underscores systematic exploitation, discrimination, and repression of the Kurds (secondary factors). The formation of a new Kurdish elite (petty bourgeosie and an intelligentsia) has permitted the creation of an organisation capable of co-ordinating the movement and linking them to outside groups. However, the four nations in which the Kurds have lived are quite dissimilar and the organisation, as well as length and intensity of Kurdish separatism, have varied accordingly. As we have seen, several characteristics have weakened their movement, especially lack of unity. They have been operating within the boundaries of each state largely independently and within each of the four countries there has been an internal political disunity. Neither has there been a consensus among the Kurds regarding their demands and their political aspirations. Moreover, there have been setbacks to the liberation struggle due to a series of political mistakes committed by the Kurdish leaders.

In spite of this, there have been some positive developments. The Kurds have increased their self-consciousness as an ethnic community and have also moved from a communal organisation to an associational one. All of this has resulted in a measure of maturity that has permitted some degree of unification of the separatist movement. The domestic ethnic conflict has developed into a broader international conflict. The Kurdish movement has received an 'instrumental intervention'[22] from governments of neighbouring states that considered the ethnic conflict as a good opportunity to promote their foreign interest. Often, the Kurds have mismanaged these foreign connections or have been deceived outright by their erstwhile foreign collaborators to the detriment of the Kurdish cause for self-determination.

Notes

1. Emmanuel Sivans, 'The Kurds: Another Perspective', *Case Studies on Human Rights and Fundamental Freedoms*, The Hague, Martinus Nijhoff, 1975, vol. 2, p. 140.
2. Martin Short, *The Kurds*, London, Minority Rights Group. Report No. 23, May 1981, p. 5.
3. Christiane Moore, *Les Kurdes aujourd'hui: mouvement national et parties politique*, Paris, Editions L'Harmattan, 1984, p. 21.
4. The Kurds in the Soviet Union are not located in the border area of the Kurdistan territory. The Soviet Kurds do not have a specific Kurdish territory—there are several Kurdish communities in the Transcaucasian Republic and Central Asia—spread between the Republic of Armenia,

Georgia and Azerbaijan. They are recognised as one of the nationalities of the Soviet Union, and are allowed to preserve their national and cultural identity through native schools, universities, publications, etc. Communication with Kurds living in other countries is infrequent (Short, *The Kurds*, p. 13).

5. Moore, *Les Kurdes*, p. 21.
6. Gérard Chaliand (ed) 'People Without a Country: The Kurds and Kurdistan', London, Zed Press, 1980, pp. 79–80; see also J. Nagel, 'The Conditions of Ethnic Separatism', *Ethnicity*, vol. 17 (1980).
7. C.J. Edmond, *Kurds , Turks and Arabs*, London, Oxford University Press, 1947, p. 6.
8. Sivans, 'The Kurds', p. 141.
9. A.H. Hourani, *Minorities in the Arab World*, London, Oxford University Press, 1947, pp. 30–1.
10. Short, *The Kurds*, p. 6.
11. Chaliand, op. cit., pp. 66–7.
12. The new Turkish regime under the leadership of Mustafa Kemal Ataturk considered the Serve Treaty inadequate to protect their interests. The Turkish territory was reduced to a Protectorate, occupied by British, French, Italian and Greek forces and their original territory was enormously reduced. That is why they rejected the guarantees offered to the non-Turkish nationalities of the Empire (Short, *The Kurds*, p. 6).
13. L.M. Von Taubinger, 'Suffering and Struggle of the Kurds', *Case Studies on Human Rights and Fundamental Freedom*, The Hague, Martin S. Nijhoff, 1975, p. 245.
14. In Turkey there are Kurds, Arabs, Circassians, Greeks, Armenians, Georgians, Lazes, Jews, Zaza; in Iran there are Armenians, Azerbaijanis, Lurs, Gashguai, Bakhtiari, Arabs, Baluchi, Shah Savans, Afshars, Dard, Turkomens, Assyrians and Kurds; in Iraq there are Armenians, Turks, Turkomens, Yazidis, Assyrians, Persians and Kurds; and in Syria there are Armenians, Assyrians, Yezidis, Alawites, Oruzes, Ismailis and Kurds (Eric Fischer, *Minorities and Minority Problems*, New York, Vantage Press, 1980).
15. Richard Tapper, ed., *The Conflict of Tribe and State in Iran and Afghanistan*, New York, St. Martin, 1983, p. 21.
16. In Turkey the use of the Kurdish language has been prohibited since 1924. The words Kurd and Kurdistan were eliminated from the Turkish vocabulary. The government suppressed from the libraries all books that mention the words Kurd or Kurdistan. The education of the Kurds continues to be implemented in the Turkish language. In 1966 the Justice Party prohibited the first socialist Kurdish magazine and all the recording of Kurdish music as well as broadcasting radio station in Kurd language (ibid., p. 114). After the destruction of the Mahabad Republic in 1946, the Kurdish language was prohibited for thirty years. The Persian language has been the only language for education and there are no schools for Kurds with an education imparted in the Kurdish language. During the Shah's dictatorship freedom of expression and the press were suppressed; the Shah closed all Kurdish printers and publicly burned all books written in Kurdish, ibid., pp. 161–2.
17. Nagel, 'The Conditions of Ethnic Separatism', p. 288.

18. In 1932, the Turkish government enacted a deportation law for its Kurdish population. This law had the objective of dispersing the Kurds through the regions of Anatolia and sending Turkish immigrants to Kurdistan (ibid., p. 101). The same policy was applied in 1958 by General Abdul Kassem in Iraq. Hundreds of thousands of Kurds were transferred from the oil region known as Kirkuk to the desert region of Dinaniya and Nisiriya. A number of Iraqi Arabs were settled in this oil region (Short, *The Kurds*, p. 16). The government of Syria inaugurated in 1962 a project known as the 'Arab Belt' that had the objective of expelling all the Kurdish population established in Djazira, bordering on Turkey, and to repopulate it progressively by an Arab population (Von Taubinger, 'Suffering and Struggle of The Kurds', p. 248).
19. Nagel, 'The Conditions of Ethnic Separation', p. 286.
20. Moore, *Les Kurdes*.
21. See Ralph R. Premdas, Chapter 1 in this volume.
22. See A. Suhrke *et al.*, 'Ethnic Conflict and International Relations', *Plural Societies*, vol. 9, no. 4 (Winter 1978), p. 3.

PART IV: EUROPE AND CANADA

11 ETHNO-NATIONALISM AND REGIONAL AUTONOMY IN CANADA AND WESTERN EUROPE

Alan B. Anderson

Introduction: Typologies of relations between political states and language minorities

During recent years many of the indigenous (non-immigrant) ethnolinguistic minorities in Europe have revealed an increasing politicisation concomitant with a renewed awareness of their sub-national identity. Throughout the European continent may be found remarkable examples of the longevity of ethnolinguistic minorities and of persistence of minority languages. Similarly, although in a more limited period of time, across the Atlantic in Canada many ethnic minorities have effectively resisted assimilation and some have recently become more active in their demands for state recognition of their languages. Ethnic separatism has regained prominence, not only among Basques, Catalans, Bretons, Corsicans, Frisians, Scottish and Welsh nationalists and others in Europe but also among French Canadians in Québec.

In this chapter, our principal concern will be to discern contrasts or similarities in the reaction of central governments towards the attempt of ethnolinguistic minorities to gain political autonomy or possibly even complete independence, or at least to reinforce their ethnic identity through further recognition of their language. In other words, how do national and, in some cases, provincial governments respond to what they have tended to view as the 'problem' of minority languages? 'Official' recognition of minority languages at the national, regional or even local levels in Canada may be instructively compared with such recognition or lack of it in various European countries.

Canada and most European countries have very complex populations in ethnic terms. While most Canadians are native-born (about 85 per cent), it is equally true that most Canadians immigrated within three or four generations, and Canada's immigration rate of approximately 100,000 a year remains one of the highest in the world. Canada has two major 'official' national languages, English and French, but the population now includes over seventy well-defined types of ethnic groups ranging in size from several millions to only a few hundreds. In fact, *every* ethnic group in Canada is a minority.

In Europe, despite the continuing prevalence of the 'nation-state' concept, most countries retain clearly defined indigenous ethnolinguistic minorities. In Western and Northern Europe there are more than fifty such varieties, excluding the additional heterogeneity introduced by millions of 'guest workers' and other immigrants. An even greater number is found in Eastern Europe. The enormous ethnic complexity of the Soviet Union is becoming evident even now with the growing ethnic unrest in several of its republics. For example, it is a striking fact that only one (Portugal) of the thirteen countries comprising *continental* Western and Northern Europe (excluding Britain, Ireland and Iceland, as well as six very small states), does not include indigenous ethnolinguistic minorities. Of course, the number of such minorities within each country varies considerably, the most complicated country in Western Europe being France, with at least ten indigenous language minorities: Breton; Flemish; German-Alsatian; Italian and Corsican; Provençal, Gascon and Languedocien (now collectively consolidated into 'Occitanien'); Catalan; and Basque.

Types of minority situations

Seven basic types of minority situations may be distinguished: first, the language minority may be situated in its own compact 'homeland' territory within a specific country. In Canada a good example of this situation is provided by the French Canadians within Québec ('Québecois'), who have tended to regard themselves as *maîtres chez nous* (masters in their own home, i.e., in Québec); French Canadian nationalists and separatists have stressed that Québec in particular is their nation-state, whereas Canada in general is at best an artificial political entity. There are many European examples: Languedocien and Provençal in France; Greenlanders and Faroese within nominally Danish but now autonomous territory; Sorbs in East Germany; Czechs and Slovaks in Czechoslovakia; Slovenes, Serbs and Croats in Yugoslavia.

Secondly, a language minority may culturally (but not necessarily politically) represent the linguistic majority in the neighbouring country; in this sense the ethnolinguistic frontier does not precisely coincide with the international boundary. In Canada the French population has 'spilled over' the borders of Québec into the adjacent provinces of Ontario and New Brunswick[1] as well as into adjacent American states. This type of situation is very common in Europe: for example, the Flemish, German and Italian-speaking populations in France respectively adjacent to Belgium, Germany and Italy; or the Gallego (Portuguese)-speaking people in north-western Spain; Flemish (Dutch), Walloon (French) and German-speakers in Belgium; German, French and Italian Swiss; French-speaking Savoyards (Aostans) and Vaudois (Waldenses) as well as German-speaking South Tyrolians in Italy; French-speaking Channel Islanders who are British citizens; the Swedish-speaking population in Finland; Germans in Poland, Czechoslovakia and Hungary; Albanians in the Kosovo autonomous region of Yugoslavia; Hungarians in the Transylvanian region of Romania; Bulgars in Yugoslavia, Greece and Turkey; etc.

Thirdly, the situation can become even more complicated when complementary minorities exist on *both* sides of an international border or as in the Canadian case the provincial border. Some examples are French in Ontario, yet English in Québec; German-speakers in Denmark, yet Danish-speakers in Germany; Italian-speaking Yugoslavs, yet Slovenes in Italy; Croats and Slovenes in Austria, yet Austrians in Yugoslavia; Hungarians in Czechoslovakian Slovakia, yet Slovaks in Hungary; Greeks and Italians in Albania, yet Albanians in Greece and Italy, etc.

Fourthly, a language minority may be essentially 'international' when it is indigenous to a specific region yet divided between two or more states. A good example of this in North America is found in the native Indian people, divided between Canada and the United States, or the Inuit (Eskimo) people of Alaska, Canada and Greenland. European examples might include the Frisians in the Netherlands, West Germany and Denmark; the Lapps in Norway, Sweden, Finland and the Soviet Union; the Basque and Catalan-speaking people in Spain and France; the Macedonian people in Yugoslavia, Greece and Bulgaria; etc.

Fifthly, certain language minorities might be widely scattered, such as gypsies, Jews, 'Volksdeutsche' (ethnic Germans), Vlachs (speaking a Romanian dialect), Pomaks (Moslemised Bulgars), Turks and Tatars in the Balkan countries, or the Romansch-Ladin-Friulian dialect groupings in Switzerland and Italy.

Sixthly, a special case might be made for interrelated language minorities enjoying ethnic and linguistic revival within separate countries. The 'Celtic Revival' is a good case in point, as it involves a revival of the Scottish Gaelic language in Scotland and Canada, Irish

Gaelic or Erse in Ireland (Eire), Manx in the Isle of Man (Mannin), Welsh in Wales (Cymru), Cornish in Cornwall (Kernow) and Breton in French Brittany (Breizh).

Seventhly, the most complicated situation is found when language minorities exist within language minorities. In a sense, the English in Québec are in this predicament: they are a thoroughly outnumbered minority in a predominantly French-speaking province which in turn is situated within a predominantly English-speaking country (Canada). A more specific Canadian case might be, for example, a Volga German Baptist settlement within a largely Ukrainian Orthodox and Catholic region in the western province of Saskatchewan. Some intriguing examples of this degree of complexity are still found in Europe: the people inhabiting the upper portion of the Val Gressoney in the Val d'Aosta region in north-western Italy speak a German dialect, although this region is an autonomous French-speaking province within an Italian-speaking country. Again, the people in several valleys of the Dolomites speak Ladin dialects; they are situated in the autonomous German-speaking region of the South Tyrol (Alto Adige) within Italy. The Voivodina autonomous region in Yugoslavia includes Ruthenians, Slovaks, Romanians, Germans and other language minorities who can attend schools in their own languages in a region which is largely Hungarian-speaking within Serbia.

Unilingualism, bilingualism, and multilingualism

Another typology relating to the political situation of ethnolinguistic minorities is based on the classification of countries as *officially* unilingual (monoglot), bilingual (diglossic), or multilingual (polyglot). However, this typology runs into many pitfalls. In Eastern Europe excluding the Soviet Union, only Yugoslavia is clearly multilingual in an official sense. In Western Europe only Switzerland is officially multilingual as a whole. In Luxembourg German and French are official while Letzeburgesch is the prevalent local dialect. Belgium is officially bilingual with Walloon and Flemish, yet grants some recognition to its German-speaking minority; similarly Finland is officially bilingual with Finnish and Swedish, yet recognises its Lapps. Several countries are officially unilingual as a whole, while they recognise bilingualism officially at an intra-national, regional level, such as in the Netherlands (Frisian/Dutch in Friesland), Italy (French/Italian in Valle d'Aosta and German/Italian in Alto-Adige) and Spain (Basque/Spanish in the

Basque Provinces and Catalan/Spanish in Catalonia). Other countries, officially unilingual at the national level, grant limited concessions to ethnolinguistic minorities short of regional bilingualism.

Sociologists, sociolinguists and other social scientists have written many papers on political implications of multilingualism within states, including theoretical and methodological insights.[2] While such general discussions are most relevant to any discussion of the political situation of ethnolinguistic minorities in Europe, the brevity of the present chapter necessitates restricting the discussion to a more succinct commentary on the present situation in several cases.

Alternative state policies

Let us now formulate and exemplify a typology referring specifically to alternative state policies concerning ethnolinguistic minorities in Canada and Europe. These policies could be placed on a continuum ranging from negative through conservative and moderate to liberal treatment of language minorities.

Clearly, there have been two basic types of very negative policies towards ethnic or language minorities. Undoubtedly the most negative position that a state may assume is to rid itself completely of a minority. This has been done by means of outright extermination (genocide), exemplified in not-so-distant history by Hitler's 'final solution' of the Jewish (and gypsy) question. A minority may also be expelled. In fact, Turkey both exterminated and expelled its Armenians. At least 15 million ethnic Germans (Volksdeutsche) were expelled or obliged to retreat from Eastern European countries, particularly Poland and Czechoslovakia, between 1944 and 1947. Many European countries have employed such policies in the past, and perhaps still do in the sense of refusing would-be immigrants 'landed' or resident status except on relatively short-term work contracts or refusing refugees entry into the country. Canada has by no means been immune to this sort of policy: witness the extermination of the Beothuk Indians in Newfoundland when that province was a British colony, or the Oriental exclusion acts aimed at keeping out Chinese and Japanese till the 1940s or, better yet, the actual deportation and imprisonment of Japanese Canadians, many of them Canadian citizens, during World War II. It should be added that another, less negative way in which a country could rid itself of a minority is to exchange this counter-ethnic (that is, different from the majority) minority for co-ethnics (that is, people of the same ethnicity or language as the majority), who were themselves a minority in another, usually neighbouring, country. This was done most extensively, for example, in the Balkans before, during and after World War I, such as the Greek minority in Turkey being 'repatriated' to Greece in exchange for Turks expelled from Greece.

The second basic type of negative policy towards ethnic or language minorities is assimilation, in which case the state still attempts to get rid of a problematic minority, yet not by deportation or genocide. Here we are referring to an explicit policy of forced assimilation. That is to say, the language minority is not permitted to maintain any cultural distinctiveness apart from the majority, therefore no allowance is made for use of a minority language in schools or other public institutions. Such a policy, in the form of Anglo-conformity, prevailed for all ethnolinguistic minorities in Canada, with the possible exception of French Canadians within, but certainly not outside, Québec and of native peoples, at least till the 1930s and in some cases longer, although it was resisted in varying degrees by the minorities. Examples of assimilatory policies still are readily found in Eastern Europe: Sorbs in East Germany, Germans remaining in Eastern Europe, Macedonians in Greece and Bulgaria, etc. Until recently, assimilation of language minorities was the prevalent policy in France, Spain and Italy.

A number of policies may be termed conservative, yet are clearly not as negative as those which we have just discussed in so far as they are not necessarily designed to get rid of a minority through genocide, deportation or forced assimilation. Thus, in countries still exhibiting fairly strong centralism, assimilation may not be as explicit as it is implicit as a desired goal. Minority languages may be recognised yet restricted to private schools in lieu of public financial support. In fact, the national state may simply choose largely to ignore the minority. In moving progressively away from Anglo-conformity, some Canadian minorities have passed through this state. Until quite recently certain European countries pursued this sort of policy: for example, Germans in Belgium, some of the language minorities in Austria, Lapps in northern Scandinavia, and still perhaps Frisians in West Germany and Denmark.

More moderate policies are found in states exhibiting limited or weak centralism. If the national government coud be termed somewhat centralist, perhaps it would have abandoned assimilation as a general policy although assimilation might still be advocated in conservative circles; and there may be evidence of limited government support of minority languages in selected public schools. Alternatively, if the government clearly exhibits weak centralism, there may be fairly generous encouragement, including financial support, of minority languages in schools, etc., and official national policy of ethnic pluralism however defined, yet no or very limited recognition of minority territorial rights, namely, regional autonomy. Québec has been guided in recent years by provincial governments, particularly by the avowedly separatist Parti Québecois since 1976, towards increasingly conservative language policies: restricting funding to English-language universities, requiring French to be the dominant language in shop signs, advertisements, and industrial companies, and forcing new immigrants to send their children to French schools. In Europe, perhaps the situations of the German minority in Denmark and conversely the Danish one in Germany are representative of the 'limited centralism' type, while the current situations of the Slavic minorities in Austria, the Romansch in Switzerland and the Lapps in Scandinavia and Finland represent the 'weak centralism' type. Romania, while somewhat pluralistic, currently falls short of recognising full regional autonomy for its language minorities.

Both the policies of regional autonomy and of ethnic federalism are obviously quite liberal treatment of language minorities. The former policy of regional autonomy implies explicit recognition of minority territorial rights; thus the minority forms a 'state within a state' and presumably is allowed to use its own language 'officially' within this territory. While not quite being granted this status by the national government of Canada, in effect the Province of Québec is regarded by its French population and the provincial government as a 'state within a state'. On a far smaller, more localised scale, Canadian history has seen some development of such ethnic autonomy, very temporarily in the one time creation of German Mennonite and Russian Doukhobor reserves and even a self-proclaimed Icelandic republic in Western Canada, more lastingly in the continuing system of Indian reserves currently being reinforced by the success of native land claims. In Europe, limited regional autonomy is now enjoyed by Basques and Catalans in Spain (but not yet by their co-ethnics or other minorities in France), by French and German minorities in Italy, Frisians in the Netherlands, Swedes in Finland's Aland Islands, as well as by Danish Greenlanders; while more far-reaching autonomy is enshrined in the Soviet constitution as the complicated system of SSRs, ASSRs, AOs and NOs.[3]

Ethnic federalism may be defined as the situation when the national state as a whole is viewed essentially as a partnership between ethnolinguistic minorities; therefore, the principle minority languages are fully recognised, probably throughout the entire country. We could consider, albeit with some reservations, the English–French bilingualism and biculturalism—since 1971 redefined as *multi*-culturalism—in Canada to be an illustration of this policy; yet better examples might be found in Switzerland, Belgium, Yugoslavia, the Soviet Union and possibly Luxembourg and the United Kingdom, though again with some qualifications.

Finally, it is at least theoretically possible for separatist forces among a minority to be successful eventually in gaining complete independence from the former majority. While we are referring here to the formulation of a new country, wherein the former minority now becomes a majority, a variation on the theme is when a former minority achieves independence from the former majority by means of irredentism: annexation by co-ethnics to a neighbouring country. In Europe irredentism temporarily 'returned' the Italian-speaking population of Istria, the Julian Alps and Dalmatia to Italy. Possibly a completely independent Québec could eventually have designs on the adjacent solidly French-speaking areas across the border in Ontario and New Brunswick. The new policy of 'devolution' in Britain is not satisfactory to the most ardent Scottish and Welsh nationalists, who have long advocated complete independence from the United Kingdom, already accomplished, of course, by the Irish republicans.

Minority reaction to state policy

A final typology relating to Canadian and European comparative study of ethnolinguistic minorities concerns the reaction of the minorities to these various state policies. Their reaction may range along a continuum from *passive* to *active*. Some minorities have seemed to be rather passive, submissive or disorganised (for example, gypsies, Tatars, certain German minorities, the Gallego-speakers in Spain, Italo-French and numerous smaller, isolated groups such as Romansch, Ladins, Sorbs, French Vaudois and German Walser in the Italian Alps, Frisians in Germany, etc.). Other minorities, while somewhat docile, are better organised and may reveal latent minority nationalism (such as Flemish-speakers in France, the Occitanien movement, perhaps the majority of the Scottish and Welsh populations, Albanians and Magyars in Yugoslavia, Alsatians, German speakers in Belgium, Lapps, the Danish–German border minorities, Frisians in the Netherlands, Aostans, etc.). Still others are both well-organised, actively mobilised and may reveal overt or manifest nationalism (for example, Basques and

Catalans in France and particularly Spain, the German minorities in the Italian Sud Tirol, Flemish and Walloons in Belgium, Bretons, principal minorities in Yugoslavia, and in Canada, French Canadian nationalism and separatism, as well as the native autonomy movement).

A special case could be made for ethnolinguistic revival combined with varying degrees of minority nationalism or separatism. This is most obviously exemplified in the Celtic Revival, ranging from the recognition of Irish Gaelic as a national language in the Republic of Ireland, to the rather successful revival of Welsh in Wales, the widespread efforts to spread Breton in Brittany and Scottish Gaelic in Scotland, or to revive almost completely extinct Celtic languages such as Manx and Cornish. Further examples are found in the revival or maintenance of the Rhaeto-Romance languages (Romansh, Ladin, Friulian) in Switzerland and/or Italy, as well as of Frisian in the Netherlands. Lastly, violent terrorism stands at the 'end of the line' in this continuum of minority reaction, utilised by such divergent radical nationalist movements as the Front de Liberation Québecois, IMRO in 'Greater Macedonia', ETA among Spanish Basques, the Breton Liberation Front, the Front National du Liberation Corsicain, etc.

A rather strange collection of discontented activists, representing a wide variety of Western European ethnolinguistic minorities and ranging from terrorists to more moderate nationalists, met secretly in Trieste in 1974. What drew them together was their shared sense of oppression by, and subjugation to, a national majority. Their common demand was for varying degrees of political autonomy, from official recognition of a minority language to full independence. Ethnolinguistic minorities throughout Western Europe, almost all of them in regions adjacent to international frontiers, have been uniting recently in a common effort to press for a 'Europe of Peoples'. A fairly novel concept of a collection of ethnolinguistic regions enjoying regional autonomy, but united economically if not politically, has rapidly been gaining popularity among these minorities. In short, what these minorities are fighting for is the right to be different in an era of increasing uniformity (Heraud 1966).

Most, in fact almost all, of the activist groups advancing this view are well to the left in political orientation. Yet even the most radical of these groups tend to be rather cool towards official Communist parties, more so those in Eastern Europe conforming to Soviet policy than those representing Eurocommunism in their own countries in Western Europe. For their part, Eastern European Communist governments, particularly the Soviet Union and Yugoslavia, have tended to be very wary of minority nationalism or separatism, which is hardly surprising in view of the potential problem of ethnolinguistic minorities which could be disruptive of national unity in those countries. Moreover, a wide variety of exiled minority nationalist organisations outside of those countries have proclaimed their desire to 'liberate' their homelands (for example, Estonians, Latvians, Lithuanians, Ukrainians, Armenians, Hungarians, Czechoslovaks, Croatians, Macedonians, etc. to name but a few). On the other hand, at the very least in theory and on paper though not so much in practice as recent events in Azerbaijan, Armenia, Georgia, Estonia, Latvia and Lithuania revealed, the Soviet Constitution is an admirable exemplification of incorporating ethnolinguistic minorities into a complex federal political structure offering varying degrees of autonomy in accordance with the size of the minority, from full republic status (SSR) to autonomous republic (ASSR), autonomous oblast, and nationality okrug. Yugoslavia similarly incorporates autonomous regions within full republics in a federation based on ethnic, linguistic and religious distinctions, but there too the ethnic tensions that developed in 1988 in Serbia and Albania demonstrated the fragility of the constitutional arrangements.

The long-cherished notion of the ethnically homogeneous nation-state in Western Europe has been increasingly challenged in recent years, not only by indigenous ethnolinguistic minorities but also by millions of immigrant *gastarbeiter* (guest workers). Contemporaneous with a trend toward pan- or inter-nationalism in developing societies is a trend in Western Europe to break up into even smaller segments, both geographic and linguistic, nations already shrunken on the scale of world influence by the loss of former empires (C.L. Sulzberger, *New York Times*, 27 January 1976). Several countries threatened by what Sulzberger calls 'neotribalism' were imperial powers within relatively recent times: in Britain, France, Spain, Italy, Belgium and Austria minority nationalists continue to work towards regional autonomy. Indeed, European neotribalism, mini-separatism, or—to put it more politely—sub-nationalism or regionalism is gaining vigour precisely when the movement for European unity seems to be reaching a new crossroads in 1992. Yet the historical background to the contemporary trend towards a reawakening of minority consciousness has been decades—in some cases centuries—of discrimination against these minorities, of apparently largely unsuccessful, forced assimilation and of imposed international boundaries which neglected minority rights or wishes.

Notes

1. The majority of French in New Brunswick are of Acadian rather than Quebecois origin.
2. See particularly papers by Deutsche, Kloss, Rustow, Simon, Mackey, Lieberson and O'Connor, Laponce, Donneur, and Friedrich in Savard and Vigneault, eds (1975); Mackey (1967); Connor in Said and Simmons, eds (1976); Petersen in Glazer and Moynihan, eds (1976); Jakobson and Deutsch in Fishman, ed. (1972); Simon, Kloss and De Meyer in Migus, ed. (1975); etc.
3. The Union of Soviet Socialist Republics consists of the RSFSR (Russian Soviet Federated Socialist Republic) and fourteen member SSRs (Soviet Socialist Republics), which in turn may include ASSRs (Autonomous Soviet Socialist Republics), AOs (Autonomous Oblasts), and NOs (Nationality Okrugs) with varying degrees of autonomy along ethnic lines.

References

Adler, M.K. (1977), *Welsh and Other Dying Languages in Europe*, Hamburg, Helmut Buske Verlag.

Allardt, E. (1978), 'Finns and Swedes as Minorities in Sweden and Finland', *Scandinavian Review*, vol. 66, pp. 17–23.

Anderson, N. (1969), 'Some Comparisons of Bilingual Communities', in N. Anderson, ed., *Studies in Multilingualism*, Leiden, E.J. Brill.

Ashworth, Georgina (1977, 1978), *World Minorities*, vols. I and II, Sunbury, Middx, Quartermain House.

Connor, Walker (1976), 'The Political Significance of Ethnonationalism Within Western Europe', in A. Said and L.R. Simmons, eds, *Ethnicity in an International Context*, New Brunswick, Transaction Books.

De Meyer, J. (1975), 'La situation juridique des sociétés polyethniques en Europe', in P. Migus, ed., *Sounds Canadian: Languages and Cultures in Multi-Ethnic Society*, Toronto, Peter Martin Associates.

Denison, N. (1971), 'Some Observations on Languages Variety and Pluralism', in J.B. Pride and J. Holmes, eds, *Sociolinguistics*, Harmondsworth, Middx, Penguin.

Deutsch, K.W. (1972), 'The Trend of European Nationalism—The Language Aspect', in J.A. Fishman, ed., *Readings in the Sociology of Language*, The Hague/Paris, Mouton.

—— (1975), 'The Political Significance of Linguistic Conflicts', in J-G. Savard and R. Vigneault, eds, *Multilingual Political Systems: Problems and Solutions*, Quebec, Centre International de Recherche sur le Bilingualisme & les Presses de l'Université Laval.

Donneur, A.P. (1975), 'La solution territoriale au problême de multilingualisme', in J-G. Savard and R. Vigneault, eds, op. cit.

Enloe, C.H. (1973), *Ethnic Conflict and Political Development*, Boston, Mass., Little, Brown.

Esman, Milton J. ed. (1977), *Ethnic Conflict in the Western World*, Ithaca, NY, Cornell University Press.

Francis, E.K. (1976), *Interethnic Relations: An Essay in Sociological Theory*, Amsterdam/New York, Elsevier.

Friedrich, C.J. (1975), 'The Politics of Language and Corporate Federalism', in J-G. Savard and R. Vigneault, eds, op. cit.

Glazer, N. and Moynihan, D.P., eds (1976), *Ethnicity: Theory and Experience*, Cambridge, Mass., Harvard University Press.

Gwegen, Jorj (1975), *La Langue bretonne face à ses oppresseurs*, Quimper, Nature et Bretagne.

Hall, Raymond L., ed. (1979), *Ethnic Autonomy — Comparative Dynamics*, New York, Pergamon Press.

Heraud, G. (1966), *Peuples et langues d'Europe*, Paris, Denoel.

Humblet, J.E. (1974), 'Reflexions sur la place du dialecte dans la vie sociale: comparasion entre le Luxembourg, le Val d'Aoste, et la Wallonie', research paper presented at a session on 'Language and National Identity', ISA Research Committee on Sociolinguistics, Eighth World Congress of Sociology, Toronto, August.

Hunt, C.L. and Walker, L. (1974), *Ethnic Dynamics: Patterns of Intergroup Relations in Various Societies*, Homewood, Ill., Dorsey.

Jakobson, R. (1972), 'The Beginning of National Self-Determination in Europe', in J.A. Fishman, ed., op. cit.

Kloss, H. (1975a), 'Pygmies Among Giants: Small Minority Groups in the Multinational State', in P. Migus, ed., op. cit.

—— (1975b), 'Democracy and the Multinational State', in J-G. Savard and R. Vigneault, eds, op. cit.

Laponce, J.A. (1975), 'Relating Linguistic to Political Conflicts: The Problem of Language Shift in Multilingual Societies', in J-G. Savard and R. Vigneault, eds, op. cit.

Lieberson, S. (1972), 'An Extension of Greenberg's Linguistic Diversity Measures', in J.A. Fishman, ed., op. cit.

—— *et al.*, (1975), 'The Course of Mother-Tongue Diversity in Nations', *American Journal of Sociology*, vol. 81, pp. 34–61.

—— and O'Connor, J.F. (1975), 'Language Diversity in a Nation and its Regions', in J-G. Savard and R. Vigneault, eds, op. cit.

Linz, J.J. (1975), 'Politics in a Multilingual Society with a Dominant World Language: The Case of Spain', in J-G. Savard and R. Vigneault, eds, op. cit.

Mackey, W.F. (1967), *Bilingualism as a World Problem*, Montreal, Harvest House.

—— (1975), 'Puissance, Attraction et Pression des Langues en Contact: Modèles et Indices', in J-G. Savard and R. Vigneault, eds, op. cit.

Massucco-Costa, A. (1969), 'Torre Pellice and Its People', in N. Anderson, ed., op. cit.

McRae, K.D. (1964), *Switzerland: Example of Cultural Coexistence*, Toronto, Canadian Institute of International Affairs.

Moodie, A.E. (1961), *Geography Behind Politics*, London, Hutchinson University Library.

Peterson, W. (1976), 'On the Subnations of Western Europe', in N. Glazer and D.P. Moynihan, eds, op. cit.

Pietersen, L. (1969), '*De friesen en hun taal*', Drachten: Lavermen N.V.
—— (1974), 'Language Ideology—National Ideology—Bilingualism: the Frisian Case', research paper presented at a session on 'Language and National Identity', ISA Research Committee on Sociolinguistics, Eighth World Congress of Sociology, Toronto, August.
—— (1978), 'Die Zukunft des Friesischen', *Language Problems and Language Planning*, vol. 1, pp. 141–52.
Planson, Glaoud and Erwan Koshaneg (1977), *Histoire de la nation bretonne*, Paris, Editions de la Table Ronde.
Rustow, D.A. (1975), 'Language, Nations, and Democracy', in J-G. Savard and R. Vigneault, eds, op. cit.
Sautter, G. (1969), 'Alsatian and Vosgian Relationships', in N. Anderson, ed., op. cit.
Simon, W.B. (1969), 'Multilingualism: A Comparative Study', in N. Anderson, ed., op. cit.
—— (1975a), 'Occupational Structure, Multilingualism and Social Change', in J-G. Savard and R. Vigneault, eds, op. cit.
—— (1975b), 'A Sociological Analysis of Multilingualism', in P. Migus, ed., op. cit.
Stephens, Meic (1976), *Linguistic Minorities in Western Europe*, Llandysul, Gomer Press.
Straka, A. (1970), *Handbuch der Europaeischen Volksgruppen*, Stuttgart.
Svalastoga, K. and Wolf, P. (1969), 'A Town in Danish Borderland', in N. Anderson, ed., op. cit.
Valussi, G. (1974), 'La fonction internationale de la frontière italo-yougoslave', *Cahiers de Géographie de Québec*, vol. 18, no. 43 (April).
Vanneste, A.M.S. (1974), 'Aspects sociolinguistiques de la Flandre Française: étude diachronique et synchronique', research paper presented at a session on 'Language and National Identity', ISA Research Committee on Sociolinguistics, Eighth World Congress of Sociology, Toronto, August.
Verdoodt, A. (1974), 'The German and German Dialect Speakers in Belgium', research paper presented at a session on 'Language and National Identity', ISA Research Committee on Sociolinguistics, Eighth World Congress of Sociology, Toronto, August.
Williams, Colin H. (1980), 'Ethnic Separatism in Western Europe', *Journal of Economic and Social Geography*, vol. 71, no. 3
Young, H.F. (1974), 'South Tyrol: New Approaches to an Old Problem', *Canadian Review of Studies in Nationalism*, vol. 2, no. 1. (Fall).
Zolberg, A.R. (1975), 'Transformation of Linguistic Ideologies: The Belgian Case', in J-G. Savard and R. Vigneault, eds, op. cit.

12 SECESSION AND INDEPENDENCE FOR QUÉBEC: HOW LEGITIMATE?

Pierre Corbeil and André Montambault

On 20 May 1980, the residents of the Province of Québec in Canada voted on a referendum for independence between the two countries. About 59 per cent of the electors voted 'No'; 41 per cent voted 'Yes'. In the light of the dominant trend towards independent statehood, this result casts doubt on the credibility of the Québecois claim to nationhood. This chapter surveys the historical background of Québec's quest for self-determination and attempts to identify those factors which support or deny the Québecois claim.

Geography and history

Québec is one of the ten provinces (plus three territories) that make up the Dominion of Canada. Looking at a map of Canada, it suggests the image of a dragon. Québec is the head of that dragon with a total area of one and a half million square kilometres (the size of India). The exact area is a matter of dispute, because Québec claims Labrador which is officially part of Newfoundland. Québec is the largest province by area; it has a population of 6 million and is therefore the next most populous province after Ontario, where the population is about 9 million. Canada's total population is 25 million. Canada as a federation has provincial legislatures which exercise certain exclusive powers while the federal government has others and some are shared.

Québec sits squarely on the Canadian Shield, the oldest mountains in the world. The climate is Nordic with long cold winters and short, hot summers. Agriculture is limited to the southern plain, on either side of the St-Laurent River which flows through the province from south-west to north-east. In fact, less than 5 per cent of Québec's area is suitable for agriculture. The northern part of Québec is very rich in minerals and provides the large, swift rivers that give Québec the electricity which is the foundation of its economic life. The population of Québec is slightly over 80 per cent French-speaking. The remaining portion is almost evenly divided between those persons whose mother-tongue is English and those who have another mother-tongue, called 'allophones' in the official and popular vocabulary of Québec.

The story of Québec begins in the sixteenth century when several European countries were striving to find new sea-routes to Asia. Spain was first in this race; the main rival was France. Jacques Cartier explored the St-Laurent and established a legal claim for France to certain territories. It was not until the early seventeenth century, in 1605 in Acadia and in 1608 in Québec, that Samuel de Champlain established permanent French colonies in America. Champlain is still honoured as the founder of Québec City. From then on, the French explored the North American continent, establishing forts from Hudson Bay to Texas and from Acadia to the Rocky Mountains. They also created trade and mutual assistance treaties with the Amerindians. From 1663 to 1763, France and England engaged in a series of wars. For most of this time, the 'Canadiens', the offspring of the French colonists, although outnumbered by the English in the order of twenty to one, using irregular warfare and many Amerindian methods, kept the English colonists on the frontier in fortified towns. All good things must end someday. So, in 1760, a new English Prime Minister, William Pitt, decided to end the French Empire in America. Québec City fell in 1759 and Montreal in 1760. The Treaty of Paris (1763) gave Canada and the Lesser Antilles to England.

But it was not the end of the 'Canadiens'. At first, their territory was limited to a narrow band from Montreal to Québec City. Numbering only 65,000 persons, they were allowed the practice of their religion and seemed to accept British rule. It was their former enemies, the American colonists, who were the instrument of fate in giving them a new beginning. The Canadiens learned from their neighbours to petition and play politics with London. To keep the Canadiens from joining the rebellious American colonists, the English Parliament adopted the Québec Act in 1774, which recognised French law in Québec, allowed the legal existence of the Roman Catholic religion and recognised the French language.

After American independence, the territory north of the new border was divided into two colonies, Upper Canada, the present Ontario, and Lower Canada, the present Québec. Each had its own governor and its own Assembly. Upper Canada was created for those Americans who had remained loyal to the Crown. In both provinces, the question of local versus imperial control soon came up in the Assemblies. 'No taxation without representation' is every British subject's birthright and the elected representatives insisted that the governor choose his advisers from among their ranks and must accept their right to make a budget.

In Lower Canada, with a half-million inhabitants, mostly 'Canadiens', this question became naturally one of nationalism, the first manifestation in Canada of this European concept. Mixed with liberal influences from France and democratic ideals from the United States, local pride of race eventually led to an armed uprising from 1837 to 1838. The 'Patriotes', the combatants for independence, proclaimed the independence of Lower Canada, but were defeated by the British.

London decided to unite the two provinces into one whose English majority would ensure loyalty to the Crown. The French language lost its official status. Yet, in uniting the two assemblies, the Imperial Government allowed the collaboration of those favourable to parliamentary control over the colonial administration. In many ways, the Canadien parliamentarians dominated the government of the Province of Canada for the next decade. However, the western part of the colony filled up rapidly with new immigrants. With their Scottish and Dissident backgrounds, they were soon complaining of 'French Domination'. By 1866, this had led to an impossible parliamentary situation, the only solution to which was the creation of the federal system which still exists. The English majority won control of the federal parliament where representation was by population. The Canadiens were compensated with the creation of the Province of Québec where they would be a majority.

However, this was not a happy ending. The Province of Québec had been hedged with safeguards for the English-speaking minority. Twelve of the sixty-five ridings were reserved for their representatives in the Legislative Council. Official institutions would be bilingual. The federal government was given the power to annul provincial laws. At the same time, French-speaking colonists outside of Québec were severely controlled. In 1872, the separate schools of New Brunswick were abolished. The French-speaking Metis of the Northwest Territories were militarily crushed in 1869 and 1885. Their leader, Louis Riel, was hanged in 1886. The Manitoba provisions for the official use of French were abolished in 1890. In 1912, the teaching of French in the Province of Ontario was made illegal. This was largely due to the rise of British nationalism in Canada.

But the Québecois, as we shall henceforth call Canadiens, fought back. The reserved ridings, under the leadership of the Church colonisation, were filled with French-speaking voters. The Saguenay and northern regions were occupied and the latter annexed in 1898 and 1912. In 1883, a judgement of the Privy Council established that the provinces were sovereign in the powers reserved to them by the BNA Act. In 1886, under the leadership of Honor Mercier, Québec developed adult education, transportation and agriculture. It sent representatives to Europe and borrowed money outside the British Empire. During World War I, the pupils of Québec gave up their prize-money to help fight for the French-language schools of Ontario where mothers, armed with long hatpins, guarded their theoretically illegal schools.

From the 1930s on, the government of Québec fought federal encroachments on its prerogatives. In 1954, the government of Maurice Duplessis created a provincial income tax. In 1962, all the power companies were nationalised and Hydro-Québec became a source of national wealth and power. In 1967, the Legislative Council was abolished. In 1974 French was declared the official language of Québec. In 1976, the Parti Separatist Québecois was elected. In 1980, the referendum mentioned at the beginning was held.

Was the election of the Parti Québecois and the ensuing referendum based on an illusion? The factors which have influenced the Québecois quest for self-assertion as a separate identity have been divided into two analytic categories: primordial and secondary.[1] Primordial factors refer to deep cleavages and attachments such as language, region, religion, etc. Secondary factors pertain to recently acquired features such as neglect, discrimination, domination, etc. These factors confer on Québecois society the traits of a unique 'nation'.

Primordial factors

Territory and people

After the cession of Canada to Great Britain by France in 1763, the Québec Act (1774) recognised the 'Canadiens' in their own territory, the Province of Québec.[2] While it is difficult to speak of Québec as a nation (20 per cent of the population comes from different ethnic groups), some 80 per cent trace their genealogies back to the original French. These were the 'Canadiens', and are still called 'French-Canadians' by the English Canadians. They may reasonably be considered to have a right by prior occupancy, a principle recognised by international law.

Culture and language

The search for a distinct Québecois culture points to language as the basic constitutive element. The fact that a group speaks, reads, writes and watches television in a language other than that of its neighbours would quite generally be accepted as evidence of distinct existence as a 'nation'. This is the case for Québec where the struggle to preserve the French language is the undeniable constant in the history of the Canadiens. Laws mark the evolution summarised above, in 1774, 1791, 1849, 1867, 1910, 1974 and 1977, when the actual Charter of the French Language was passed into law.[3]

Other aspects of culture are more difficult to pinpoint. There is evidence that the values of the Québecois are unique.[4] Today, the Québecois watch their own productions on television more than American imports, a fact which distinguishes them from their Anglo-Canadian neighbours and which is affirmed in the Caplan-Sauvageau report. Joel Garreau (1981) identifies Québec as one of the 'nations' or cultural regions of North America, the only one that coincides with an existing state, and the only part of Canada distinguishable from the United States.[5]

Religion

Religion was also for a long time a distinguishing trait of Québecois culture. Almost 100 per cent of the Québecois were Roman Catholics who were a minority in all other states of North America. Moreover, the Catholic Church played in Québec the role of a national religion, supplying education and health care, organising programmes of national import and often negotiating with the imperial or federal authorities.[6] The Church in Québec was present in almost all fields especially political ones, and much of the modernisation of Québec has been a rejection, prudent or not, of the ideological and administrative models long used by the Church. It is true that modern Québec has seen a drastic decline in religious practice, but baptism into the Church is still the normal, legal form of civil registration for children.[7] Values on sex or work are more closely related to the Catholic vision of the world than to a Protestant one.

A distinct legal system

A distinct legal system is deeply embedded in Québec society. Québec's Civil Law, codified in 1861 and modified in 1981, is quite different from the British civil law that governs the rest of Canada. This Civil Law is an outgrowth of the old 'Coutume de Paris', which governed the colony in the days of the French Empire. There were, for example, no lawyers allowed in the colony before 1763. The Canadiens insisted on the preservation of their law, from the terms of capitulation of Montreal in 1760 to the implementation of the British North America Act in 1867.

The codification of the law in 1861 was George-Etienne Cartier's proudest achievement as political leader of Lower Canada (Québec). The Civil Law of Québec has absorbed many elements of the Code Napoleon and is a major barrier between the administration of Québec and the other provinces. Only Québec has notaries, for instance, whose profession is the making and breaking of contracts, including divorces between consenting parties. It is noteworthy that the different legal system was a major element in the inclusion in the new constitutional agreement of 1987 of a clause recognising Québec as a distinct society.

Non-primordial factors

In addition to the fundamental bases of nationhood just explored, and which clearly seem to validate the Québecois claim of a separate society, what of the secondary or non-primordial factors, those real or perceived wrongs and grievances that can acquire the power to mobilise opinion in favour of independence?

The negative economic consequences of federalism

One of the major bases for the emergence of a self-determination movement in Québec in recent history has been the conviction that the federal system has been a disadvantage in terms of economic development. What are the grounds for this indictment? It was the purpose of the so-called National Policy propounded by the federal government in 1879, to build a viable Canadian market and an industrial base. A protective tariff was introduced to limit access of US products to the Canadian market, and to encourage native industrial growth. Transcontinental rail links were developed to create an East–West Canadian trade axis. Up to that time, Canada's economic development had relied primarily on the export of staples (fur, timber and wheat). The National Policy was intended to reduce the dependence on such exports and develop manufacturing.

It was at the National Policy that Québecois spokesmen directed their criticism. Its objective was to promote 'national' development at the expense of any given particular region.[8] Any ensuing regional disparities would eventually be levelled by factor mobility. But one cannot assume factor mobility other than by ignoring Québec's cultural and linguistic specificity. This policy penalises Québec by disallowing it its own development strategy.

Few deny the fact that Québec's economic structure is weaker than that of neighbouring English-speaking Ontario, whose per capita industrial output is 20 per cent higher and level of unemployment lower. But this difference, say some observers, is not due to the National Policy, but to Québec's own development and resource structure.[9] Others have simply argued that all of Central Canada benefited from the National Policy, only Québec less so than Ontario. The real losers were the other regions.[10]

Apart from the National Policy, Québec questioned the federal government's numerous long-term policy decisions that have tended to weaken Québec's position.[11] They referred to such policies as the building of the St-Laurent Seaway that allowed ships to bypass Montreal on their way to the United States or the US–Canada Auto pact that concentrated 90 per cent of Canada's automobile industry in southern Ontario. The claim that the federal government has equated 'national' development with southern Ontario is widely accepted in Québec.

It is also argued that Canada's short-term stabilisation practices have been insensitive to Québec's needs. The 'national' approach to fiscal policy, in particular, runs counter to the country's highly differentiated regional economic structure. Many critics of federal policy, and not just in Québec, have suggested that the present federal system is no more than an administrative arrangement. The real Canada is to them made up of five 'regions'.[12] Many economists agree that the pan-Canadian approach to stabilisation policy is flawed. In a recent fourteen-year period, Ottawa's stabilisation policies have been shown to oppose Québec's needs seven times out of eleven.[13] The federal government may counter-argue the need for 'national' considerations.

Just before the 1980 referendum the Parti Québecois government of Québec published figures showing that Ottawa spent less in Québec than it had received in taxes.[14] This was not a new theme. However, the Parti Québecois produced a new study of national accounts that showed a net loss for Québec of at least Canadian $4.3 billion over the last fifteen years. The federal government immediately published figures showing a net gain of 1.7 billion.

Another point close to the Québecois mind pertains to income disparities. The 1969 report of the Royal Commission on Bilingualism and Biculturalism revealed that in 1961, incomes of French-Canadians throughout Canada were 20 per cent lower than Anglo-Canadians. In Québec, the difference reached 35 per cent, prompting some economists to speak of two distinct labour markets.[15] To many Québecois, however, this was proof that Canada was another place where discrimination and segregation were the lot of the minority. The figures revealed by the Commission's report only confirmed what had been known for a long time. But this is one area where the Québecois seem to have made real progress. Figures for 1981 showed that income differences fell to 3 per cent, probably lessening popular support for the independence movement.

Loss of political and economic control

A driving force behind movements for self-determination is a people's conviction that the political and economic framework that regulates their affairs deprives them of decision-making powers.[16] In the case of Québec, we must consider both the question of the power of the federal goverment and that of the foreign presence in industry.

The British North America Act of 1867 was the culmination of British Imperial attempts to unite Canada. The supporters of the BNA Act argued that Confederation was a clever ploy to give to French-Canadians a homeland in which they were the majority. The English-speaking inhabitants of Québec felt in 1867 that they had been sold out however.[17] Since 1867 autonomist opinion in Québec has decried subsequent federal government practice which allegedly pursued a policy of centralisation.[18] The BNA Act did give the federal government power to disallow provincial laws, but gave it powers for 'order and good govenment'. However, these powers were eroded by several judicial decisions which recognised that the provinces were sovereign within their jurisdiction (*Hodge* v. *The Queen*, 1883).

The problem of centralisation grew after World War I when the federal government wrung from the provinces agreements to cede taxing powers in return for help with their severe economic problems. Ottawa was thus able to gain control of unemployment, broadcasting, transport and many aspects of life from which it was hitherto excluded. Since the 1960s, the Québecois have learned to look to the provincial government for most matters of import. On these terms, the federal government was viewed as a block to Québec's progress.

A concomitant question has been Québecois representation in federal decision-making. Ethnic under-representation occurred both in the federal cabinet and civil service.[19] In 1946, Québecois representation was less than half its proportional numbers. The Trudeau government (1968–84) partially corrected the imbalance. The federal scene is still perceived, on these grounds, with much suspicion by many Québecois.

The second source of outside control has been foreign ownership of Québec's industry. This became an issue in the 1930s with Barbeau's *La*

Mesure de notre taille (1936). In the 1970s several studies revealed that barely one-fifth of sales in the manufacturing sector originated with francophone-controlled firms and that these were concentrated in traditional low-technology industries serving local markets.[20] It seems reasonable to state that since the cession of Canada to the British in 1763, the Québecois have lost control over their economy. The major export industries (fur, timber and wheat) fell into the hands of British firms. To be sure, there were successful Québecois businessmen,[21] but they were not powerful. Recently it was shown that Anglo-Canadian interests still account for 40 per cent of manufacturing sales.[22] Only in banking do francophones control about 50 per cent of assets, due to the development of a powerful network of credit unions.

The roots of francophone exclusion are deep.[23] Foreign control adds a 'dual-dependency'.[24] American capital accounted for 75 per cent of all foreign investments in Canada. American control of Québec's industries became as great as Anglo-Canadian. However, while American presence came to be economic imperialism in English Canada, in Québec reaction has been positive. Québec governments have tended to favour foreign, especially American, investments. Not only is this true of the Liberal and Union Nationale governments since 1990, but the Party Québecois also opposed the federal attempts to control foreign investment. American investors were seen as a lesser threat to Québec's autonomy than their Anglo-Canadian rivals. The Parti Québecois moved, at the end of its eight years in power, towards encouraging new Québecois entrepreneurs to develop an indigenous capitalism, as part of an integrated North American economy. Their policy called for continued economic association with Canada after independence.

Another factor influencing the independence movement has been French-Canadian under-representation in the business world. They were over-represented in the liberal professions, including religious orders.[25] For some, this was due to Québec's rural traditions and the Québecois value system. Many authors have, however, attributed this business 'inferiority' strictly to the political domination subsequent to the cession of 1763. It has also been suggested that the Québecois rejected capitalist values in the nineteenth century as being Anglo-Saxon in origin.

The sense of economic inferiority contributed to frustration in the Québecois elite. Today, however, there has been a veritable surge of Québecois entrepreneurship. Already, Québec's management schools account for over 30 per cent of all business and management students in Canada.[26] Numerous business periodicals have appeared on the stands and half-a-dozen television programmes now cater to these new tastes. In a survey of Québecois business activity since colonial times, Toulouse (1980) has tried to extinguish the myth of economic inferiority. He notes that there have always been people in Québec with a 'well-developed business sense'. The present surge of private entrepreneurship certainly draws upon a rich reservoir of business talent. There is even a new phenomenon of note — Québecois multi-national corporations.

The impact of this upsurge of entrepreneurship on the independence movement cannot easily be assessed. If it does favour the growth of national self-confidence, it will give encouragement to self-determination. On the other hand, if businessmen can accomplish so much within the federal framework, they may not feel the need to support the creation of a sovereign state.

Finally, we examine demographic aspects of Québecois separatism. In Québec, demography and language have always been inseparable. The survival of Québecois culture on a continent dominated by the English language required a minimal population base. Also, political power at the federal level required numbers, since the distribution of seats in the federal House of Commons was based on population. Francophones have been a minority in Canada since Confederation (1866). But Québec's share of the population has fallen from 32.3 per cent to 25.8 per cent. About 10 per cent of Québec is of British ancestry, creating thus a minority within a minority. The Québecois demographic decline is due to the combined effects of Québecois emigration to the eastern United States from 1850 on, and the waves of immigration that increased Canada's population. Between 1946 and 1982, Canada received nearly 6 million immigrants, raising the population to over 25 million. Québec received less than 16 per cent of the total, 10 per cent less than its demographic weight.[27] Nationalists in particular have been loud in denouncing this slow and subtle form of marginalisation.

For a long time immigration came mostly from Great Britain. The federal authorities saw no reason to help Québec recruit immigrants from French-speaking lands. A high birth rate, the highest in the Western world, guaranteed numbers, but this was offset by heavy out-migration. Ironically, when immigration did come to Québec, it was not welcomed. Economic conditions caused the Québecois worker to see the newcomer as a competitor. Most immigrants did not learn French, but there was some integration. Common social conditions and religion, as with the Irish and the Italians, did produce Francophone Québecois with Italian or Irish names. Most Québecois consider encouraging the birth rate preferable to encouraging immigration. Québec and the federal government have in recent years agreed on more control over immigration for Québec.

The demographic threat is today fought in Montreal. The British minority in Québec has fallen from 25 per cent in 1867 to 7.7 per cent in 1981. In fact, 110,000 Anglophones left the province between 1976 and 1981.[28] However, Montreal has been receiving large numbers of immigrants who tended to prefer the English language for reasons of mobility. Some see Québec as a way station to Ontario, or even the United States. These immigrants now form over 10 per cent of the population of the province, and a much larger percentage of the population of Montreal.

Québec's initiatives sought to strengthen the French language within Québec. Friction between Francophones and Anglophone immigrants came to a head in Montreal in 1968, when a school board decided to offer only French schooling to immigrant children. Laws were enacted to deal with this question, culminating in the Charter of the French Language (Law 101), which limited access to English schools to children whose parents or elder siblings had attended English schools. The Charter also set out to promote the use of the French language in business and public life in general. Several clauses of this law have, however, been overturned by judicial decisions based on the federal charter of rights (1982).

Thus, within an eight-year period (1969–77), Québec had given itself a sophisticated language policy that had favoured a 'territorial' approach, according to which the individual must adapt to the dominant language of a region.[29] The proportion of Anglophones using only English in the workplace has fallen from 64 per cent to 32 per cent and the proportion of allophones using only French is now greater than that using only English.[30]

Clearly Québec has been able to take a bold and determined approach in controlling its linguistic destiny. The results are not only statistical, they are seen and felt. These changes, as well as the emergence of Francophones in all levels of business, are giving the French language a new vitality undreamed of twenty years ago. Given these developments, it is difficult to assert that French cannot come into its own without full political sovereignty.

The modern independence movement

A will to collective survival as a nation is embedded in the history of the

Québecois. A collective sense emerged soon after the Treaty of Paris had ceded Canada to Britain. As early as 1764, some ninety-five persons petitioned the king requesting the preservation of French law.[31] Similarly, the debate on elected assembly for the colony led to a meeting of 300 people in Montreal in 1788, when the population of the city was only a few thousand. The Assembly created in 1791 for Québec was soon the scene of parliamentary battles between representatives of the French-speaking majority and the appointees of the governor. By 1814, the Parti Canadien was putting in writing the distinction between the population they represented and *les Anglais*.[32] By 1834, the Patriotes, the national party, voted in Assembly (fifty-six to twenty-three) Ninety-Two Resolutions which mentioned the under-representation of 'Canadiens' and other grievances. This led to the war of 1837–8. The British army defeated the Patriote militia and destroyed the farms of all the Canadiens on their route of march. In February 1838, a Patriote leader, Robert Nelson, led a force of 300 men from the United States and proclaimed the independence of Lower Canada. Nelson was defeated, but he had been testimony to the will for nationhood. Throughout the nineteenth century, it was manifested repeatedly by leaders like Lafontaine in 1840 or Mercier in 1886. Other notable cases include that of Mederic Lanctot, who campaigned in 1867 for an independent Québec, and Jules-Paul Tardivel, in 1904, suggested that Canada was an unstable arrangement that should be dissolved. Then there was the Ligue Nationaliste of Henri Bourassa, who helped to maintain the confusion between the English and French meanings of 'nation' by defending the autonomy of Canada within the British Empire.

The secession of Québec became alive again after World War I, starting with the Motion Francoeur debated in the Legislative Assembly of Québec in 1918.[33] The agitation helped foster a new sense of social and economic resentment by the more urbanised Québecois, and resulted in the election of governments who were more concerned with Québecois self-affirmation: Duplessis and then Lesage (1944–60, 1960–6).

The latest resurgence of the secessionist movement dates back to 1957 with the creation of the Alliance Laurentienne. This, and its successors, would create the most serious political crisis since Confederation. Beginning in 1963, a new form of action appeared: violent terrorism. This new current was the product of several small groups of extremists, loosely identified with a left-wing revolutionary ideology and collectively known as the Front de Liberation du Québec (FLQ). The early groups took essentially symbolic actions, such as bombing historical monuments. But in 1970, one group kidnapped a British diplomat and assassinated a Québec minister. This event brought considerable public discredit to the FLQ and allowed the federal government, then headed by Trudeau, to resort to the War Measures Act in an attempt to discredit all secessionists and left-wing opposition.[34] The FLQ has since disappeared along with terrorist methods.

It is on the more conventional political terrain that the new wave of secessionism would produce its greatest results. Coinciding with the so-called Quiet Revolution, the movement would go, within barely a decade, from marginal groupings to the creation of a full-fledged political party. In accomplishing this, the movement had gained a very broad popular base, a coalition including the labour unions and most of Québec's artists. The Parti Québecois , as it is called, was largely the work of one man, Réné Levesque, who assembled its various components and led it to power in 1976. At that time, the new government had promised to hold a referendum on the question, linking sovereignty for Québec with economic association between it and Canada. In the referendum, the government asked only for a mandate to negotiate 'sovereignty-association', but the verdict, as we have seen, was negative (though francophones gave the 'Yes' a slight majority).

What are the options now given to the population of Québec with respect to their political relationship to Canada? At one end of the spectrum still remains the unitary state, which is not a serious possibility. Next comes updated, renegotiated federalism, but one that would maintain the vision of 'one Canada'. Put at its best, this would mean creating a larger polity, though not necessarily a 'melting pot'. In practice, this has often been the 'unhyphenated' nationalism of the English-Canadian majority.[35] A second vision amounts to a recognition that the 'one Canada' is an unworkable dream. It imagines a Canada where Québec would have a 'special status' owing to its cultural specificities. This allows for a large zone of negotiation around this concept of 'special status' including the two-founding-nations approach.

Beyond the special status alternative, we enter the realm of scenarios implying varying degrees of sovereignty for Québec. These can range from the Parti Québecois's concept of 'sovereignty-association'—political sovereignty coupled with economic association—to unconditional independence. These positions can be defended on purely ethnocentric grounds or out of a conviction that a sovereign Québec would be the best solution for both Canada and Québec.

Notes

1. See Ralph R. Premdas, 'Secessionist Politics in Papua New Guinea', *Pacific Affairs* (Spring 1977) and the theoretical chapter in this volume; also C. Geertz, ed., *The Integrative Revolution*, Glencoe, Ill., The Free Press, 1963.
2. M. Brunet *et al.*, *Histoire du Canada par les textes*, Montreal, Fides, 1963.
3. F. Angers, *Les Droits du français au Québec*, Montreal, Editions du Jour, 1971.
4. M. Rioux and Y. Martin, *French-Canadian Society*, Toronto, McClelland and Stewart, 1964.
5. J. Garreau, *The Nine Nations of North America*, New York, Avon Books, 1981.
6. J. Hamelin, *Histoire du Québec*, St Hyacinthe, Edisem, 1977.
7. N. Eid and M. Brunet, 'Faut-il oublier l'histoire religieuse du québec?' *Critre*, vol. 32 (1981).
8. B. Landry, *Economie et Independence*, Montreal, Les Editions Quinze, 1977.
9. A. Faucher and M. Lamontagne, 'Histoire de l'industrialisation', in R. Durocher et P.A. Linteau, eds, *Le Retard du Québec*, Trois-Rivières, Boral Express, 1977.
10. D.F. Walker, *Canada's Industrial Space Economy*, Toronto, Wiley, 1980.
11. J.P. Charbonneau and G. Paquette, *L'Option*, Montreal, Les Editions de l'Homme, 1978.
12. Ibid.
13. Landry, *Economie et Independence.*
14. R. Tremblay, *Presentation des comptes economiques du Québec*, Québec, MIC, 1977.
15. A. Raynauld, 'La Communauté politique Canadienne', in *Economie and Independence*, Montreal, Les Editions Quinze, 1977.
16. See the theoretical chapter by R. Premdas in this volume.
17. P. Corbeil, 'L'Influence des representants anglophones sur la politique québecoise de 1874: une Re-Valuation', *Revista de Historia de America*, vol. 102 (1986).
18. Charbonneau and Paquette, op. cit.
19. R.G. Breton *et al*, *Les Frontieres culturelles et la cohesion du Canada*, Toronto, Institute for Research for Public Policy, 1981.
20. A. Raynauld, *La Propiété des entreprises au Québec*, Montreal, Les Presses de l'Université de Montreal, 1974.
21. J.M. Toulouse, *Reussités québecoises*, Montreal, Les Editions Agence D'Arc, 1980.
22. P. Frechette *et al.*, eds, *L'Économie du Québec*, Anjou, Que., Holt-Rinehart-Winston, 1975.
23. Brunet, *et al.*, op. cit.
24. M. St-Germain, *Une Economie à liberer*, Montreal, Les Presses de l'Université de Montreal, 1973.
25. R. Durocher *et al.*, *Le Québec depuis 1930*, Montreal, Boral Express, 1986.
26. Forchette and Vzina, op. cit.
27. Durocher, *et al.*, op. cit.
28. G. Mathews, *Le Choc demographique*, Montreal, Boral Express, 1984.

29. R.Y. Bourhis, ed., *Conflict and Language Planning in Quebec*, Montreal, Multilingual Matters Ltd., 1984.
30. Mathews, op. cit.
31. Brunet *et al.*, op. cit.
32. D. Vaugeois, *L'Union des deux Canadas 1791–1840*, Trois-Rivières, Le Bien Public, 1962.
33. Hamelin, op. cit.
34. M. Bellavance and M. Gilbert, *L'Opinion publique et la crise d'octobre*, Montreal, Editions du Jour, 1971.
35. J. Morchain and M. Wade, *Search for a Nation*, Toronto, J.M. Dent and Sons, 1967.

13 THE CANADIAN WEST: A CASE OF REGIONAL SEPARATISM

Don Ray and Ralph R. Premdas

Only a decade ago, the literature on political integration was largely confined to Third World countries. It is now realised that many developed countries suffer from similar traumas of internal fragmentation.[1] Note Audrey and David Smock: 'No continent and virtually no nation is now immune to the impact of claims for special status and privileges made on behalf of communal groups'.[2] Among developed countries, Canada has long been seen as an exception to the claim that the industrial North was blessed with a culturally homogeneous population sharing a common consensus on fundamental issues. Often, however, it was the province of Quebec which was perceived as the source of Canadian disunity. Outside Quebecois ethno-nationalism, Canada was seen as unified. Not much is often heard of the regional assertion and periodic claims for separation from Western Canada. Yet, this region has had a long history of discontent and has quite credibly threatened Canadian unity from time to time.

But what does one do with a movement that does not assert a claim for separation on ethnic distinctiveness? Are separatist movements constituted only of sub-state entities practising a distinct language or religion? We do not think so. Strong secondary factors, such as discrimination, exploitation or neglect, can by themselves (often along with weak and transparently fictional primordial claims) encourage the demand for autonomy.[3] This chapter deals with one such separatist movement. It refers to an autonomist movement whose values, religion, race and language are generally similar to that of the original state from which separation is sought, but because of alleged discrimination — and domination — claims have emerged for self-determination.

Anthony D. Smith discussed this territorial-regional aspect of a separatist movement, noting that:

> What is important and critical is the differences between 'ethnic' and 'territorial' separatism. In the latter case, the basis of the unit and its leader's sense of apartness, is geography. There may be other differences like color or dialect, but the separatist movement is ultimately staking its claim in virtue of its remoteness and territorial distinctiveness of their unit.[4]

Although based primarily on geography, regional separatists may bolster their arguments on mythical primordial attributes. In the case of Western Canadian separatism, various organizations have made special appeals to history and culture. The firmest foundation, however, is erected on secondary factors. Regional separatism, as Colin Williams has noted, 'is most often linked with some attribute of land in terms of environmental hazard to be overcome or some developmental potential to be realised'.[5] The primordial factors are not forgotten: 'The separatist group thus conceives of itself to be in an unsatisfactory dependent status and this essentially economic factor may be coupled with racial, cultural, and social factors as well'. This is not to say that, unlike primordial factors, the secondary bases are accurate and objective. They could be equally unfounded. In the following sections we separate the West's claim to a unique historical and culturally derived identity (primordial factors), from its economic and political complaints (secondary factors) and discuss each in turn. We begin, however, by giving an overview of the West as a region. The final part of the essay discusses the contemporary aspects of Western separatism.

The West: an overview

The western part of Canada stretches from just west of the Great Lakes to the Pacific Ocean. Canadians have thought of the west as including the three prairie provinces of Manitoba, Saskatchewan and Alberta as well as the mountainous Pacific-rim province of British Columbia. However, some Westerners, including the separatists, have attempted to include the north. According to this definition then, Western Canada would extend north from the border with the United States all the way to the North Pole. This 'West' would comprise about half of Canada and would be one of the largest countries in the world, in terms of territory.

About a third of Canada's people live in the West (by any of these definitions), concentrated in a few cities. Ethnically, the major cleavage has been between the indigenous peoples and the immigrants drawn mainly from Europe. Except for the North-West Territories, the indigenous peoples form a minority who have been shunted off the public conscience and on to official and unofficial reservations. In recent times, the salient cleavages in the West have been within the European immigrant communities. Discrimination against immigrants from eastern and southern Europe by those from north-west Europe has nearly ended. Anti-French feeling by most white English-speakers in the

West is a fact of life, serving as one of the triggers for the emergence of the Western separatist movement.

The notion of 'Western Canada' has been made possible only by the creation of Canada as an internally self-governing country from three of Britain's remaining North American colonies in 1867. Canada's evolution into a sovereign state has been one of accretion: Federation in 1867; full control over foreign affairs and defence from the 1870s to the 1930s; full judicial domestic control of the Constitution in 1982. In the meantime, Canada expanded westwards from its eastern origins, commencing during the 1870s.

In a race with the United States for western North America, Canada consolidated its sovereignty over what became the West in a series of national integration tasks. Between 1867 and 1905, it acquired the West by purchase and treaty, established Canadian administration, suppressing two rebellions in the process, and finally created the provinces of Alberta and Saskatchewan in 1950. Manitoba had been created in 1870 and British Columbia (BC) joined in 1871. The Federal government consolidated its control with an economic strategy for the West called the National Policy. Railways were built across the West to stimulate immigration. The new settlers would export their agricultural products on these railways and import manufactured products from central Canada.

Settlers from Europe, central Canada and the United States poured into the West. The West's contribution to the Canadian economy is overwhelmingly in the production of natural resources, mostly for export, with little industrialisation apart from Winnipeg, Manitoba. The Western economy is dependent on economic forces located outside the region and outside of Canada. This dependency has long rankled in the minds of Westerners and has contributed to the rise of a series of populist and radical initiatives aimed at reducing external domination. The contemporary Western separatist movement is, in large part, the latest in this series of movements produced by these economic circumstances.

Evidence of the contemporary version of Western alienation can be traced to the end of the 1960s. The frustrations of certain Westerners boiled over in the 1970s into various separatist organisations. The most prominent of these were the Independent Alberta Association and several BC-based organisations. These separatists saw the Liberals as being not only communist-led, but also dominated by the 'French'. These attributes were personified by Pierre Trudeau, Federal Prime Minister from 1968 to 1979 and again from 1980 to 1984. Trudeau's resurrection on 18 February 1980 led to the creation of two major separatist organisations in May 1980: Western Canada Concept (WCC) and West-Fed (Western Canada Federation). These gained significant, if minority, memberships throughout the West.

Western separatist movements appear to assume various forms and exhibit the wave-like pattern of other secessionist movements with peaks of activity followed by troughs of quietude.

The West: bases of a separate identity

Regional and cultural factors

The West, and in particular, the core prairie West, has evolved a consciousness of itself as a separate and unique unit within the Canadian federation. W. L. Morton goes so far as to say that 'the West was a region of political and material differences sufficiently significant to give it the character of a sub-society'.[6] A collective consciousness of a separate identity seemed to have been forged into existence. Western academic David Smith has underlined that while 'the region's geography, economy, and people set it apart from the rest of the country . . . it is at the level of public consciousness that the region has achieved its lasting identity'.[7]

The objective elements that provide the foundations of a separate identity are ecology, people, culture and history. The most unique aspects of the West pertain to the mystique of the frontier and the distinctive features of the environment: the vastness, the isolation, the weather and the landscape.[8] Indeed, the saga of Western settlement has set aside the environment for much lamentation and lyric.[9]

The ecology apart, the population of the West was also different. The indigenous peoples and the Metis (mainly offspring from native Indians and French settlers) supplied the original communities. The settlers who came to the West were in many respects different from those who occupied central and eastern Canada. The 'charter' settlers of central Canada were the English and French. On the frontier, however, an ethnic kaleidoscope was grafted on, so that to the indigenous peoples and the Metis were added waves of English, Scottish, Irish, German, Russian, Ukrainian, Polish, Belgian, Dutch, Scandinavian and Icelandic peoples. Whereas in the east, the French and English groups constituted over 80 per cent of the population, in the West they were barely 50 per cent or less.

Some observers suggest that the West is marked off from the rest of

Canada by a body of unique beliefs and outlooks. If this is so, then the crucible from which these developed was the West's experience in settling the frontier. For most Westerners, their roots go back only to the turn of the twentieth century when immigrants came looking for a new life. From this relatively brief history, the distinctive experience was in part distinguished by alleged discrimination and exploitation. In turn, the frustrations unleashed a steady procession of protests and radical ideologies. To Louis Riel, the Metis' leader, is assigned the historic role of resistance against federal incursions. Writes Morton: 'The beginning of the process [of subordination] was the resistance of the Metis of Red river to the annexation of the Northwest by Canada in 1869.[10]

The Metis sought protection of their 'language, faith, and existence as a group' demanding a separate province with entrenched guarantees of their rights.[11] While provincial status for Manitoba was granted in 1870, it was denied control over its land and natural resources, unlike other provinces. 'This', Morton remarked, 'was the beginning of the bias of prairie politics'.[12]

When the West was annexed to Canada from the Hudson Bay Company by the Rupert Land Act of 1868, a vast area about five times the size of the original confederation was added to the Canadian state. The annexation established a hinterland colony in the service of central Canada. The National Policy promulgated in 1879 to facilitate the opening up of the West bestowed most benefits to central Canada and much burden to the West. A tariff wall was erected to protect Canadian manufacturers mainly located in central Canada and to raise revenues for a transcontinental railway. This resulted in high prices for farm equipment and services needed by Western settlers. To the West, the tariff soon became a symbol of subordination and exploitation by the federal government on behalf of central Canadian industrialists, banks and transport monopolies.[13]

Such ill-treatment meted out to the West laid the foundations for what came to be called 'Western alienation'. It initiated a tradition of protest and radicalism that became a permanent fixture in the West's participation in the confederation. The heart of Western protest was political subordination and economic dependency. But political protest was only part of a larger package of institutions that characterised the West. Other outlooks and values would also emerge. We look at these now. We remind ourselves, however, that claims to uniqueness of cultural identity need not always be consistent with objective facts. In forging a collective consciousness, the role of myth and folklore is vital.

Saskatchewan's David Smith argued that the struggle to settle the

West produced 'a unique set of attitudes, beliefs, values, skills'.[14] Former Prime Minister Trudeau felt that 'there is a different culture in the West than there is in Central Canada . . . it is not a different civilization, but certainly it is a different form of culture than exists elsewhere'.[15] Stanley agreed saying that 'the people of the West have remained fundamentally unchanged. They have not become Canadians of the same kind as those of other provinces'.[16]

What exactly did these writers mean by suggesting that the West was culturally different from the rest of Canada? Did they mean that a distinct society had evolved or that a sub-society with its own regional themes had emerged but which was fundamentally part of a larger overarching Canadian cultural identity? From the literature on the West, an array of unique social, political, cultural and attitudinal traits have been assigned to Western people. At the socio-cultural level, references abound about the evolution of mutual aid and co-operation among the early settlers, especially those on the prairies. This was reflected institutionally by the emergence of an infrastructure of co-operative societies and farmers' associations. Farming on nucleated homesteads in a harsh climatic environment under conditions of isolation and scarce economic resources compelled collective co-operative behaviour for survival. Wilmott argued that 'for in all this mutual aid and joint activity, a supportive value system was bound to emerge'.[17] It was also claimed that the environment moulded a unique Western personality. Thus Stanley argued that 'the characteristic spirit of the Westerner is that of independence, self-reliance, willingness to strike out on a new path'.[18] Unique political traits included egalitarianism, non-partisanship and dislike for titles, honours and distinctions. Finally, socially, the West allegedly displayed distinctive mores of common courtesies expressed in a 'civilized tempo of life' within an environment of clean air and water.[19] Together, these traits moulded a unique Western identity. It will not be part of our task here to evaluate these ascribed traits of Westerners for their objectivity or mythological content. It is enough for us to indicate that many Westerners do believe that they share, at a minimum, a separate regional life style.

On the subject of values, a few comments are required on the stereotypes traditionally assigned to Westerners. To the West have been attributed the stereotypes of cloddishness, parochialism and bigotry. To the central Canadian, the Westerner was a farmer, a country hick and a person lacking cosmopolitanism and culture. Even some Westerners have come to incorporate these stereotypes in their own intra-community insult vocabulary. A Western nationalist remembers how in school his teacher scolded his unacceptable behaviour by saying, 'Don't be a farmer!'[20]

The farm–hick–parochial–clod image persists, despite the fact that the contemporary Westerner is an urbanite with thorough exposure to cosmopolitan culture. The other aspect of Western stereotypes is bigotry, most particularly expressed in anti-French antipathy. Westerners feel that their anti-Francophone prejudices derive from attempts by the Federal government to force them to accept costly services for French language instruction when, on an ethnic distribution basis, the need in the West is more for special facilities in Ukrainian, Hungarian, Polish, etc. Westerners argue that the federal programme of bilingualism and biculturalism is suitable only for those parts of Canada, apart from Quebec, where the Quebecois population is significant, such as Ontario, Arcadia, New Brunswick and Manitoba.[21] Further, Westerners argue that the assertion of Quebecois nationalism has diverted attention and resources from Western demands and needs. The Western perception of Quebec is therefore seen as not entirely ethnocentric or racial but points to a contest over resources.

The cumulative impact of Western alienation has been described by Western nationalist George Melnyk as lack of complete self-esteem among many Westerners.[22] A cadre of Western intellectuals has emerged to rewrite Western history and literature 'to control their own destiny'.[23] Western educational and cultural institutions all play up Western motifs and contributions in literature, art, and life style. An intelligentsia, political leadership, folklore, literature and other assorted paraphernalia firm up the claim that a unique Western identity exists. To the territory, landscape, economy, immigrant diversity and lifestyle are attached special sentiments of a primordial nature, however fabricated, far-fetched, or mythological it may be.

Secondary factors: economic grievances

Tariffs and transport

Underlying the economic grievances of the West is disparate regional development within Canada. Central Canada (Toronto and Montreal mainly) has emerged as the centre of the country's industrial and financial strength so overwhelmingly that this feature imparts the impression of a structural metropolis–colony relationship. A populous industrial-financial heartland overpowers and exploits a sparsely populated agricultural and mineral-resource hinterland. The West is part of the exploited periphery and, over a century of economic change, this cleavage has not been bridged but consolidated and exacerbated.

The historical record indicates that the opening up of the West was intended to create a hinterland that supplied raw materials to promote Canada's economic development. Note Richards and Pratt: 'the prairie West was consciously settled and developed as an economic hinterland. This colonialism was no accident of history. It was imposed as an act of policy'.[24] Under the National Policy of 1879, three programmes were promulgated: (a) a protective tariff to stimulate industrialisation; (b) an immigration initiative to attract settlers to the West; and (c) a subsidised transcontinental railway to penetrate the Western frontier and promote agricultural and mineral production. It was the costs that came with the tariffs and transport policies that furnished the fuel of Western disenchantment.

While the protectionist tariff succeeded in promoting industrial growth, it concentrated most industries within central Canada. This was inevitable in a capitalist market economy since central Canada had the largest and most skilled population concentration to sustain an industrial sector, and an infrastructure of financial, communications and energy supports.[25] In effect, underdevelopment in the West was not conspiratorial, for 'hinterland regions do not become industrial centers in a market economy'.[26]

To many Westerners, however, the evidence pointed not entirely to the role of disinterested market forces. The tariffs created virtual monopolies for certain industries resulting in higher costs of goods and services for Western residents. In a free-trade competitive system, these additional costs would be eliminated. Given the marginality of the first settlers in the West and their greater reliance on imported farm equipment, the tariffs placed an inordinate if unequal burden on them.[27] Many Westerners also believed that without the tariffs, foreign industries would have been built in the West to capitalise on the specialised demands for certain goods. Despite evidence that many Western industries today survive because of the tariff, what loomed largest in the West's view was that it had to bear high prices of manufactured goods for an indefinite period well beyond that justified for incubation and maturity of infant industries. The tariffs constituted a permanent subsidy by the periphery to central Canadian industrial uncompetitiveness and inefficiency.

Finally, Western nationalists point out that a tariff is a double-edged device. While it protects a country's industry from foreign competition, it encourages other nations to erect retaliatory tariffs to protect their industries from competition. For the West, which is an exporter of raw material, foreign tariffs limit access of its goods to these markets and also make them less competitive. Western Canadians, then, are exposed to double jeopardy, first from high internal prices of domestic manufactures, and second from restriction of market opportunities for its exports.

If Western grievances germinated from tariffs, then their handmaiden was transport practices. Essentially, this complaint revolved around the monopoly rights the Federal government granted the Canadian Pacific Railroad (CPR) which allegedly charged what the traffic could bear. Under the regulated freight rates on products to and from the West, a 'fair discrimination price' was levied.[28] In practice, this meant that the railroad operated at a loss in the eastern transport corridors in competition with alternative transport facilities, but was permitted to recuperate the loss by charging a high rate from Western customers. The West attempted to establish its own railways, but its legislation to this end was disallowed by the Federal government. Persistent protest bordering on outright rebellion finally yielded the Crowsnest Pass subsidised rate for wheat.

Oil, gas, energy, and other natural resources

Fundamental to the conflict over natural resources are two sets of separate rights conferred respectively on provincial and Federal governments. On one hand, under Section 109 of the British North America Act, which was Canada's Constitution, the provinces possessed exclusive ownership and control over natural resources. On the other hand, powers were assigned to the Federal government over taxation and the regulation of trade and commerce. Clearly, these powers overlapped and depending on how they were used they affected Western resources. The West felt that it was victimised on the issue of land and natural resources from the very moment Western territories acceded to provincial status. Manitoba, which became a province in 1870, and Saskatchewan and Alberta, provinces in 1905, were all denied control over their land and resources, unlike other provinces which obtained full ownership and control. British Columbia, a Western province, on attaining provincial status had full ownership and control except for large tracts of land which were set aside for the development of the Pacific Railroad. The Federal government justified its withholding of land and resources on the rationale that it needed to provide incentives for Western settlement and development. When the Western provinces finally wrested full control in 1930, much of its land and natural resources were already alienated to private persons and corporations.

The natural resource issue again raised its controversial head in the 1970s over petroleum. Alberta and Saskatchewan were endowed with considerable energy resources, especially Alberta. Following the international oil crisis in 1973, petroleum prices escalated. Alberta (and the resident American multinational companies which controlled much of the oil and gas resources) stood to reap a bountiful windfall. The Federal government felt that it should receive a 'national patrimony entitlement' from the profits. That apart, it felt that the oil boom was creating immense regional disparity in wealth. Furthermore, the high prices of fuel had overly inflated the Federal budgetary deficit resulting in a massive national debt. Using its taxation and regulation of trade and commerce powers, the Federal government tapped into the Western oil revenues. It taxed oil exports and simultaneously restricted the price of oil sold on the domestic market so that it was well below world prices.

Western leaders reacted to the National Energy Policy (NEP) 'as an unparalleled assault on Western resources and ownership rights'.[29] Among the Western populace, not only sentiments of disenchantment were expressed, but also opinions about the need to secede from the Confederation. To the West, taxation of provincial oil also represented a violation of an old practice whereby one level of government did not tax another level. The entire experience with the Federal energy policy reaffirmed Western feelings of powerlessness.

Political grievances

When the Western provinces were incorporated as a part of the Canadian Confederation, the political framework and the economic system dominated by central Canada had already been established. The political subordination of the West to central Canadian interests would feature in practically every grievance that would arise. Operationally, political subordination meant several things. To begin with, it denied control over land and natural resources to the Western provinces when they acceded to provincial status. Political subordination also meant the disallowance of provincial laws by the Federal government. The power of disallowance permitted central Canadian interests to nullify efforts by the Western provinces, led by Manitoba, to break up the exploitative railroad monopolies. Political subordination further institutionalized Western powerlessness through the electoral system, which awarded power to the most populous provinces—namely, Ontario and Quebec in central Canada, with about two-thirds of the total Canadian population. Finally, political subordination implied that the Federal government controlled by central Canadian interests made laws on vital subjects such as agriculture, trade and commerce that dictated life in the West. In practice, this meant that the tariffs, freight rates, interest rates and access to export markets—all crucial to the West's well-being and survival—were at the mercy of central Canadian industrial and financial interests. Because of the one-sidedness of federal legislation against Western economic interests, a main precondition of rebellion was quickly laid: a sense of powerlessness.

From the exploitation and discrimination, Western protests built up to a crescendo of openly organised defiance which came to the boil by 1921. An assortment of voluntary associations proliferated, ranging from trade unions and political-religious movements to political parties and co-operative societies: 'It was a time when the political evolution of Western Canada struck out on a new path, when the prairies emerged as a full-fledged and a regionally distinct actor on the Canadian political scene.[30] Some concessions were granted such as the Crowsnest Pass Agreement but new circumstances, including the Great Depression, kept the prairie fire of protest alive and burning. Into the 1920s and 1930s, the assertion of Western regional sentiments continued. Major political changes were instituted. Third parties were established which uprooted and displaced the two (Central Canada-based) traditional parties. These included the Progressive Party of Canada, the Social Credit Party of Alberta and the CCF of Saskatchewan, which had captured power in the Western provinces. The West had asserted itself and had inscribed protest as its distinctive regional medium of political expression. It successfully modified aspects of the freight rate and transport costs, eliminated Federal disallowance of provincial ownership and control of their lands and natural resources.

But fundamental structural features remained, underscoring the continued subordination and vulnerability of the West to central Canada. The tariff walls remained and the discriminatory freight-rate structure persisted in relation to non-wheat products shipped to and from the West. The West also remained a preponderantly primary-producing economy (wheat, oil, gas, potash, etc.) relying on export markets organised for it by the Federal government. Above all, the political system that accorded controlling power in the Federal parliament to central Canada remained untouched. In the 1960s these residual areas of grievance erupted again in the West but under a different set of circumstances. The new element that emerged was the rise of Quebecois nationalism, which eclipsed Western Canadian demands for Federal government attention.

In the shadow of Quebec's nationalist assertions, the West found itself neglected again as Federal politicians devoted most of their time to the issue of Quebec's participation in the Confederation. The rise of the separatist Parti Québecois and the threat that a part of Canada, which constituted about one-third of its population and covered a vast territory, would secede demanded federal priority.

Western alienation appeared to be embedded in the region's relationship to the Federal government and central Canada. To rectify the lack of effective power, several proposals have been advanced. Among these were: (a) a Federal Senate (upper house) elected by the provinces on an equal basis and endowed with powers almost equal to that of the House of Commons; (b) an electoral system of proportional representation that will allow the established two parties, particularly the Liberal Party, the opportunity to obtain some of the seats in the West; and (c) further devolution of powers to the provinces. These prescriptions may not necessarily pacify the protest proclivities of the West any more than the shift of people from the rural to urban areas did. Western alienation appears permanently engrained in the territorial expression of the regional peripheries of the Canadian Confederation. Regardless of whether the West is poor (pre-World War II) or prosperous (post-World War II), it protests.

Contemporary Western separatism

In this section, we provide a sketch that describes the form Western alienation is assuming today. We emphasise that the situation is very fluid and, at times, murky. But the separatists are alive and well, taking different organisational forms but pronouncing on familiar themes of Western alienation. Recent Federal parliamentary elections have exposed the extent to which the three major parties have become regionalised (Table 13.1). The Progressive Conservatives and the New Democrats share the West and the Liberals have their political base largely in East. This regionalisation of the parties was reflected in the virtual exclusion out of Western-elected representatives from Trudeau's Federal cabinet. Many Westerners felt that they lacked real power under the Liberals.

Organized Western separatists such as the Independent Alberta

Table 13.1 Canada: distribution of seats in Federal parliament, 1984 and 1988

	1984			1988		
	Total seats (no.)	West* seats (no.)	Percentage of West seats	Total seats (no.)	West* seats (no.)	Percentage of West seats
Progressive Conservatives	219	61 (76.3)	75.1	169	48 (53.9)	57.3
Liberals	40	02 (2.5)	14.2	83	08 (9.0)	28.1
New Democrats	30	17 (21.2)	10.7	43	33 (37.1)	14.6
Total	289	80	100.0	295	89	100.0

Source: Maclean's, 5 December 1988, p. 15.
*West includes Yukon (1 seat) and North-West Territories.

Association had existed since the early 1970s in Calgary and other parts of Alberta. The significance of the fall of Joe Clark escaped nearly all analysts at the time—except the separatists. Elmer Knutson, the leader of the separatist organisation, West-Fed, argued that Clark's fall was an alarm signal to Anglophone Canadians. Trudeau's victory was alleged to mean that the English language was to be wiped out in Canada. In order to remove this threat to Anglophone power, Knutson suggested that either Quebec or the West had to leave Canada.[31] The defeat of the independence option in the Quebec referendum of 20 May 1980 prompted Knutson and some other alienated Western Conservatives into action. If Quebec was not going to separate, then the West should. On 23 May 1980, armed with the knowledge that he had a substantial number of people behind him, Knutson launched West-Fed. Its goal was to forge a western Canadian federation out of the four western provinces. Branches were formed across the West. The West-Fed or 'Western Canada Federation' platform attempted to negotiate a host of demands ranging from the end of bilingualism to the abolition of metrication. In effect, West-Fed held that separation of the West would not be necessary if central Canada would yield a more favourable relationship with the West. However, the argument went, if central Canada obstinately refused to end its colonial domination of the West, then West-Fed would seek to implement its last resort: separation.

Within a week of West-Fed's founding in Alberta, a like-minded group called Western Canada Concept (WCC) was established in

British Columbia by Doug Christie, a lawyer from Victoria, BC. He brought his uncompromising message declaring that he was a separatist and that separation was the *only* answer to the ailments of the West. Christie urged that the four western provinces form an independent unitary Western Canada.

Through the summer and fall of 1980 both organisations spread the sparks of separatism. The fire started smouldering in meeting after meeting in small towns and village halls across Alberta and throughout the West. Reverberating with ideological echoes of the 1930s Social Credit, these rallies afforded a rural base for the urban small business leaders of the movement.[32]

Prime Minister Trudeau's relentless post-1980 drive to provide Canada with a new constitution inadvertently further fanned the fires of separatism. Many Westerners had deep reservations about any constitution created by a Liberal Party with only two elected Western representatives. The controversy over the Constitution became enmeshed with the issue of Western oil revenues. Many disillusioned Westerners believed that Clark's defeat had been paid for by Liberal promises of a Federal grab for Western resources. They believed that the fact that Liberals had coldly calculated the scarceness of Liberal votes in the West meant that they could afford to sacrifice the West for electoral gains on Ontario.

Some Westerners, such as Dr Ruth Gorman, went so far as to regard Trudeau's 1980 Constitutional proposals as a further way of stealing Western resource revenues.[33] In her speeches at separatist meetings, she argued that the Federal Liberal government's omission of entrenched property rights in the new Constitution was not accidental but part of what she perceived as Trudeau's commitment to socialism. Therefore, her argument went, Western Canadians should be concerned about property rights. Many members of her audiences went one step further and concluded that secession was necessary in order to protect their property rights, especially the wealth derived from oil. This analysis ignored the fact that property rights had not been entrenched before, and in any case property rights had been a provincially-controlled matter and would remain so in the new Constitution, well out of the control of the Federal government.

The Federal government's budget of October 1980 and its National Energy Program (NEP) added to the other frustrations of certain Westerners. The budget increased the federal government's share of oil and gas revenues from 10 per cent to 24 per cent. This was achieved at the expense of the oil companies, the share of which decreased dramatically from 45 per cent to 33 per cent, and the provincial government, which had its part of the pie trimmed from 45 to 43 per cent.

The Federal government designed the National Energy Program to accomplish several goals. Until this time, the oil industry had been massively dominated by foreign interests; now a series of tax concessions only for Canadian-owned companies were to be the instrument for the 'Canadianisation' of the oil patch. The Federal government also acquired new revenues, which might be used to decrease its budget deficits. Finally, the federal government obtained control over that strategic commodity, oil.

The Calgary-based oil industry was enraged when it realised that its revenues were to be slashed by more than 25 per cent. Alberta Premier Peter Lougheed began to cut back the production of oil intended for central Canadian markets. The various oil-sands megaprojects ground to a halt in the resulting uncertainties. Oil companies began shifting their exploration funds and oil rigs into the United States. Oil industry executives began to talk seriously of separatism as a possible weapon to combat the Federal measures. Some, drawn from the small, independent oil service companies, took over the Calgary branch of the West-Fed and began to organize for separation if necessary.

In public, the oil industry responded very cautiously to the proposal for separation, probably viewing it as a possible tactic to gain energy policy concessions from the Federal government. The major international companies never endorsed separatism, but a number of small oilmen did. But the industry's fears of and protests against the National Energy Program's impact on their wealth, stoked higher the fires of separatist sympathies. Separatists had already argued that the proposed Constitution's omission of the entrenched right to own property was an attack on the right to own property. They concluded that socialism had taken yet another stride forward in Canada.

On the evening of 20 November 1980, before the largest audience ever to listen to a separatist leader, the WCC's Doug Christie argued that central Canada regarded the West as an economic colony. He portrayed Western Canadians as lacking any effective power in the Federal government. He stirred up feelings of frustration, anger and a pride in being a Western Canadian.[34]

The separatists were not able to keep up the excitement and momentum, however. At times it seemed that the movement was dying. Large rallies were not possible. In the fall of 1981, the acrimony between Alberta and Ottawa toned down as they publicly resolved their differences over the two major issues that sustained the movement: energy and the Constitution. To many, Albertans and the Western interests were no longer mortally threatened. Separation need no longer be considered as an alternative.

During 1981 two internal organisational problems crippled the separatist movement: leadership and policy. The plans and policies for an independent West were hazy and ill-defined by both parties. Even though the policies of most political parties were often incomplete, sometimes contradictory, and frequently showed little thought on how goals were to be achieved, the Western separatist organisations were particularly lacking in this respect. The Western Canada Concept at least was unequivocal about separation. All other future policy was to be decided by the parliament of the new country. To be fair, the movement did take steps in 1982 as well as 1983 to establish some sort of view of the future, but its policies were not elaborated until after the movement had peaked.

The movement's fortunes were at their lowest in 1981. It had lost its earlier mass support and consequently its public profile and was torn by internal conflicts. Its smaller urban base seemed to have melted away. The movement had come to depend on smaller rural meetings of around fifty to a hundred people and on meetings at core members' houses in the cities. Commentators dismissed Western separatism as being dead, burnt-out. But they were wrong; Western separatism was renewed by the WCC victory in the Olds-Didsbury by-election. This led to a resurgence of separatist support in Calgary and across the province.

Its Olds-Didsbury victory was taken as final proof that West-Fed's strategy of working for change through other political parties was no longer necessary. Olds-Didsbury had proved that an avowedly separatist party could gain enough public acceptance to win an election, if not yet a separation referendum. West-Fed, the largest separatist organisation up to then, advised its members to join the WCC instead. The Western separatist movement had resolved a major strategic choice about organisation. The competition between the leaders of the WCC and West-Fed for members and for dominance, was resolved at that time in favour of the WCC. The separatist movement in Alberta emerged for a short while as a consolidated force and an expectation that it would win the provincial government. Even Conservative sources were afraid that the WCC might win twenty seats at the next provincial election.

The Conservatives won seventy-five of the seventy-nine seats in the Legislature. Nevertheless the WCC results are somewhat impressive. In just over two years of organising in Alberta, the WCC established registered constituency associations in all seventy-nine of the province's ridings, had candidates in all but one riding and won nearly 12 per cent of the popular vote. If seats had been allocated on the basis of a party's share of the popular vote, the WCC would have received nine seats. The WCC seemed to have emerged from the election with a province-wide, battle-tested organisation, a substantial popular base, but no high-profile candidates.

The election results provoked more factional fighting over personalities and the question of when, or even if, to separate. Despite the efforts of the WCC leadership and members to recover the initiative that the 1982 by-election had given them, the party's decline continued. Support for Western separation hovered at the level of 3 to 12 per cent, not enough to elect another separatist in the provincial elections of all four Western provinces nor at the 1984 Federal election.

Significantly, secret polls have shown that although Western separatism *per se* had little support, a majority of Westerners still expressed feelings of Western alienation from what they perceived as the political and economic masters of Canada, based in central Canada. While Trudeau resigned from politics in 1984, and while a Conservative Federal government was elected in 1984, the feelings of regional ideological and economic alienation remained alive. This was especially true in Alberta, which never fully recovered from the 1980 fall in oil prices.

A number of political leaders have tried to marry Western populism to Western alienation. West-Fed was reincarnated, this time as a party, the Confederation of the Regions Party (COR). COR gathered some organisational and electoral support, but no elected members, on a platform similar to that of West-Fed. In 1987 the son of a former Alberta premier tried to re-create his father's party, as the Reform Association of Canada, even to the extent of using Social Credit's colour, green. Underlying these attempts is a sense of belonging to a distinctive regional bloc by capitalists and political leaders, who believe that their interests have been subordinated to those of the central Canadian rulers and that the Federal government is the mechanism that enforces this subordination.

Notes

1. See Milton Esman, ed., *Ethnic Conflict in the Western World*, Ithaca, NY, Cornell University Press, 1976.

2. D.R. Smock and A.C. Smock, *The Politics of Pluralism*, New York, Elsevier, 1975, p. 2.
3. For a discussion of the two categories of causes which tend to be associated with separatist movements, see Ralph R. Premdas, 'Secession and Political Change: The Papua Besena Case', *Oceania*, vol. 47, no. 4 (June 1977), pp. 265–83.
4. A.D. Smith, 'Nationalism, Ethnic Separatism, and the Intelligentsia', in Colin H. Williams ed., *National Separatism*, Vancouver, University of British Columbia Press, 1985.
5. C. Williams, 'Introduction', in *National Separatism*, op. cit., p. 1; Smith, 'Nationalism, Ethnic Separatism, and the Intelligentsia'.
6. W.L. Morton, 'The Bias of Prairie Politics', in D. Swainson, ed., *Historical Essays on the Prairie Provinces*, Toronto, McClelland and Steward, 1970, p. 300.
7. D. Smith, cited in R. Gibbins, *Prairie Politics and Society*, Toronto, Buttersworth, 1980, p. 11.
8. J. Barr, 'Beyond Bitterness', in J. Barr and D. Anderson, eds, *The Unfinished Revolt*, Toronto, McClelland and Stewart, 1971, p. 24.
9. G.F.G. Stanley, 'The Western Canadian Mystique', in David P. Gagan, ed., *Prairie Perspectives*, Toronto, Holt, Rinehart and Winston, 1970, p. 20.
10. Morton, op. cit., pp. 293–4.
11. Ibid.
12. Ibid.
13. See J. Richards and L. Pratt, *Prairie Capitalism*, Toronto, McClelland and Stewart, 1979, p. 15.
14. D. Smith, 'Western Politics and National Unity', in D.J. Bercuson, ed., *Canada and the Burden of Unity*, Toronto, Macmillan, 1978, pp. 150–1.
15. Cited in Gibbins, op. cit., p. 5.
16. Stanley, op. cit., p. 18.
17. D.E. Wilmott, 'The Formal Organizations of Saskatchewan Farmers, 1900–1985', in A.W. Rasporich, ed., *Western Canada: Past and Present*, Toronto, McClelland and Stewart, 1975, p. 37.
18. Stanley, op. cit., p. 23.
19. Barr, op. cit., p. 21.
20. Ibid.
21. J.A. Archer, 'The Prairie Perspective', in R.M. Burns, ed., *One Country or Two?*, Montreal, McGill University Press, 1971, p. 24.
22. G. Melnyk, *Radical Regionalism*, Edmonton, Nu West Press, 1981, p. 18.
23. Barr, op. cit., p. 13.
24. Richards and Pratt, op. cit., p. 15.
25. K.H. Norrie, 'Some comments on Prairie Economic Alienation', in C. Caldarola, ed., *Society and Politics in Alberta*, Toronto, Methuen, 1979, p. 132.
26. Ibid., p. 138.
27. See G. Stevenson, *Unfulfilled Union*, Toronto, Gage Publications, 1979, p. 71.
28. See T. G. Regehr, 'Western Canada and the Burden of National Transportation Policy' in Bercuson, ed., *Canada and the Burden of National Unity*, op. cit., p. 116.

29. L. Pratt, 'Whose Oil Is It?' in *Prairie Capitalism* edited by Richards and Pratt, op. cit., p. 158.
30. Gibbins, op. cit., p. 37.
31. See *Calgary Herald*, 20 February 1980.
32. Interview with Elmer Knudson, Edmonton, 19 October 1981.
33. Interview with Ruth Gorman, Calgary, 22 October 1981.
34. CBC Radio, 20 November 1980.

INDEX